IMAGES
of America

SHEBOYGAN FALLS

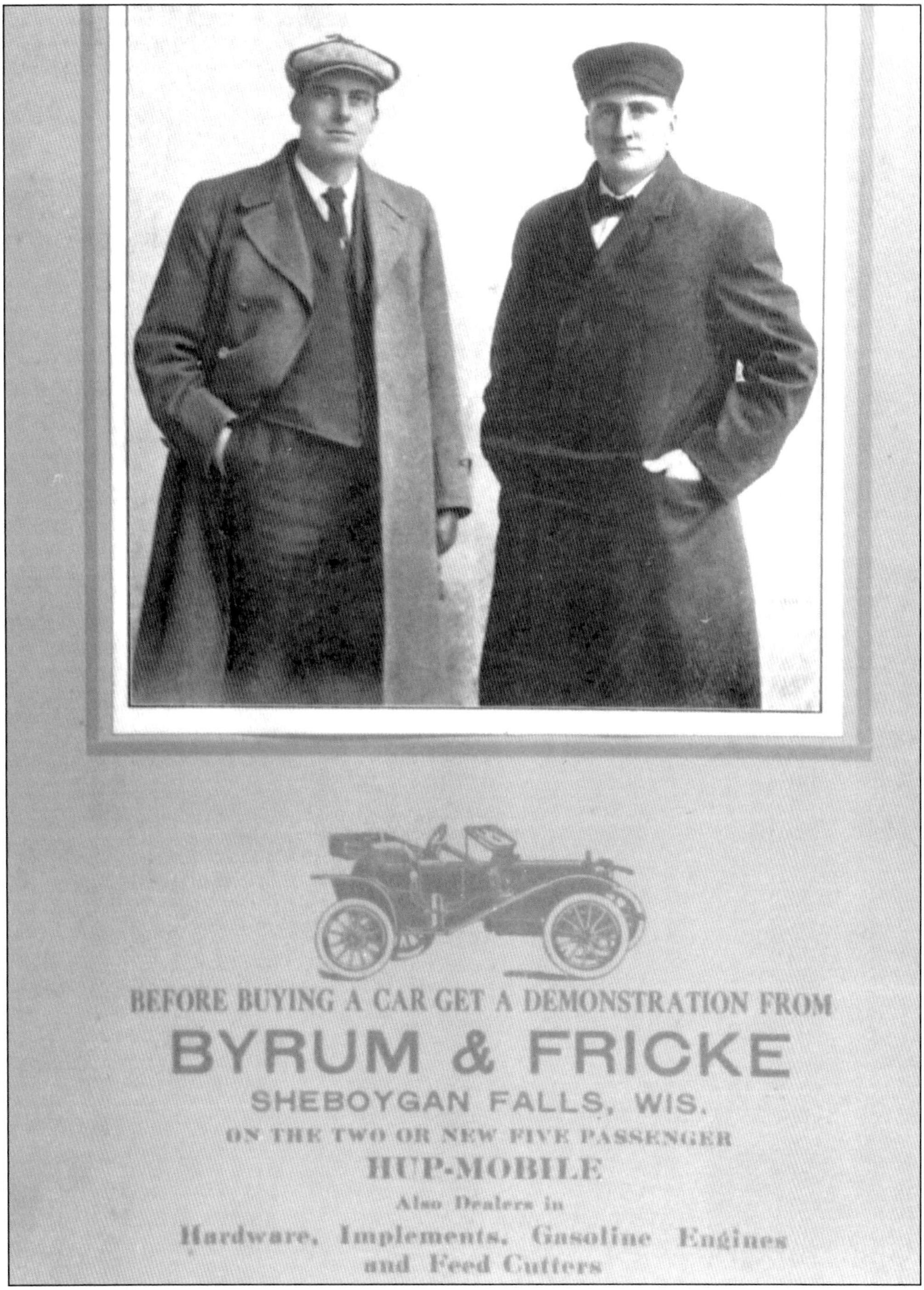

BYRUM AND FRICKE ADVERTISEMENT. This is an ad for the Byrum and Fricke Hardware Store and Hupmobile dealership in 1912. The business lasted only a short time. Later Henry Fricke went into the garage business with his son, Clarence. Hupmobiles were built from 1909 to 1940 by the Hupp Motor Company of Detroit, Michigan. The Hupmobile is pictured on the back of a United States ten dollar bill.

IMAGES
of America

SHEBOYGAN FALLS

The Sheboygan County Historical Research Center

ARCADIA
PUBLISHING

ISBN 978-0-7385-3384-1

Published by Arcadia Publishing
Charleston, South Carolina

Printed in the United States of America

Library of Congress Catalog Card Number: 2006540386

For all general information contact Arcadia Publishing at:
Telephone 843-853-2070
Fax 843-853-0044
E-mail sales@arcadiapublishing.com
For customer service and orders:
Toll-Free 1-888-313-2665

Visit us on the Internet at www.arcadiapublishing.com

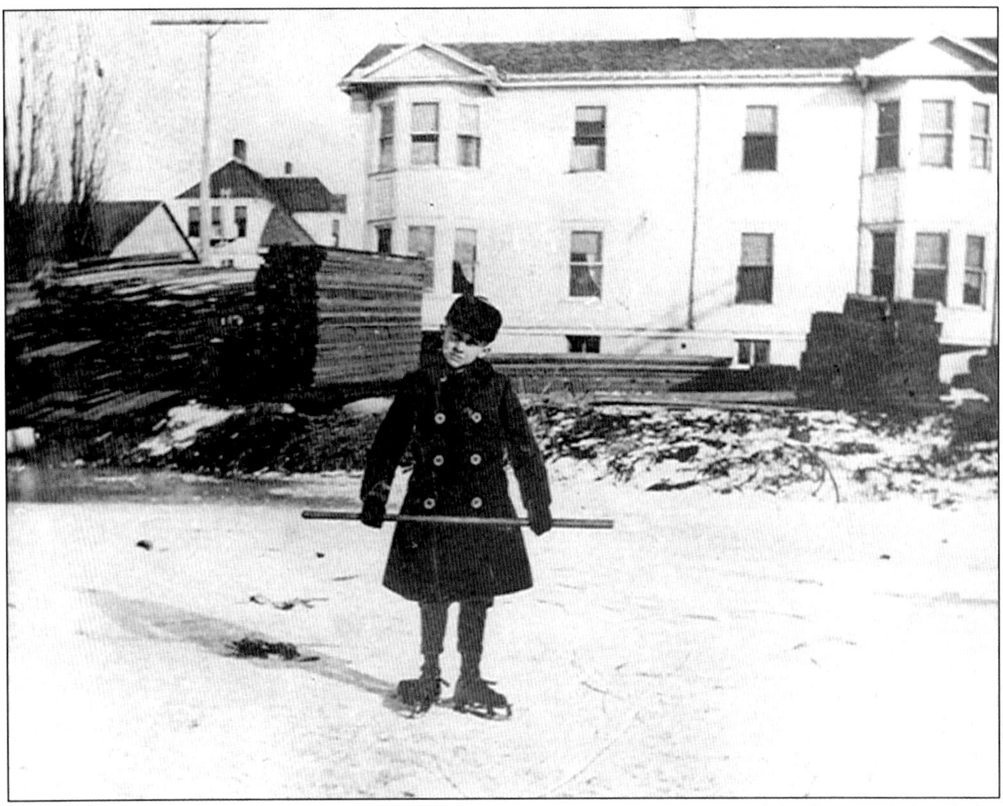

SKATER. Burton Leavens, as a child, is seen skating on a frozen portion of the lagoon behind the R.H. Thomas Lumber Company. The A.E. Henry homestead is seen in the background.

Contents

ACKNOWLEDGMENTS

Local history is nearly always undervalued, but if we examine it closely, we see it is the basis for all other history. It is precious information to be valued for what it is: the record of the daily lives of ordinary people doing ordinary things.

Sheboygan Falls is fortunate to always have had visionary people who understood the importance of documenting the "Here and Now." One of those visionaries was Burton Leavens. Leavens, a 1916 graduate of Sheboygan Falls High School, collected early area photos, and then in the 1950s began taking pictures duplicating earlier scenes in Sheboygan Falls. He preserved the chronology of the main buildings and homes in the city. The Sheboygan County Historical Research Center houses his collection of street scenes, homes, people, and activities, taken in and around Sheboygan Falls from the 1860s through the 1950s. The collection consists of more than 1,000 photographs and is at the core of this publication. We thank Mr. Leavens for his vision.

We also wish to thank the following organizations and members for supporting this local history project:

F.K. Bemis Family Foundation
Bemis Manufacturing Company
Peter and Verena Bachmann
The Jerome Bersch Family as recognized by Cindy and Mike Kuehn
Clicquennoi Family Foundation
Feldmann Engineering and Manufacturing Company
The Leavens, Lumsden, and Matheson Families

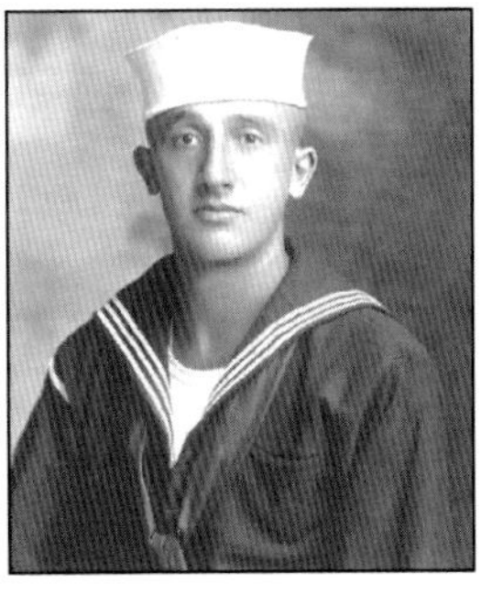

BURTON LEAVENS. Mr. Leavens, renowned local photographer, is shown here while enlisted in the U.S. Navy, 1918–1919.

INTRODUCTION

One often wonders why a town is situated where it is. Why did people settle here when so many locations were available? Well, in the case of Sheboygan Falls, that is quite an easy question. It was the river and the natural falls of the Sheboygan River that drew early pioneers to this spot. Water meant power and transportation. It meant a suitable place for settlement. Water for drinking, cooking, cleaning, and supporting livestock was readily at hand. Water meant the promise of a prosperous future.

In the early 1830s, the land that would become Sheboygan Falls was on the western frontier of the United States. The Native Americans of the area had, for the most part, been moved further west across the Mississippi River. The land was newly surveyed during the winter of 1834–1835, and opened to the public for purchase and settlement. Over the next ten years, the remainder of the county would grow slowly, with a number of setbacks. Real settlement from the east came only in the mid-1840s, when immigrant life began to pour in from the Erie Canal and the Great Lakes. Once Sheboygan Falls began to grow, it never stopped.

Sheboygan Falls, 1835–1976, written by the Sheboygan Falls Bicentennial Committee, states:

> *The town site of Sheboygan Falls was acquired at a public land sale held in Green Bay in November, 1835. The founder of Sheboygan Falls was Col. Silas Stedman, a New Englander, who came to Sheboygan County in 1835. He made his way on foot northward from Chicago. When he reached the Sheboygan River, he passed the night at the Farnsworth mill, the only structure in the county, and started the next morning to explore the country "up river." At Sheboygan Falls he heard the sound of unseen falling waters and descending a steep declivity through dense woods and underbrush saw the "rapid waters of the Sheboygan River dashing down a very rocky ledge." He recognized it was an ideal location for a sawmill and town site, and the best natural water power in the entire county. He returned to the lake and then continued his journey in company with the mail carrier, northward along the lake shore to Green Bay where he found that the sale of lands in Sheboygan County, including the present sites of both Sheboygan and Sheboygan Falls, would take place in November.*
>
> *Obtaining a sectional map of the area around Sheboygan Falls prepared by a government surveyor, Stedman returned to Milwaukee and late in October started once more for Green Bay in order to be on hand for the land sale. He visited the Falls enroute, and with the aid of his maps ascertained the section which contained the Falls. Stedman bid as high as $13.50 an acre, and succeeded in obtaining the land.*

A plat was made of it, which was prepared by H.S. Wright and bears the date of March 31, 1837. This plat was not recorded, and is no longer in existence. Upon this first plat a public square was designated, bounded by Broadway, Maple, Buffalo and Pine Streets; but in 1846 when the village was resurveyed and a new plat made, the public square was eliminated according to Frank Denison. Both the original plat and the replat described the town as Rochester. The United States postal department officially changed the name Rochester to Sheboygan Falls in 1850 and the state legislature confirmed the change by statute the same year.

After the purchase of the Sheboygan Falls town site in 1835, Col. Stedman hired businessman David Giddings to erect a sawmill. Lumber was bringing $50.00 per thousand board feet, at the time, and Stedman saw the business opportunity in this. The mill was located on the south side of Monroe Street at the east approach to the bridge. In a corner of the sawmill Stedman installed a set of stones for grinding flour and grist. It supplied the flour for all the surrounding communities for a number of years. Until it was swept away in the flood of 1883, the Stedman mill at one time or another housed a number of businesses such as the Quinlan rake factory, the Mattoon Chair and Spindle Company, the Taylor Brothers sash, door and blind factory, and the Prentice Woolen Mills.

In 1842, Charles D. Cole started another sawmill and gristmill on the east side of the river south of the old Stedman mill. The Cole family was instrumental in the growth of Sheboygan Falls, opening the first general store, the first temperance lodge and many other firsts. Other pioneers with the names Stedman, Giddings, Trowbridge, Rounseville, Leighton, Denison, Smith, and Leavens provided the "sturdy stock" with which to populate and grow Sheboygan Falls. These early settlers brought their families and friends to the western edge of America in search of a better life and more opportunities for their children.

About 25 years ago, when historic preservation, conservation, and adaptive reuse were terms used only by architects and historians, a few far-sighted residents of the area understood the concept and what it could mean for the city. Thankfully, instead of tearing down most of the beautiful buildings in Sheboygan Falls, the renovations of the 1940s, 50s, and 60s tended just to cover up the historic features. Whether it was frugality or just luck, once the plywood and corrugated metal siding of those past eras was pulled off the Greek Revival-style beauties of the city, their true potential could be seen. After the first building or two in the city was rehabilitated, there was no turning back. The photos included in this book show the good, the bad, and some of the ugly. They are here to show from whence we came. The properties were beautiful to begin with. Then they fell on tough times, but now they're back, more beautiful than ever. Enjoy the changes. Enjoy the travel through time and remember this is only a handful of the images available.

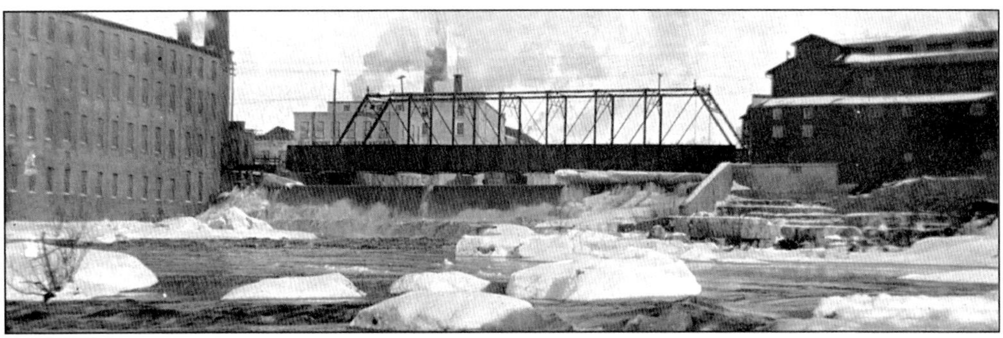

Lower Falls Looking Upriver. This winter scene of the ice-clogged Sheboygan River running through Sheboygan Falls at Monroe Street shows the Brickner Woolen Mills on the left. The Brickner Woolen Mills warehouse is seen on the right. This photo predates the 1905 flood.

One

PIONEERS

The earliest pioneers in the area were Yankee trailblazers from New England and New York, well-settled descendants of English immigrants, already residents of the United States for some 200 years by the time they arrived in Sheboygan County. In 1848, Sheboygan Falls was 12 years old, but growth had been slow for the first six years. In 1842, there were only four families and as many houses there. These were the residences of Silas Stedman, the Rochester Lumber Company mill house, where 12 people lived, the home of Charles Cole where 12 more people lived, and across the river, the David Giddings home on the southwest corner of Broadway and Pine Streets. The river had been bridged in 1841, it being the source of power which drew the settlers to the city. The population grew steadily after this point in time. A June 1849 *Sheboygan Mercury* article written by the editor, Mr. Gillett, stated, " To close we will state Sheboygan Falls contains about 700 inhabitants with as few idlers as can be found in any place in the west. These inhabitants are possessed with energy and enterprise. The place must become one of importance."

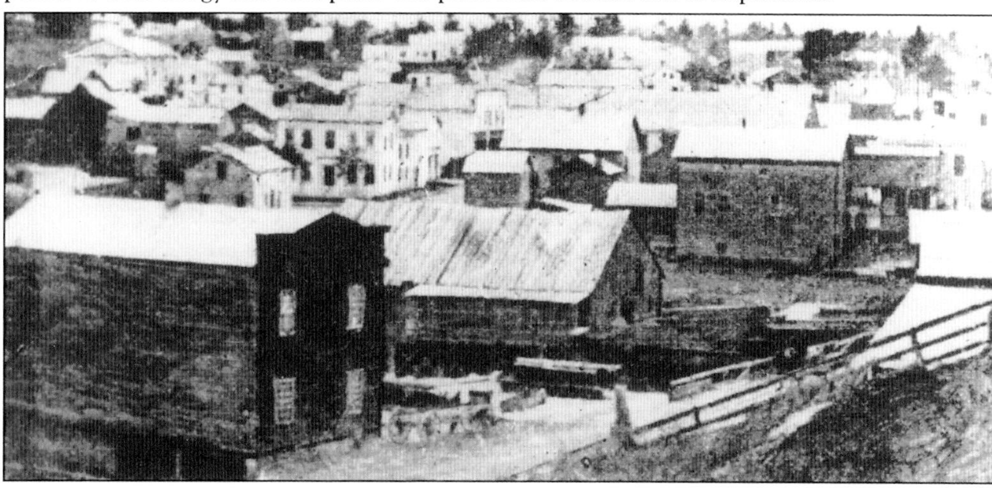

EARLIEST STREET SCENE OF SHEBOYGAN FALLS. This is the earliest known photo of Sheboygan Falls. It was reprinted from a daguerreotype taken by William Henry Paine in the early 1850s. The view is from the elevation of the east side of the Sheboygan River looking southwest. The Methodist church is visible in the left center of the photo. The two-story building, slightly off center, with five windows across the front, was the home of David Giddings, located on the southeast corner of Pine and Broadway. It burned in 1879.

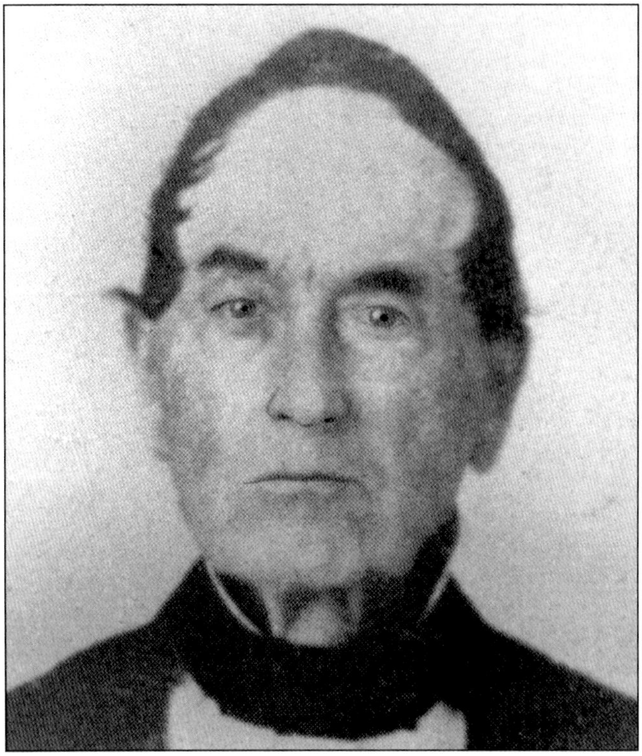

SILAS STEDMAN. The first man to purchase land in what would become Sheboygan Falls and settle here was Silas Stedman. A native of Massachusetts, he purchased the land in 1835 and arranged to have the first sawmill built. It was located on the east side of the river at the site of the falls. This was the first business in Sheboygan Falls, then called Rochester.

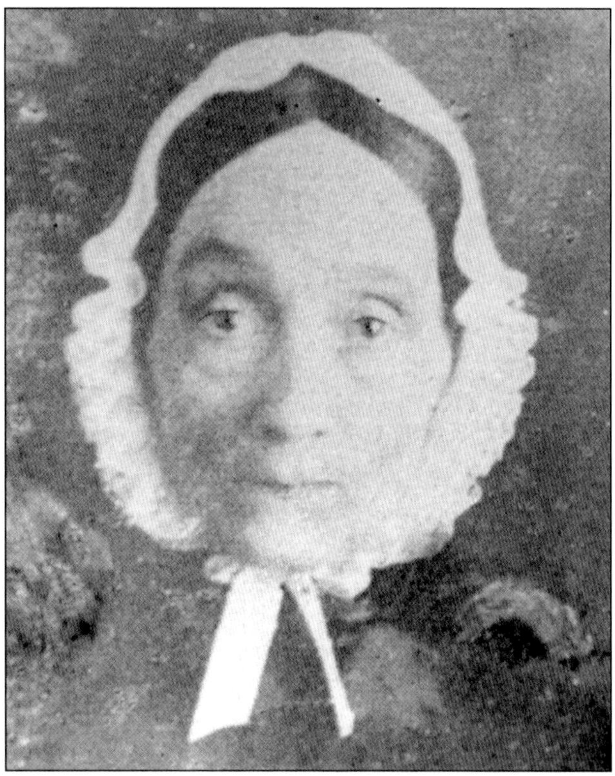

BETSY BOLLES STEDMAN. Elizabeth Bolles Stedman, Silas' wife, followed her husband to Wisconsin in 1836. The couple had no children and the first years in the village must have been very lonely. Contemporaries remember her as a well-groomed lady always wearing a dainty lace cap tied around her neck.

CHARLES D. COLE. Probably the most important settler in Sheboygan Falls was Charles D. Cole. As the second postmaster of the county, Cole convinced many fellow New Yorkers to move to the county, including his mother (after the death of his father), sisters, brothers, and his wife's family. He was a trader, store owner, farmer, financier, government land agent, registrar of deeds, and founder of the first Temperance Society in Wisconsin.

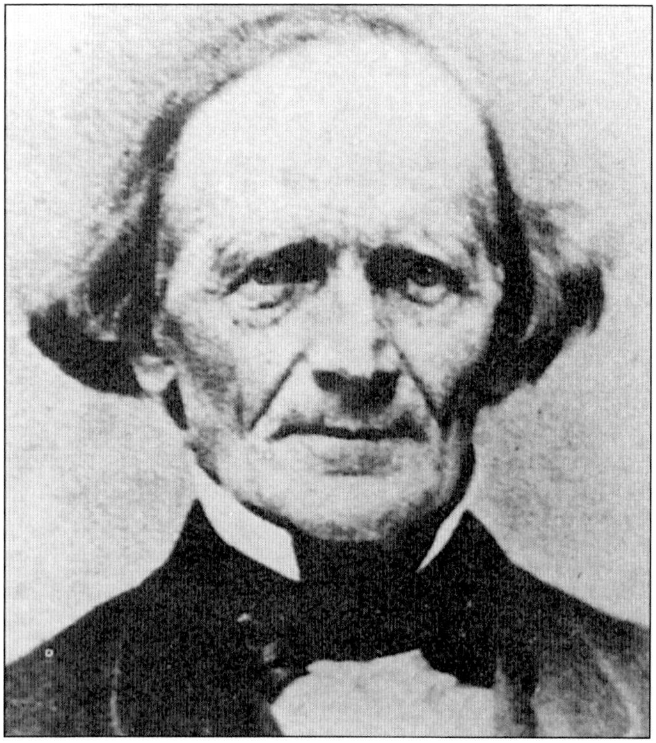

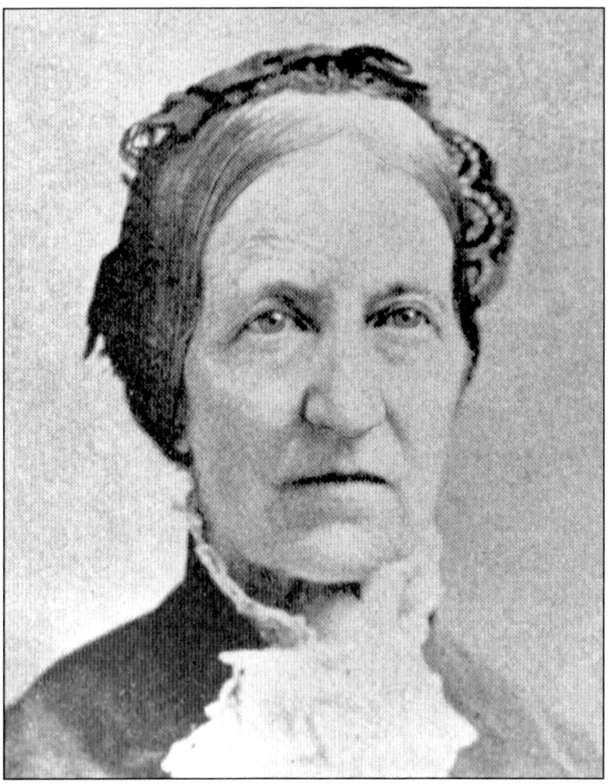

SARAH TROWBRIDGE COLE. Charles Cole's wife, Sarah Trowbridge, was a guiding light in the small community, teaching school in her home. She was a founding member of the First Baptist church congregation begun in 1838. Her parents and siblings followed the Coles to the Wisconsin Territorial wilderness.

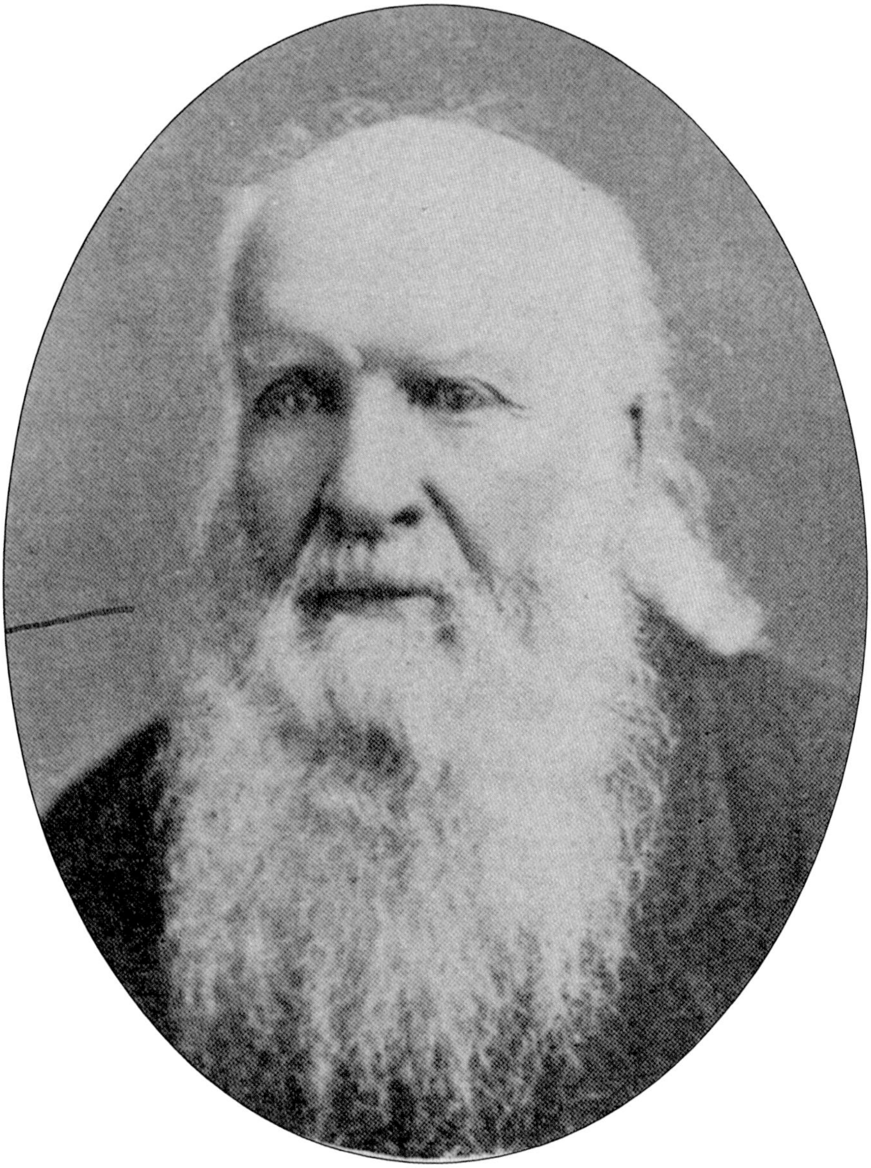

DEACON TROWBRIDGE. Born October 16, 1790, in Massachusetts, Deacon William Trowbridge married Dorothy Chapin in 1812. The couple had eight children. The family came to Sheboygan Falls in August of 1837 from their home in Tompkins County, New York. The family made the entire trip to Sheboygan County by the Great Lakes, and at the end of four weeks their vessel anchored in the lake opposite the site of Sheboygan, where they were transferred to shore in an old scow. Trowbridge purchased land from his son-in-law and daughter, Charles and Sarah Cole. Mr. Trowbridge is considered the first man to operate a farm in Sheboygan County, establishing a farm along what is now Highway C about one-and-a-half miles west of Sheboygan Falls. He was also a blacksmith, whitesmith, and lay preacher, being one of the founders of the Baptist Church. Trowbridge was the first preacher in the county who held regular services, from his arrival until his death in 1880. Deacon William Trowbridge died on November 20, 1880, in his 91st year, at the residence of his son, James L. Trowbridge.

DAVID GIDDINGS. David Giddings moved to Sheboygan Falls in 1838 where he purchased a half interest in Stedman's sawmill and almost 400 acres of land. He surveyed a large area of Wisconsin, served in the territorial legislature, and was a member of the House of Representatives. In 1839, he surveyed the road and later built the first bridge across the Sheboygan River at Sheboygan Falls. He established the Giddings farm which remained in the family until 1907.

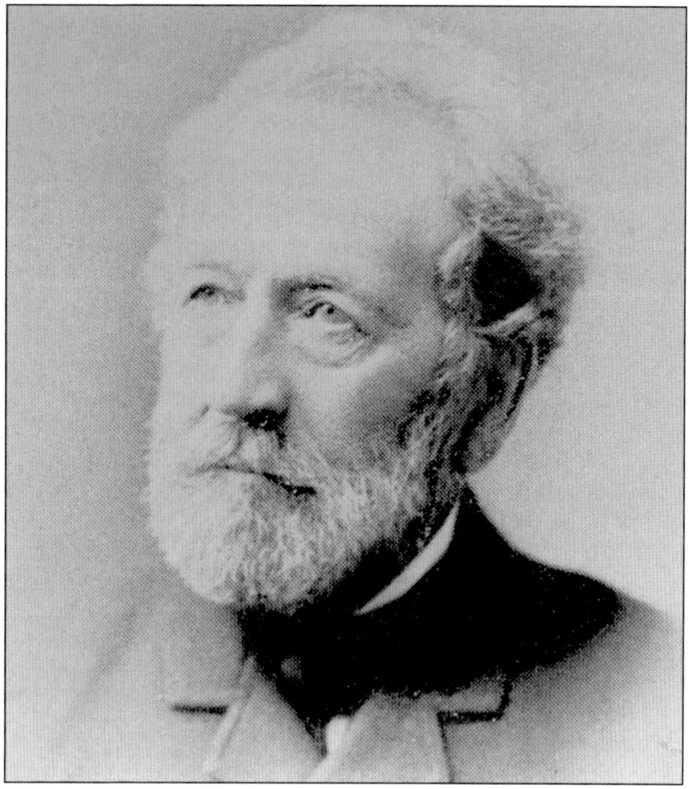

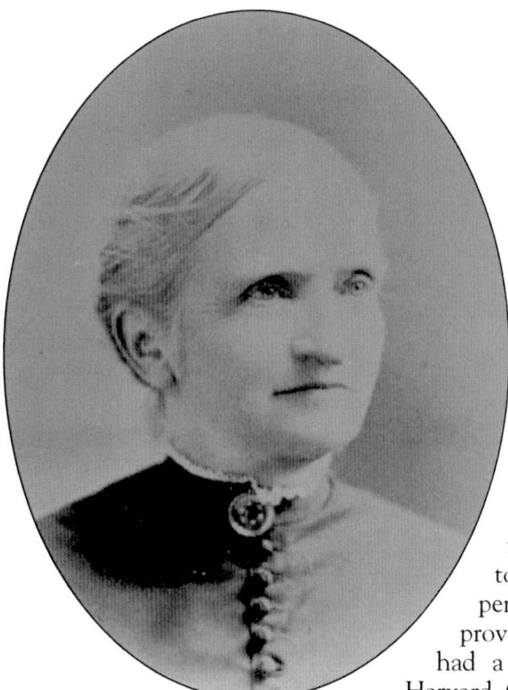

DOROTHY TROWBRIDGE GIDDINGS. Dorothy Trowbridge and David Giddings were married June 7, 1842, and the whole village turned out for the festivities. The celebration was held on Deacon Trowbridge's farm located just west of the village on what today is County Highway C. The Deacon performed the ceremony, with neighbor ladies providing the wedding feast. Dorothy and David had a long, happy marriage and three children, Harvard, Clara, and George.

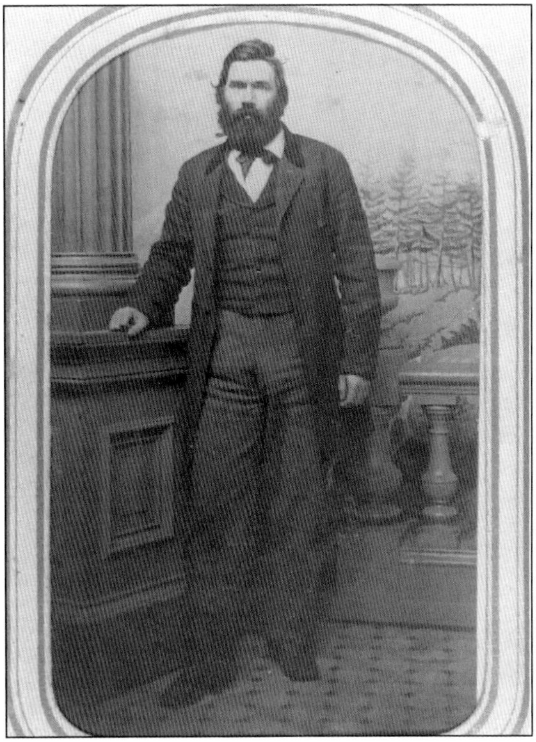

SAMUEL ROUNSEVILLE. Samuel Rounseville came to the Falls in 1841, following his half-brother Albert and Albert's wife, Lucy Trowbridge, daughter of Deacon Trowbridge. Rounseville taught school in the first schoolhouse in 1842 and 1843. He went on to operate one of the first plant nurseries in the area, on 100 acres along what is now the Curt Joa property on Fond du Lac Avenue.

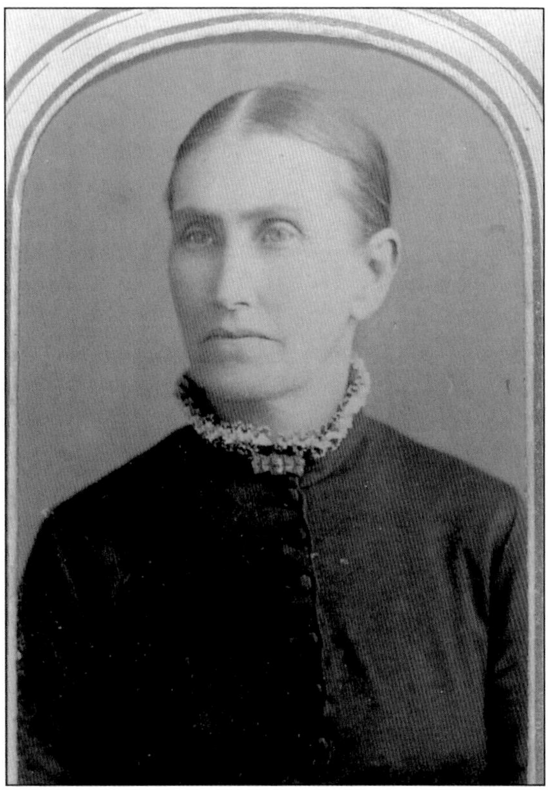

NANCY KITTELL ROUNSEVILLE. Samuel Rounseville returned to New York in 1847 to marry his love, Nancy Kittell. Nancy and Sam had 12 children, two of whom, Daniel and Hoyt, became connected with the Chicago and North Western Railway. None of the Rounseville sons were interested in the family business, so in 1878, their extensive property was sold to James Crocker. The couple operated a small farm south of the falls in the town of Wilson until their deaths.

JONATHAN LEIGHTON. Jonathan Leighton, born in Maine, was orphaned at a young age and made his way working on a farm, doing carpentry, and working as a joiner. In the spring of 1844, the Leightons arrived in Sheboygan Falls. Joining his father-in-law, Leighton went into the lumbering business. Later, the two built a sawmill on the west side of the river at the lower dam. In 1855, he purchased 127 acres along the river at what is now Kohler. His heirs sold the property to Walter Kohler in 1915. The property is known as Riverbend today.

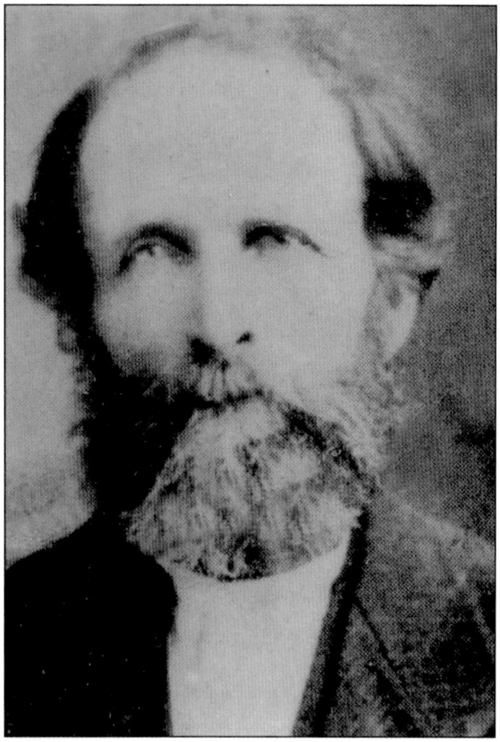

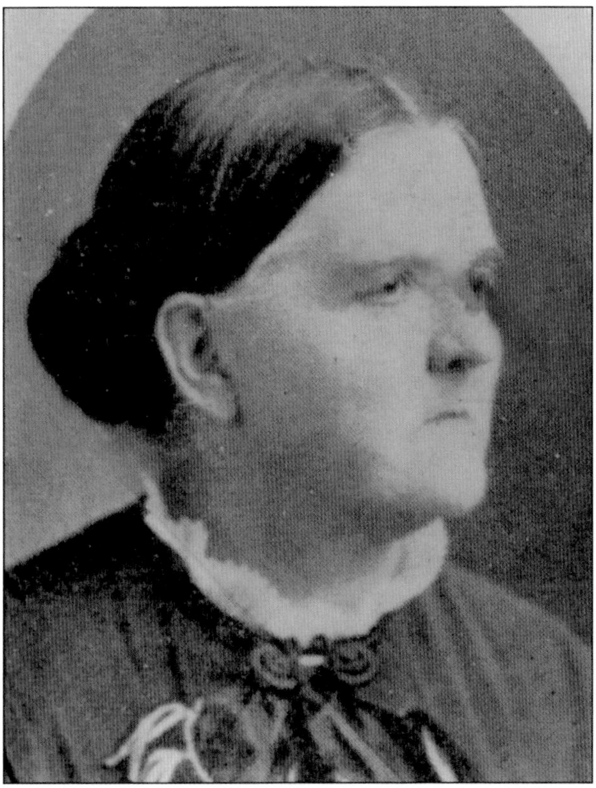

ELIZABETH LEIGHTON. Elizabeth Littlefield Leighton and Jonathan married in 1839. They had eight children; six survived into adulthood. Jonathan went west to look for gold in 1863 and didn't return for seven years. Elizabeth was left to run the farm and raise their children alone. She was successful in both endeavors, and upon his return home the couple lived happily until their deaths. Jonathan died in 1897 and Elizabeth in 1913. Both are buried in the Sheboygan Falls Cemetery.

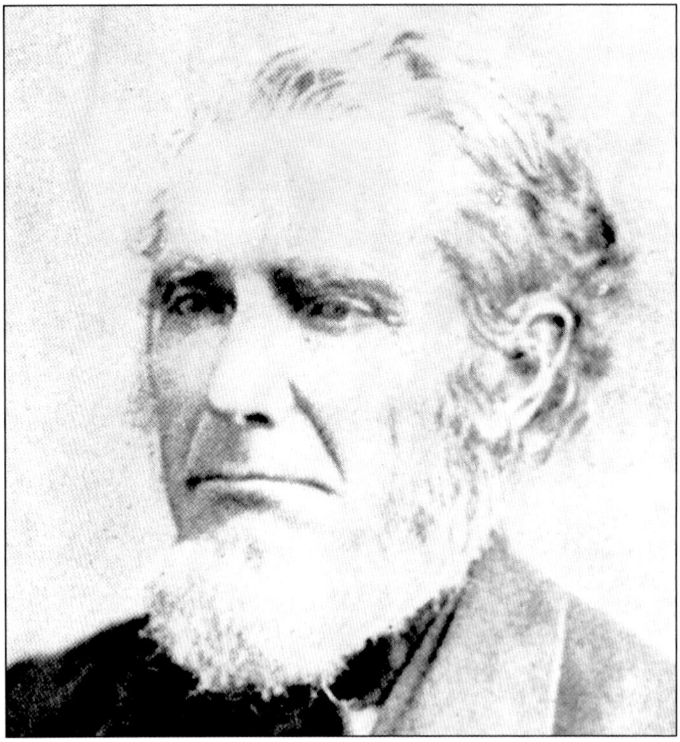

JAMES DENISON. James H. Denison was born in New York in 1817. He married Louisa Cole in 1846, and shortly thereafter the couple moved to Sheboygan Falls. Denison followed his trade as carpenter for six years, then purchased an additional 80 acres to join his 160 acres and turned to farming. He was an astute farmer, recording climatologic information, crops grown, and the results. In his later years, he turned to historical writing and contributed many articles to newspapers and historical atlases, as well as publishing his memoirs.

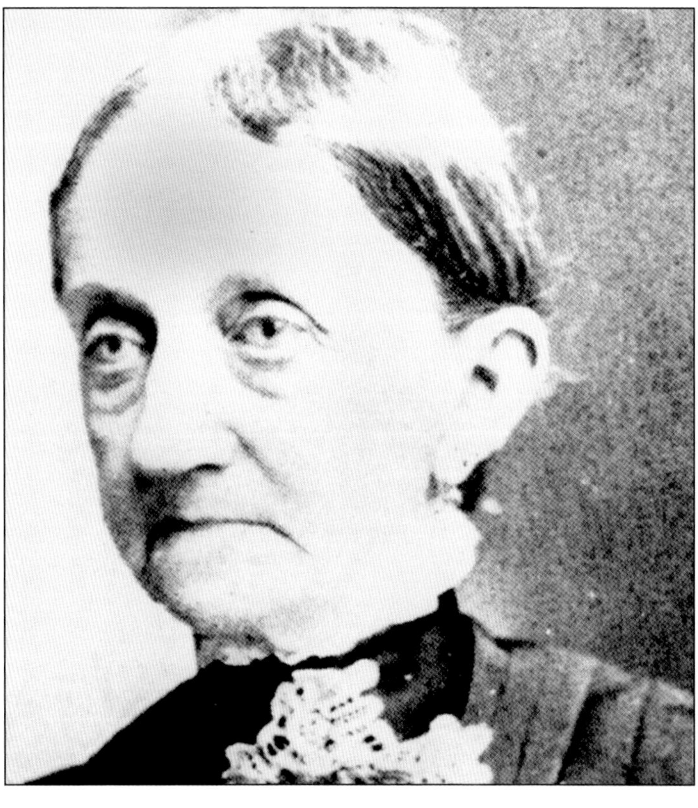

LOUISA COLE DENISON. Louisa Cole Denison and her husband James had six children; all of them married into other pioneer families. Mary married into the Leavens family, and Gertrude into the Bemis family. Their grandchildren married into the Giddings, Laun, and Schreiber families, all early settler families.

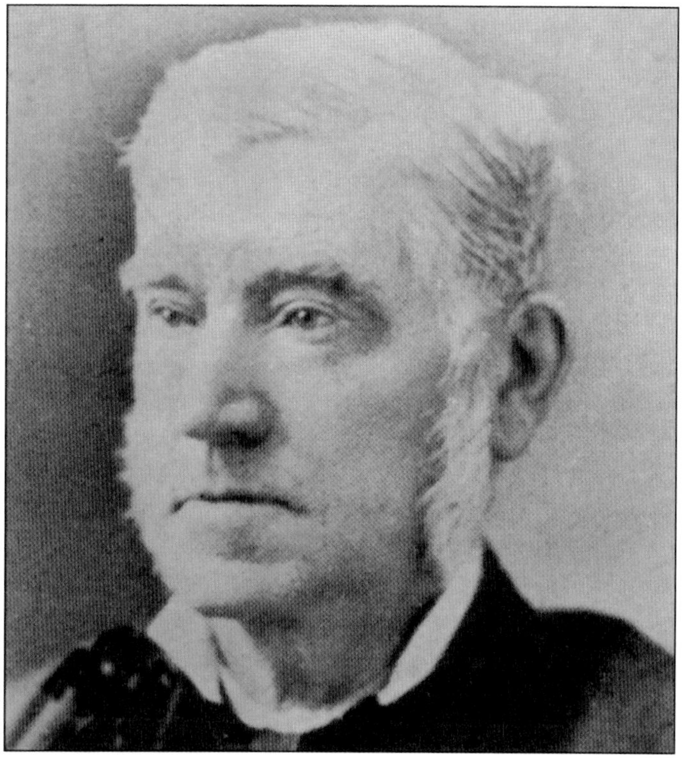

HIRAM SMITH. Hiram Smith came to Sheboygan Falls in 1847, settling near the village with his family. He commenced dairying in a small way in 1858, making some cheese and butter. He started the first creamery in the county in 1880. It was run by treadmills worked by horsepower. He is credited with being the man who did the most to make the college of agriculture at the University of Wisconsin-Madison a mecca for dairy scientists.

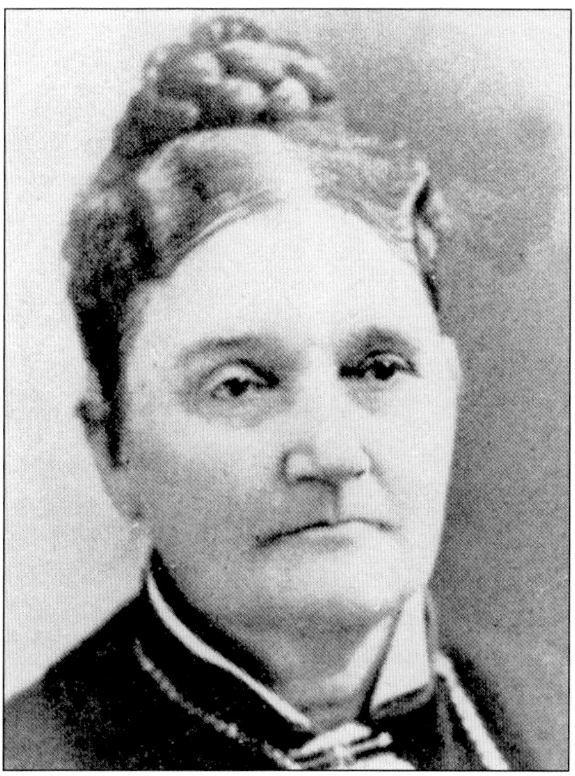

CATHERINE CONOVER SMITH. Smith married Catherine Conover in 1845. They had two children: a daughter, Lizzie, who married H.K. Loomis, and Henry, who died at the age of 14. In their later years, Hiram and Catherine lived with their daughter and son-in-law in Sheboygan Falls.

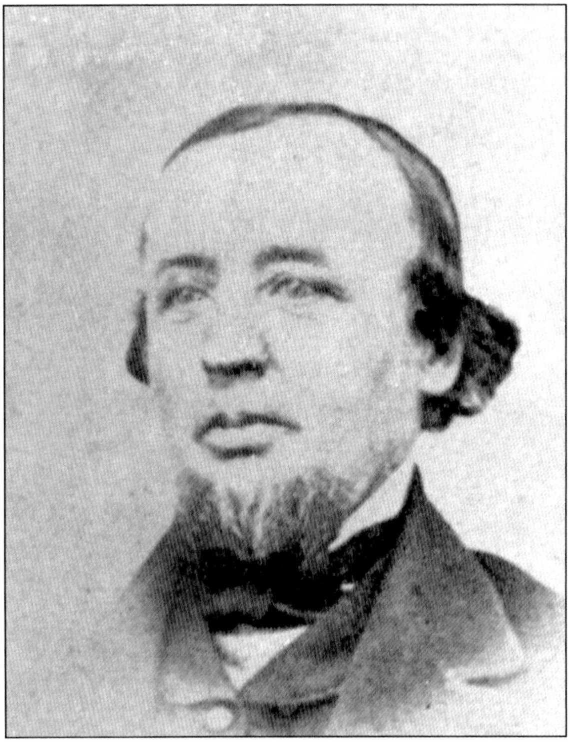

DARIUS LEAVENS. Darius Leavens came from Vermont shortly after his marriage to Hulda Bayley in 1848. He was a master carpenter and joiner and had a farm on Leavens Avenue. He and his wife raised a family of three children, Fred, Hannah, and Almon; all three married into other pioneer families of Sheboygan Falls. The Leavens homestead, a landmark, burned in 1995.

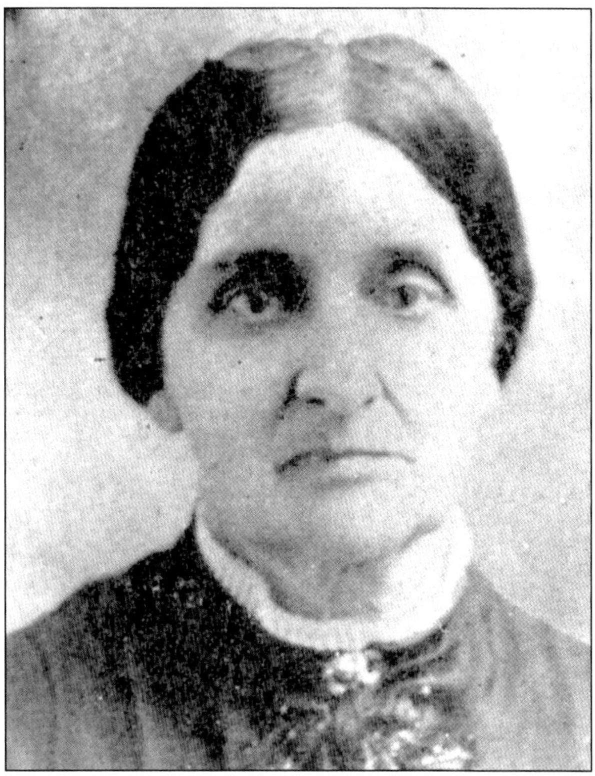

HULDA BAYLEY LEAVENS. Hulda Bayley, wife of Darius Leavens, was widowed in 1868, and in 1879, went to live with a married daughter in Greeley, Colorado. Her remains were brought back to Sheboygan Falls for burial beside her husband in the Falls Cemetery.

Two

CHURCHES AND RELIGION

Religion is a quiet constant in the lives of the citizens of Sheboygan Falls. Two churches, the Baptist and the Methodist, were not only the first congregations in the county, but also in the State of Wisconsin. Churches were central to the daily lives of the residents, and each ethnic group brought their own distinct denomination with them, creating a wonderful diversity in the community that remains to this day. The churches, along with being the center of religious life, were the centers of social and family life. Meetings of all kinds were held in church halls. Some of the churches ran their own parochial schools, ensuring that the spiritual lives of these early settlers were well cared for. Included here are photos of all the known houses of worship that have been located in Sheboygan Falls. Many have made a number of moves. Happily, a church is a church, no matter the faith.

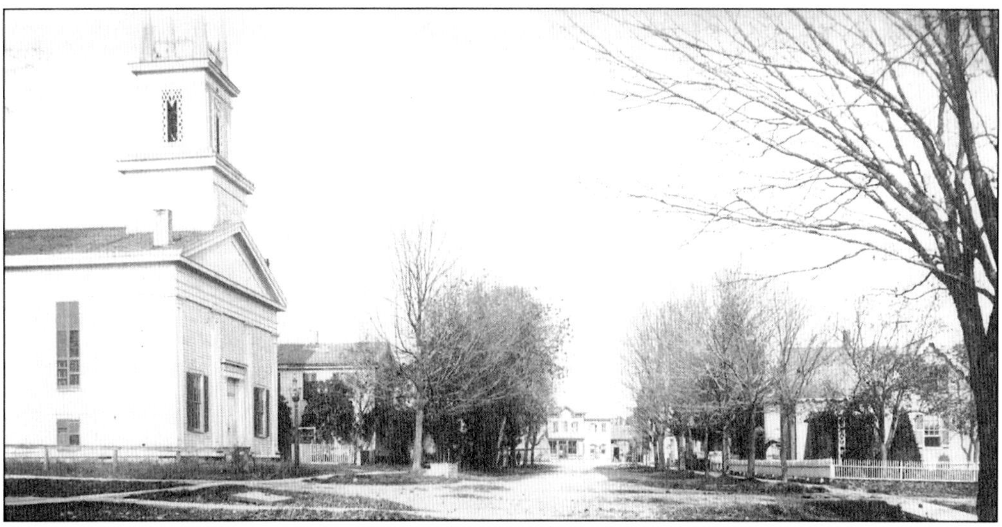

METHODIST CHURCH WITH ITS FOUR SPIRES. This image shows an early street scene of Sheboygan Falls; this is Detroit Street looking north past the Methodist Church toward Pine Street. This early fall photo, probably taken in the 1880s, shows the dirt streets, plank sidewalks and young trees of a prosperous village.

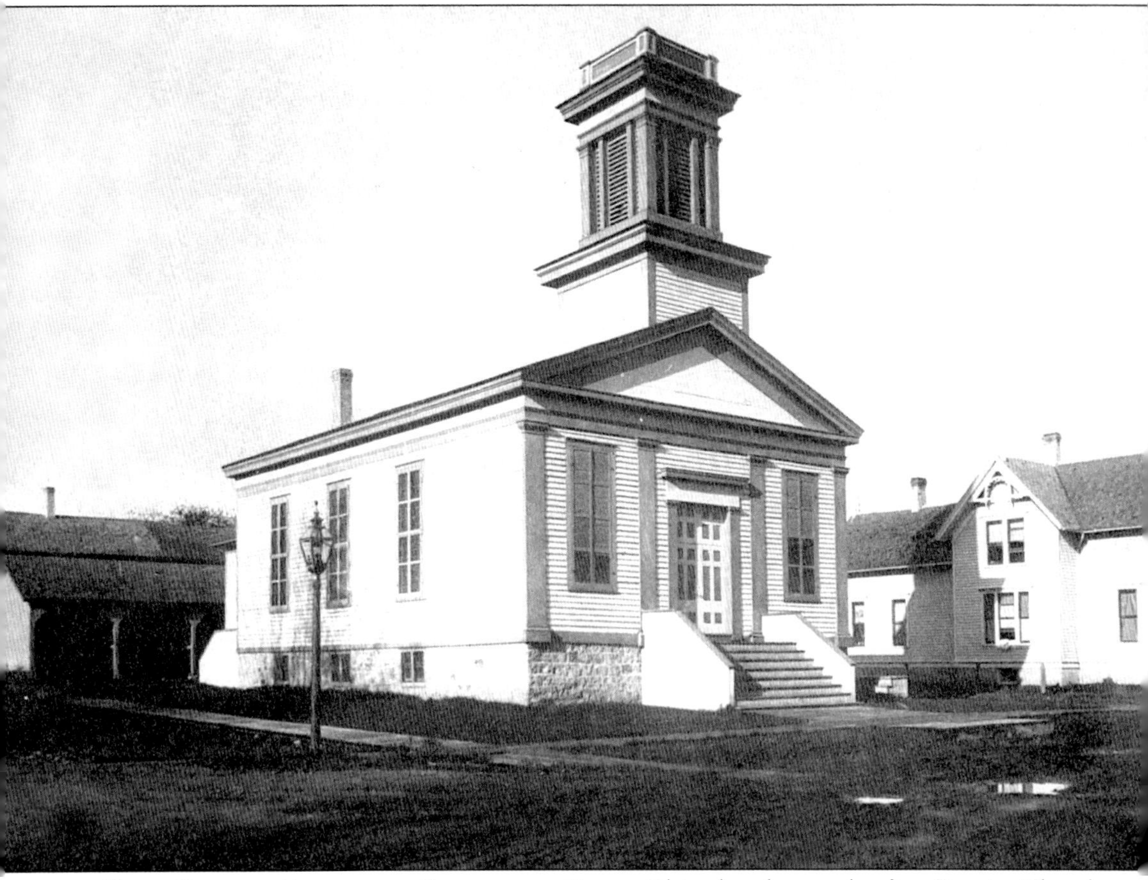

First Baptist Church of Sheboygan Falls. This church was the first Baptist Church established in the State of Wisconsin and the oldest congregation in Sheboygan County. Organized in Sheboygan at the home of A.S. Dye in 1838, the following year it moved to Sheboygan Falls. Meetings were held every Sunday, first in members' homes, then in the schoolhouse, and finally, a church building was erected in 1849–1850. This picture, dated 1898, is the second site of the church. Originally, it was built along the river near what became known as Baptist Bay, for the baptisms performed there, on the site of today's Wells Fargo Bank. On summer evenings it was reported that the croaking of the frogs could drown out the ministers' sermons. Later, the railroad was built near the church, and the constant rumblings of the trains shook the building and threatened to topple it. The building was jacked up, put on rollers, and moved down the street to its present location at 633 Buffalo Street.

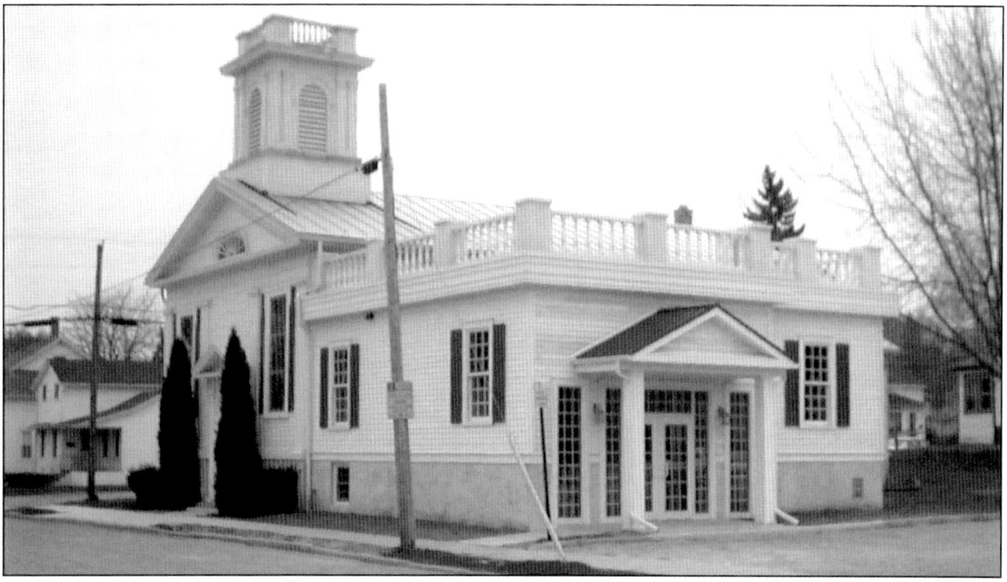

Falls Community Church. In 1993, First Baptist Church became the Falls Community Church. The name change reflected the diversity of the congregation, which welcomed everyone, but retained its ties with the American Baptist Denomination. In 2000, the first major change to the structure of the church occurred when an addition was built to accommodate handicapped-accessible bathrooms and an elevator. The Rev. Marty Carney serves the congregation as of 2004.

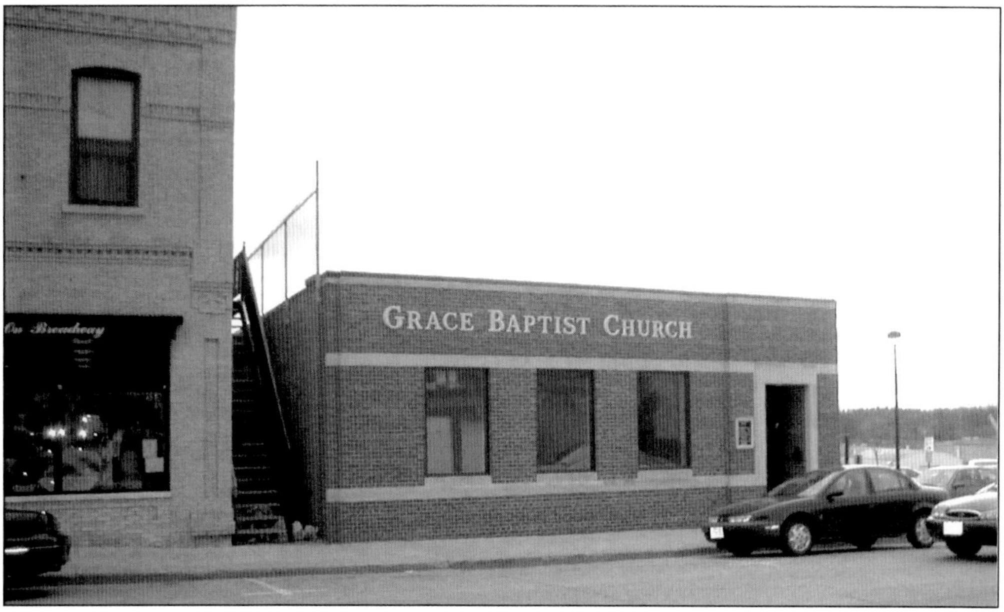

Grace Baptist Church. Begun by Pastor Larry Taylor, associate pastor at the First Baptist Church in Sheboygan Falls, this group began meeting in the cafeteria of the middle school and then the local YMCA in 1997. In 1999, the congregation purchased the old telephone company building at 614 Broadway. As it is an independent Baptist church, the pastor stresses a more fundamentalist emphasis on the Bible and its teaching, preaching, and application of the Bible to everyday situations and everyday life.

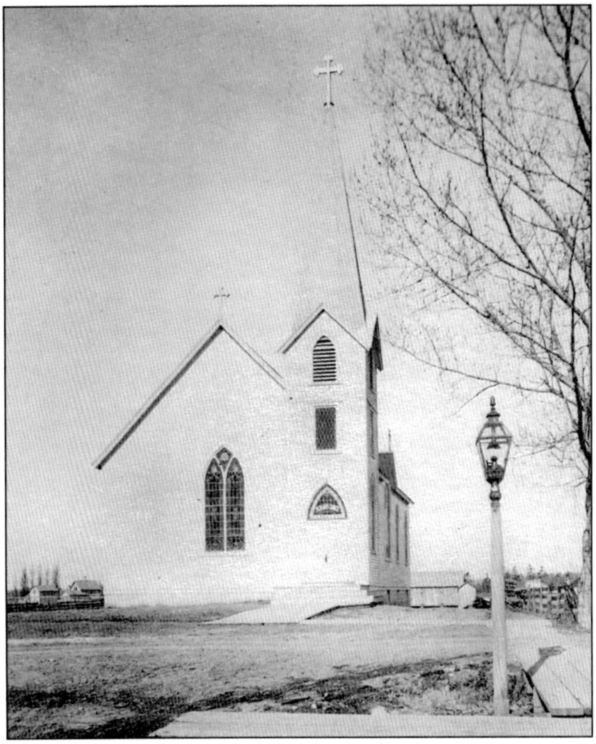

ST. MARY CATHOLIC CHURCH. The St. Mary congregation was organized largely through the efforts of George H. Brickner. The first mass in the church was said by Father Thill on January 1, 1897. This 1898 image shows the original 1896 white wood and clapboard church built on Giddings Avenue. In this photo, the streets were still dirt, the walkways were boardwalks, and the lighting was kerosene.

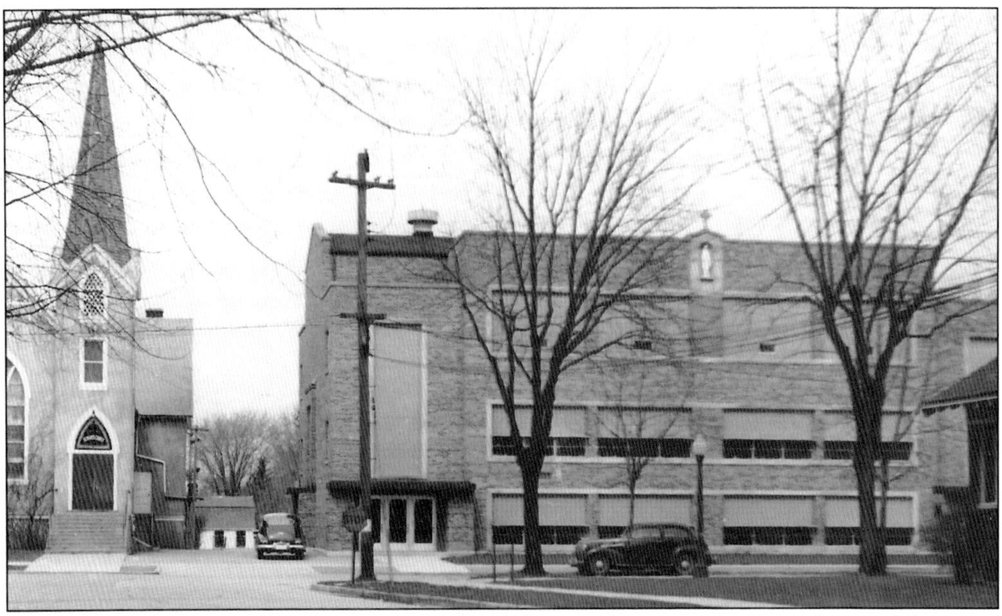

ST. MARY CHURCH AND SCHOOL. Growth of the parish soon necessitated remodeling and expanding the church building. The church was remodeled in 1920 for $15,000. Work on a parish parochial school began in spring of 1950, and it was completed and ready for its more than 300 students on September 5, 1951. By the mid-1960s, the church was crowded again, and three Masses were needed on Sundays with two more on Saturday nights to accommodate the large congregation.

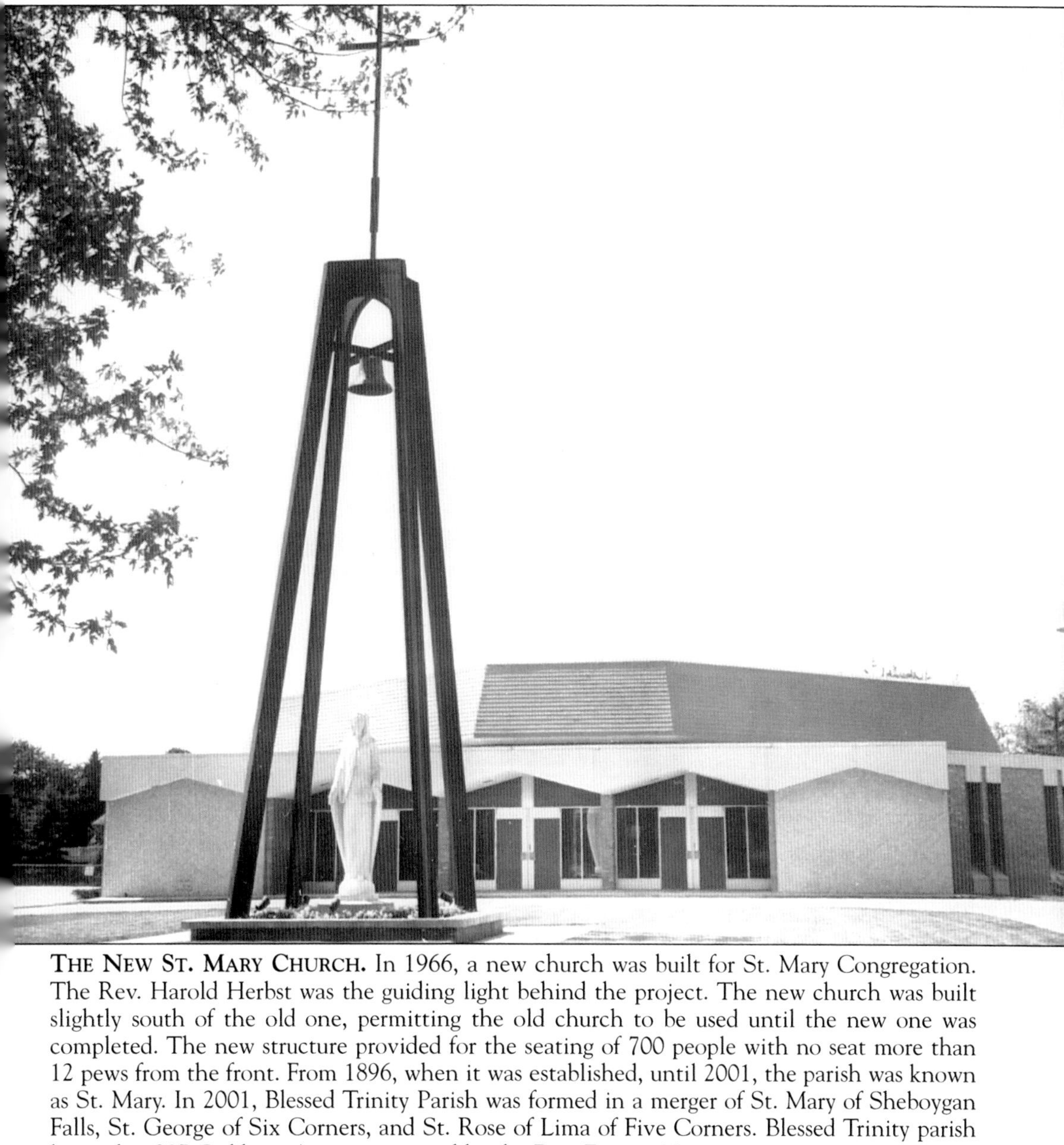

THE NEW ST. MARY CHURCH. In 1966, a new church was built for St. Mary Congregation. The Rev. Harold Herbst was the guiding light behind the project. The new church was built slightly south of the old one, permitting the old church to be used until the new one was completed. The new structure provided for the seating of 700 people with no seat more than 12 pews from the front. From 1896, when it was established, until 2001, the parish was known as St. Mary. In 2001, Blessed Trinity Parish was formed in a merger of St. Mary of Sheboygan Falls, St. George of Six Corners, and St. Rose of Lima of Five Corners. Blessed Trinity parish located at 327 Giddings Avenue is served by the Rev. Eugene Neuman.

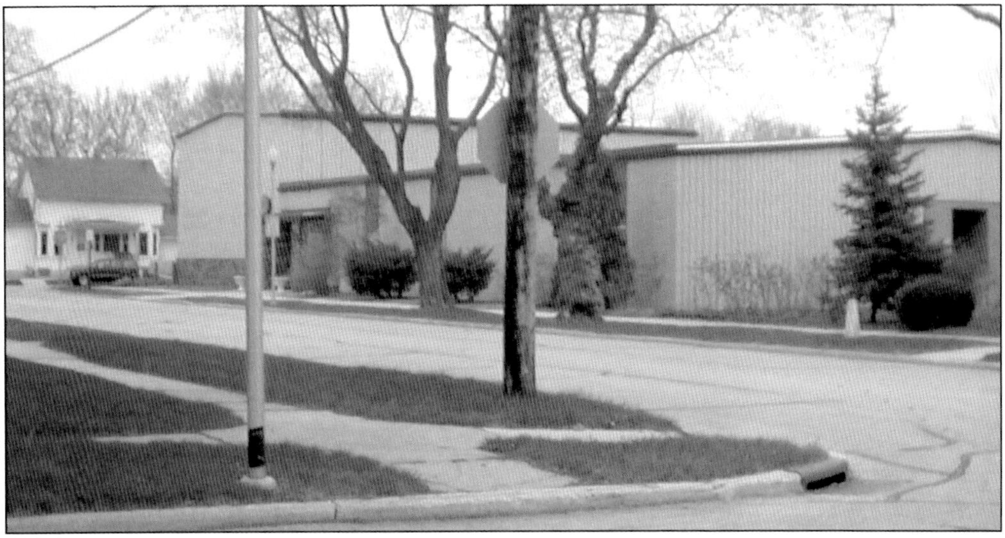

WORD OF GRACE. Word of Grace Community Church was established by the Rev. Kirby Andersen in 1990, evolving from the Faith Fellowship which began about 1980. Rev. Andersen's leadership caused the membership to soar. The church had moved to the former telephone company switching station at 614 Broadway in 1989. In September 1994, they began renting the St. Paul Education Center for meetings. In 1996, the church moved into the Education Center, leasing it from St. Paul congregation. St. Paul sold the Education Center and the former 1869 parsonage to Word of Grace.

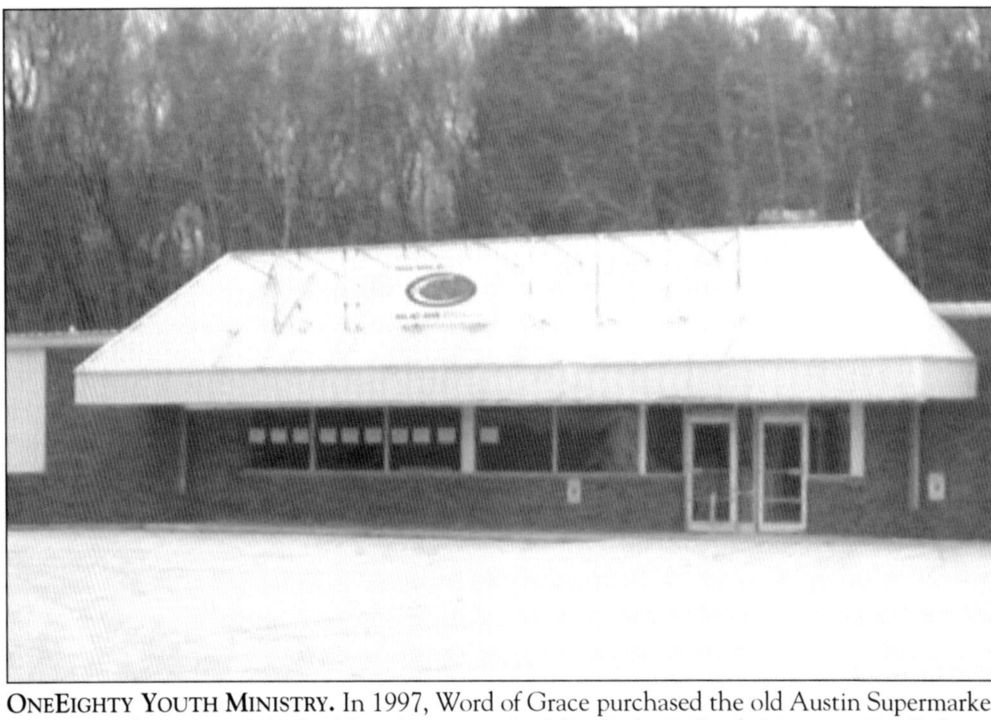

ONEEIGHTY YOUTH MINISTRY. In 1997, Word of Grace purchased the old Austin Supermarket building and renovated the building for use as the "OneEighty" Youth Ministry. OneEighty is located at 837 Buffalo and the Word of Grace Church remains at 121 Cedar Street.

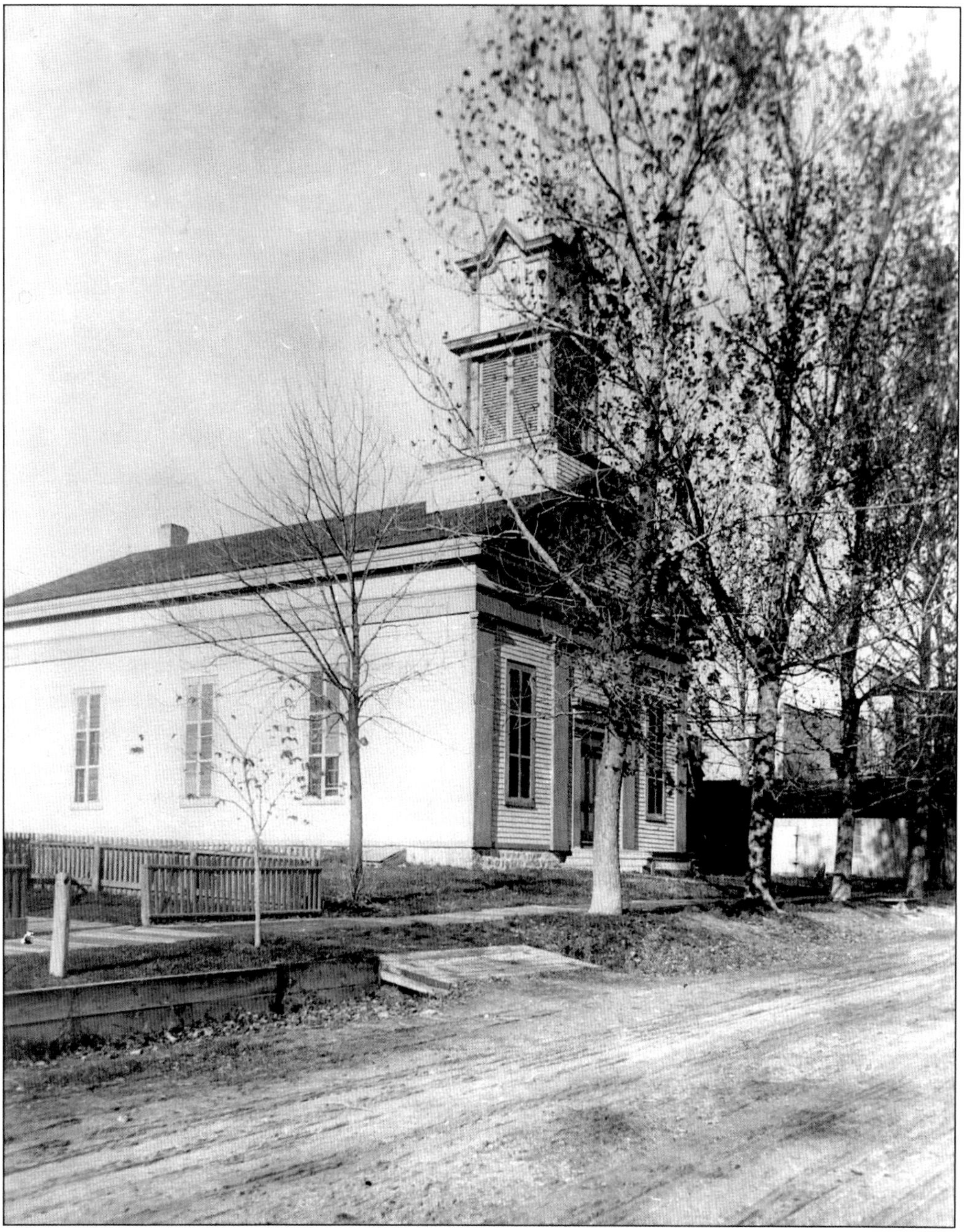

CONGREGATIONAL CHURCH. The Congregational Church was established in 1847 under the leadership of the Rev. Hiram Marsh. The thirteen members began meeting in the schoolhouse, until 1854 when they erected their own church building at 621 Broadway. Membership eventually rose to 250 people but began dwindling in the 1880s. The membership then disbanded. The building was sold for $1,050 and converted into a Lutheran Church. Members of St. Paul used the church until they built a new church in 1915. They sold the old building to the Thomas Lumber Company on Buffalo Street. The steeple was removed and the building became the meeting place of the Farmers Equity Society of Sheboygan County. In later years the building was used to store ice, before it was finally razed.

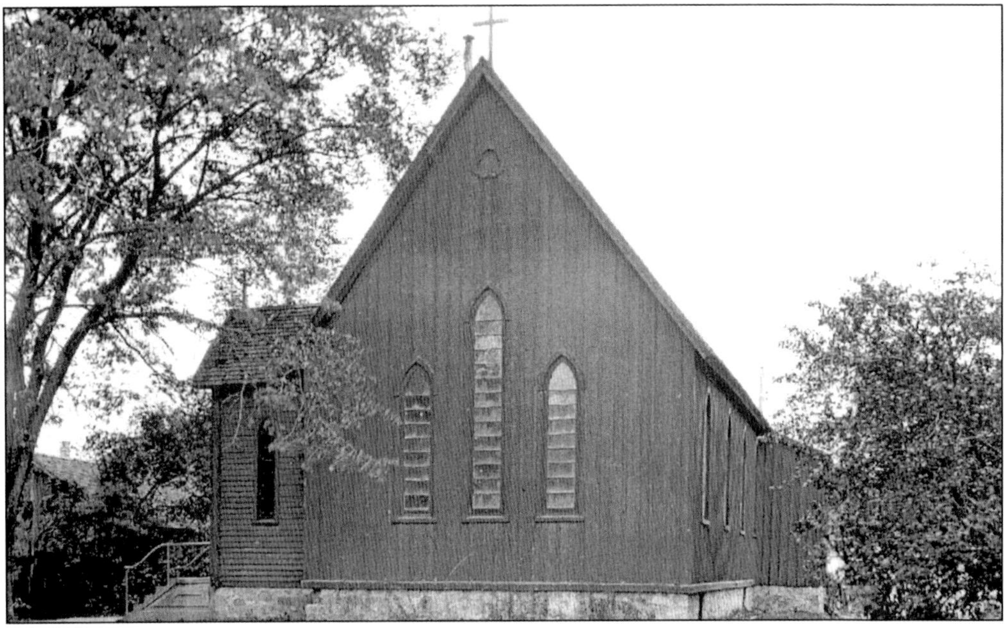

ST. PETER EPISCOPAL CHURCH. St. Peter Church was established as a mission congregation of Grace Episcopal Church, Sheboygan in 1864. The Rev. Robert Blow was the first priest to serve the mission. The first services were held in the Free Hall. Later services were held in the schoolhouse and in Chamberlain Hall. The cornerstone of the first church was laid June 8, 1869. This first church was built on Broadway on a bank above the river. Subsequent spring floods washed away much of the lower bank and the church was in danger of sliding down the embankment.

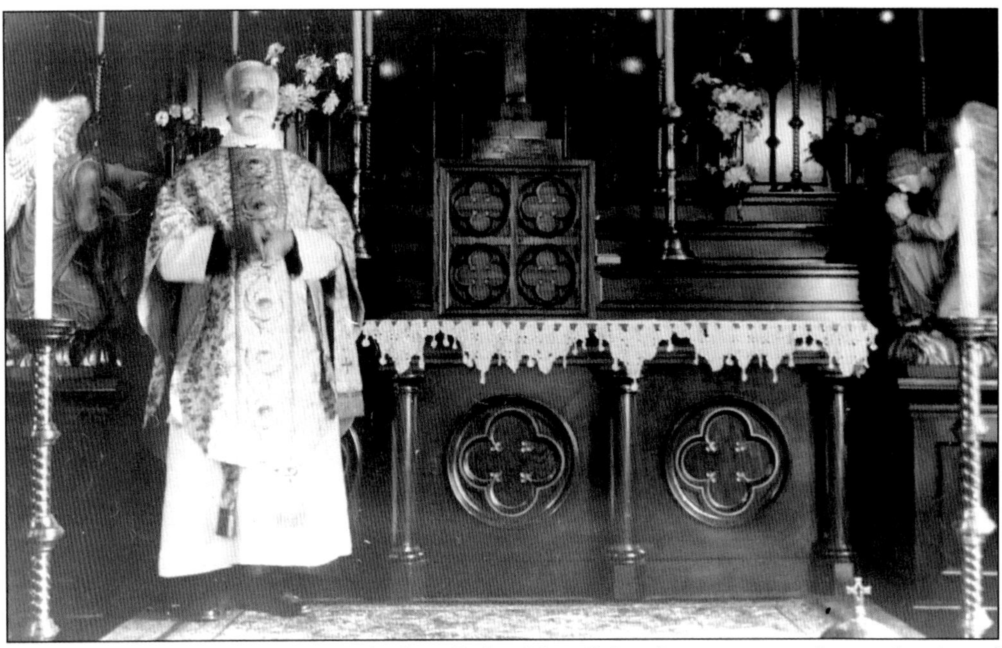

ST. PETER EPISCOPAL INTERIOR. The Rev. Father Newell Stanley is seen standing at the altar of the first St. Peter Episcopal Church in this c. 1910 photograph. Father Stanley came to St. Peter Church in 1885 and remained until 1920. He was the first resident priest of the church.

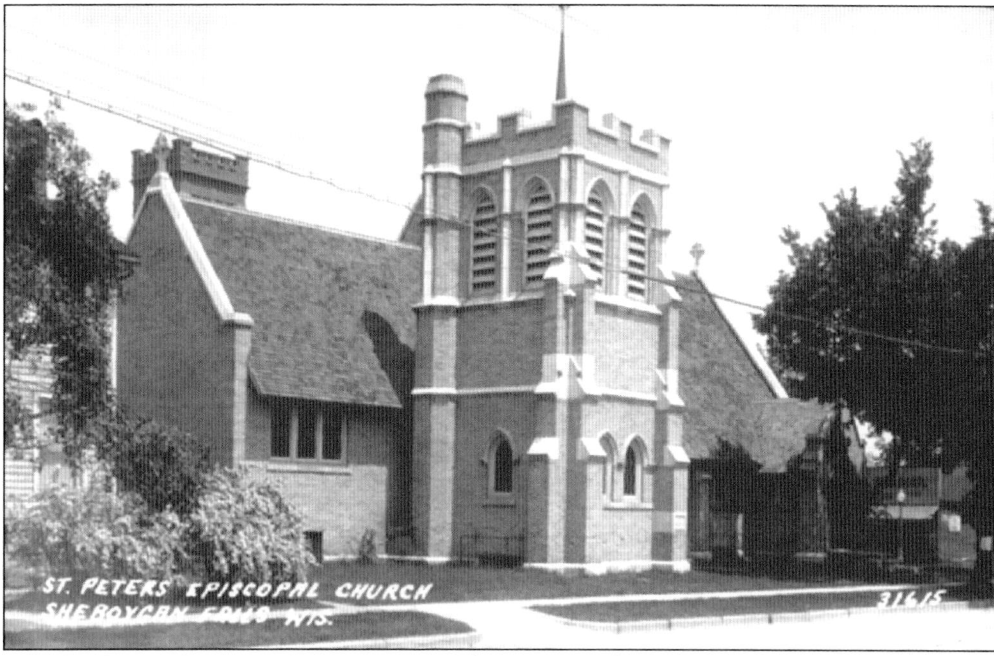

New St. Peter Church. At a meeting in February 1925, the vestry voted to build a new church. Ground was broken in August, the cornerstone laid in October, and the building was consecrated on September 12, 1926. The English Gothic building stands at 104 Elm Street. On Palm Sunday in April 1998, the church was devastated by fire. Damages were set at $500,000. The congregation vowed to rebuild and by Christmas, the church reopened. The following April, the church's 135th anniversary was celebrated. The church is served by the Rev. Father Samuel Nsengiyumva.

St. Paul Evangelical Lutheran Church. Organized in 1855, The Rev. Stecher, pastor of Trinity Lutheran Church, Sheboygan, gathered the several Lutheran families in Sheboygan Falls and organized a congregation. The first services were held in private homes, and later in the school house. The first church was erected in 1858 and cost $400. When the congregation outgrew this building, it was sold to John Kerskamp and used as the back part of his foundry. The second church was the former Congregational Church on Broadway which was purchased from the trustees for $1,050 in 1890.

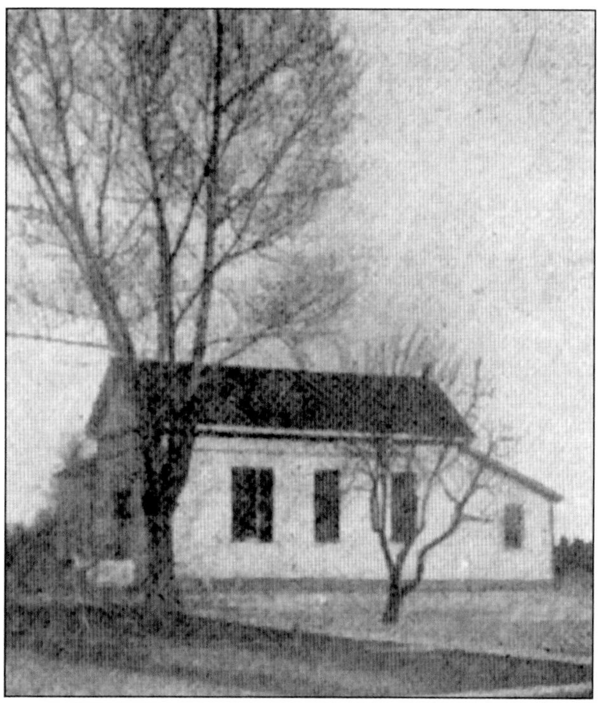

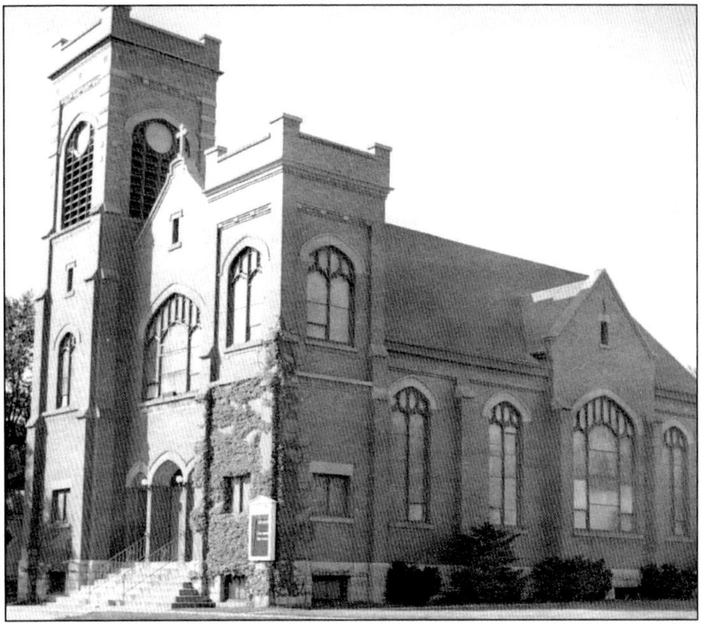

ST. PAUL EVANGELICAL LUTHERAN CHURCH. The third home of St. Paul Church was the site of the old Congregational Church in 1915. The completed brick church cost $25,000. Services were conducted in the German language until 1917. The first English service was held in the fall of 1917. A new education facility was built in 1978. In addition to classrooms, it had a kitchen and gym. In 1990, the planning committee proposed to build a new church.

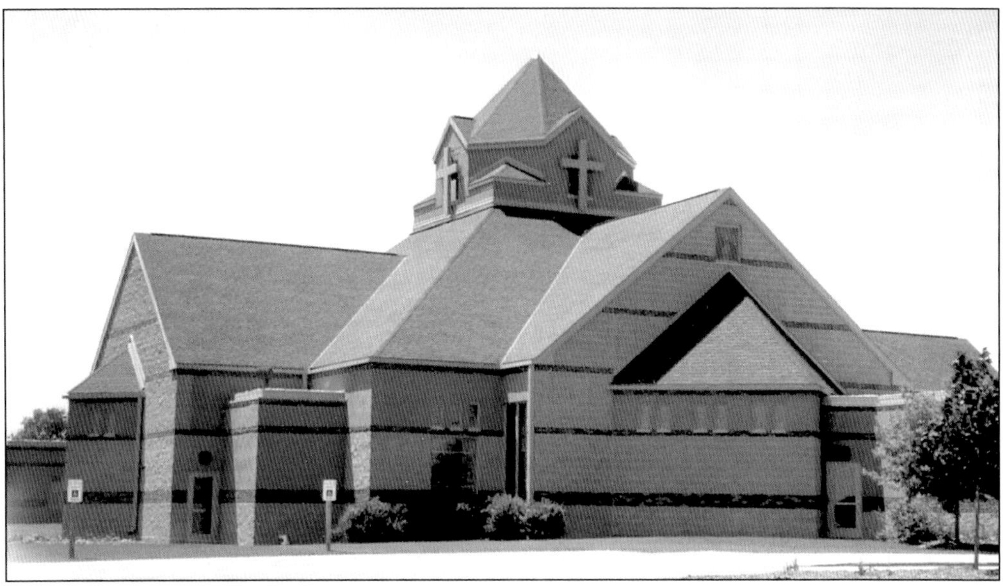

NEW ST. PAUL LUTHERAN CHURCH. Construction for a new church facility began in the fall of 1994. Phase one of the 17,000 square foot building was dedicated October 21, 1995. Seating is available for 500 worshipers and there is also an administration office suite, a gathering area, small offices, a library, and a 225 vehicle parking lot. Phase two, known as the new Christian Life and Learning Center was dedicated December 4, 1997. The congregation is served by the Rev. Thomas Gudmundson and is located at 730 County Road.

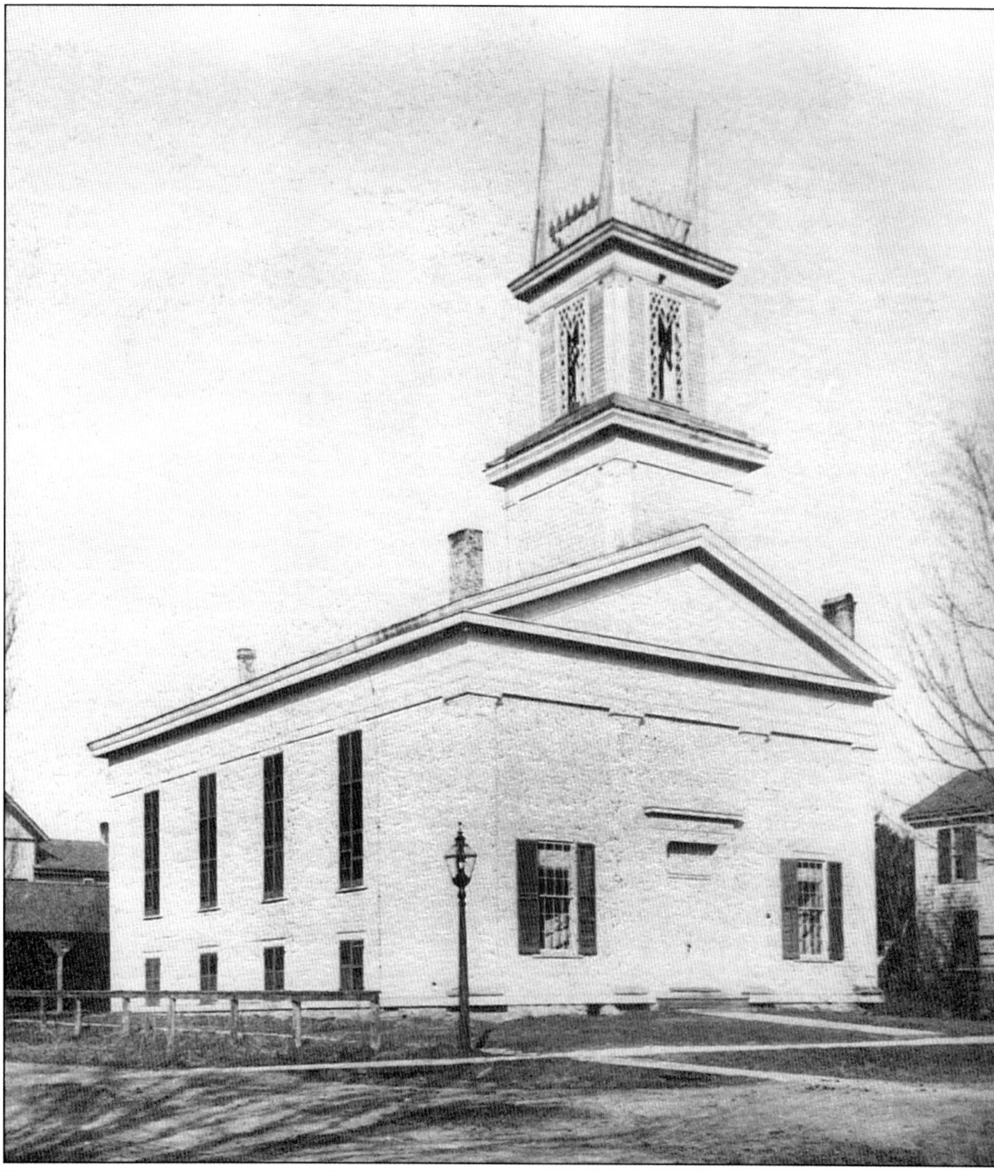

FAITH UNITED METHODIST CHURCH. The second church to be organized in Sheboygan Falls was the Methodist Church. In the early days of settlement, circuit ministers served the area, coming as early as 1837. By 1846 there were about 13 members of the Methodist-Episcopal Church in Sheboygan Falls. Rev. L.S. Prescott became their pastor. In 1847 lots were purchased for a church and a parsonage. Services were held in the schoolhouse, private homes, and Chamberlain Hall. In 1851, members of the congregation built their church. They drew the plans, cut the lumber from local trees and made the spindles, altar rail, and cherry wood turnings at the nearby Quinlan rake factory. The single story edifice, 40 by 60 feet, had a full basement. The foundation was of field stone and mortar. It is considered the finest Greek Revival-style building in the city today. The bell tower is unique to the church. It is topped by four spires, one at each corner of the tower. An addition was put on in 1967 for a religious education unit. Outside of the addition to the rear of the church and updating the church, it looks the same as it did in 1851.

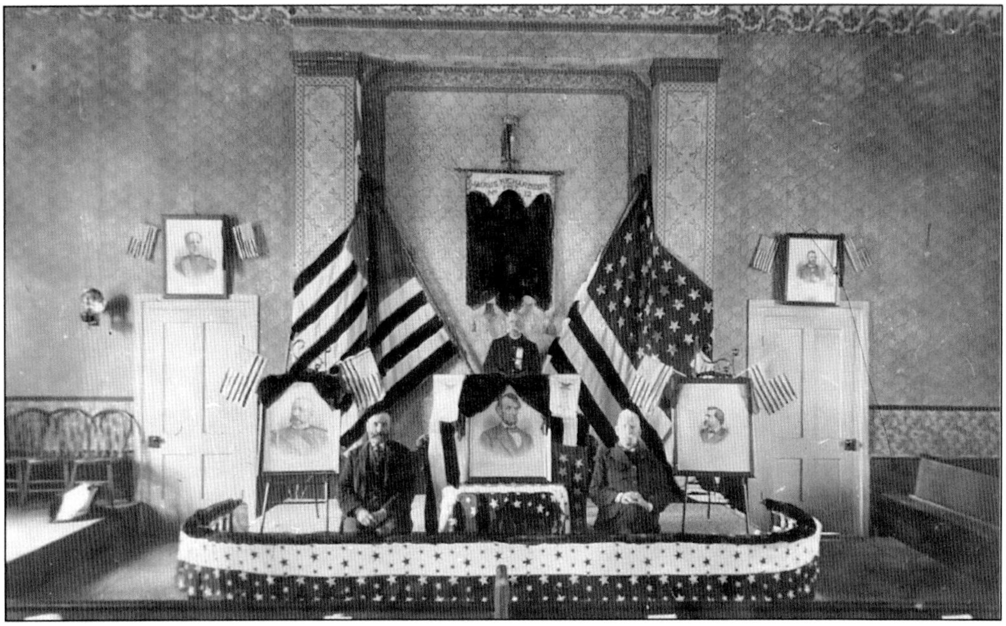

METHODIST CHURCH INTERIOR. Pictured here is the original altar area decorated for Memorial Services by the G.A.R. in 1921. Seated, from left to right, are Charles Hermann, Charles Marsielje, and William Burges. Today the pastor is the Rev. Donald Drollinger. The church is located at 633 Detroit Street.

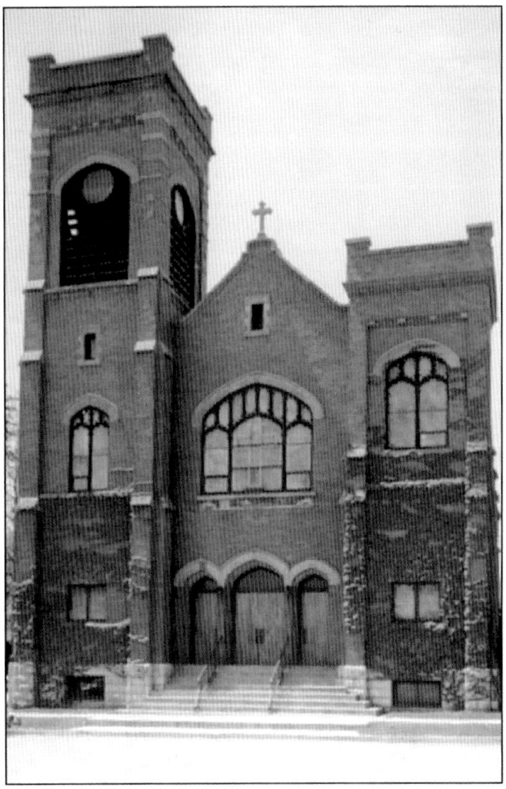

FIRST PENTECOSTAL CHURCH. The First Pentecostal Church of Sheboygan Falls was begun in Plymouth by a small group of citizens in 1986. In 1988, the congregation purchased land to build their own church. In October 1990, the first service was held in the new building. As a means of fundraising, the cooks of the congregation made and sold peanut brittle. By 1996, the congregation was outgrowing its simple building, and purchased the old St. Paul Church in July of 1997. Located at 621 Broadway, the First Pentecostal Church is now served by the Rev. Lowell Snow.

THE FIRST REFORMED CHURCH. The First Reformed Church of Sheboygan Falls was organized on July 21, 1856. In 1866, a site on Buffalo Street was purchased for $220, with the first church being built in 1883. This building at 314 Buffalo Street served as a place of worship for the next 68 years. The first resident pastor, the Rev. Fred J. Zweemer, was called in 1898. This church later housed numerous businesses and still stands today, across from the YMCA.

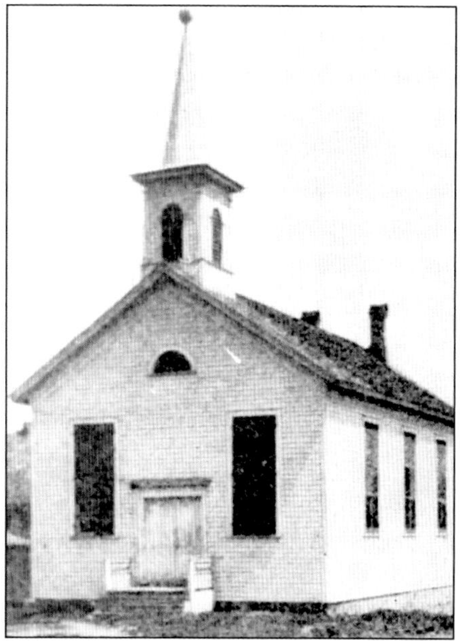

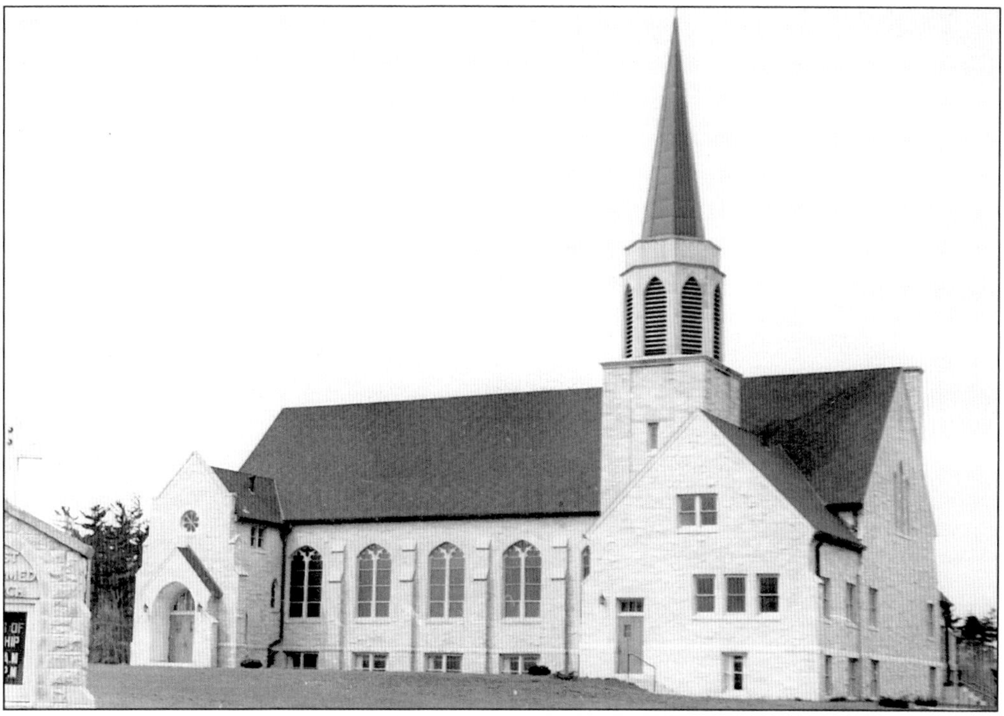

NEW FIRST REFORMED CHURCH. Plans were started in 1948 to replace the long-outgrown first church building. The new church was dedicated November 27, 1951. An extension to the church was made in 1985. Another, made in 1999, added 22,000 square feet for a family life center containing a new library, fellowship area, three offices, and a work room. Lightning struck the south side of the sanctuary on August 6, 2000. Damage was estimated at $150,000, but the church was quickly repaired. The Rev. Jeremiah Fyffe serves the church located at 527 Giddings Avenue.

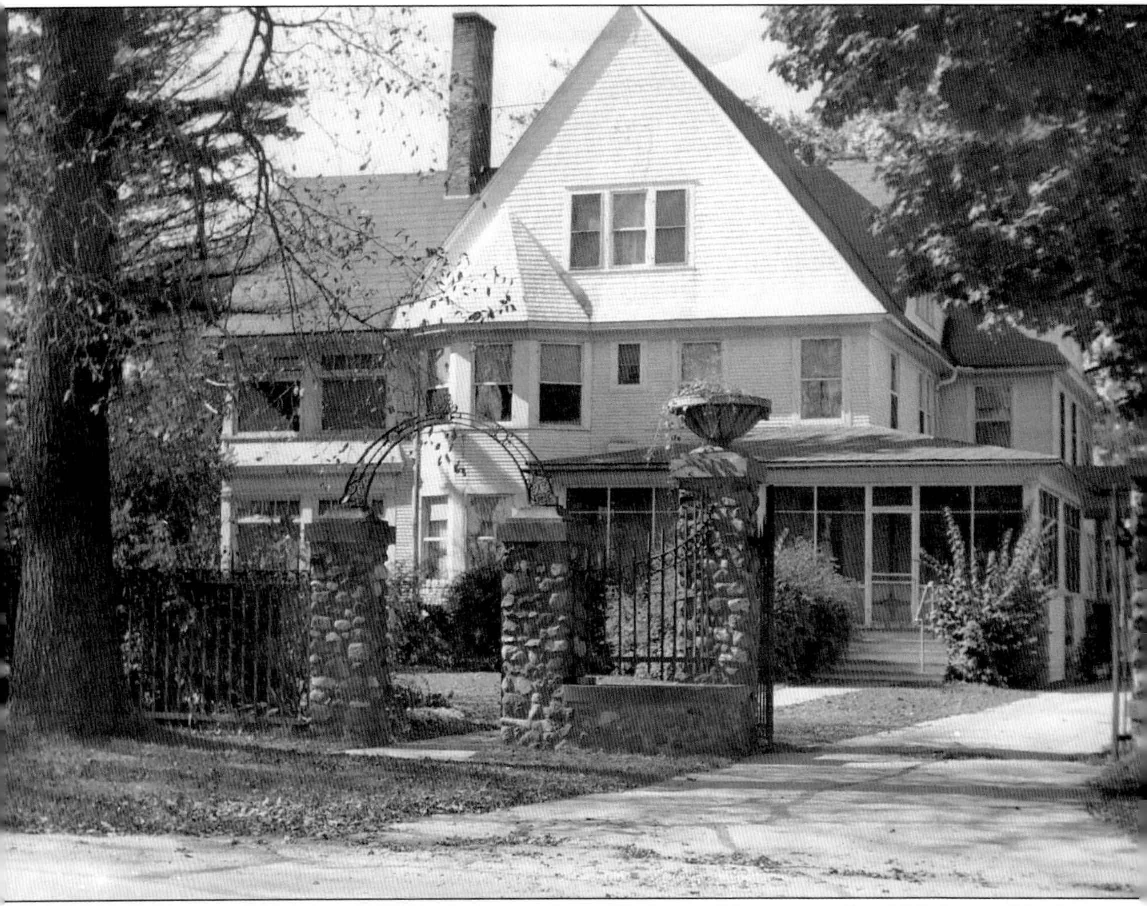

PINE HAVEN CHRISTIAN HOME. Located on Highway 32 just north of Highway 28, Pine Haven Christian Home is operated by 18 Reformed and Presbyterian churches on the site of the former Peter Reiss summer home in Sheboygan Falls. Along with this home, another 37.5 acres was purchased from Pinehurst farms. Started in 1950, single rooms initially cost $85 per month, and doubles were $75 each. The facility accommodated 12 residents. In 1958, the first expansion project was completed. Many more followed. Because the Reiss summer home became obsolete for use as a nursing facility, Pine Haven sold this home to neighboring First Reformed Church in 1976. In 1985, Pine Haven Residential Center was dedicated as a licensed community residential facility. Today it serves more than 300 residents. This photo, taken in 1955, shows the original retirement home.

Three

SCHOOLS AND EDUCATION

Settlers coming to Sheboygan Falls were alert to the importance of education for their children. Prior to the establishment of public schools, children were taught at home or in private schools. The teacher was usually someone from the neighborhood who was well-versed in reading, writing, arithmetic, and a few other essentials. Few had true academic credentials. Education was so important, even to those involved in federal government, that Congress gave the territory of Wisconsin the ability to sell land to make money to support a new school system. Section seven of the August 6, 1846 Act of Congress said that revenue from the sale of land in section sixteen of each township in the state was earmarked for schools. In many townships Section 16 remains, to this day, "The School Section." Land had to be sold in at least 40-acre tracts and could be sold for as much as possible, but for no less than $1.25 per acre. These land sales commenced May 1, 1850. This type of foresight provided a priceless base for the Wisconsin education system.

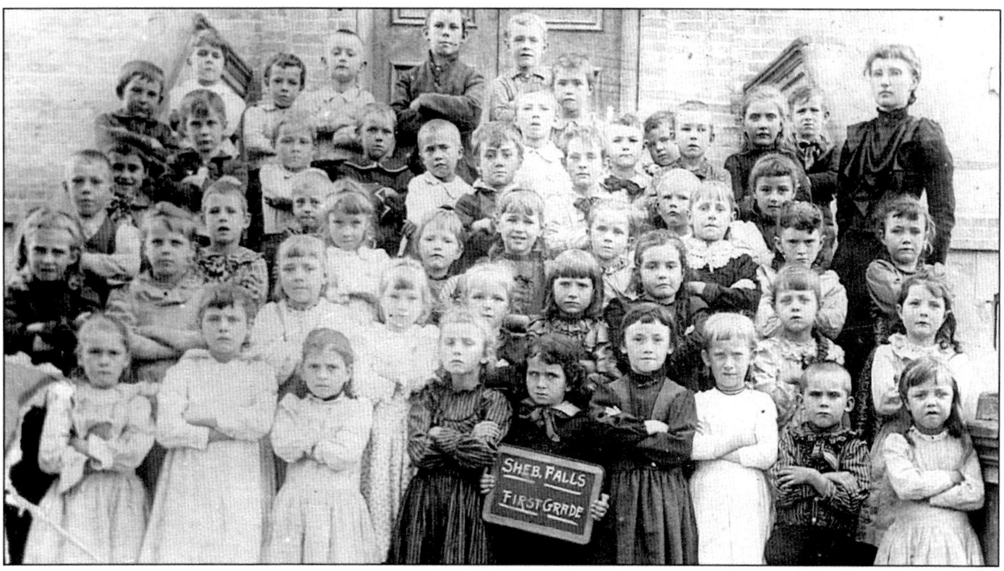

EARLIEST DAYS OF A YOUNG EDUCATION. These stern little faces show the trepidation of a student's first days in school. This photo is of Miss Lila Quinlan's first grade class at Sheboygan Falls Elementary School on September 13, 1893.

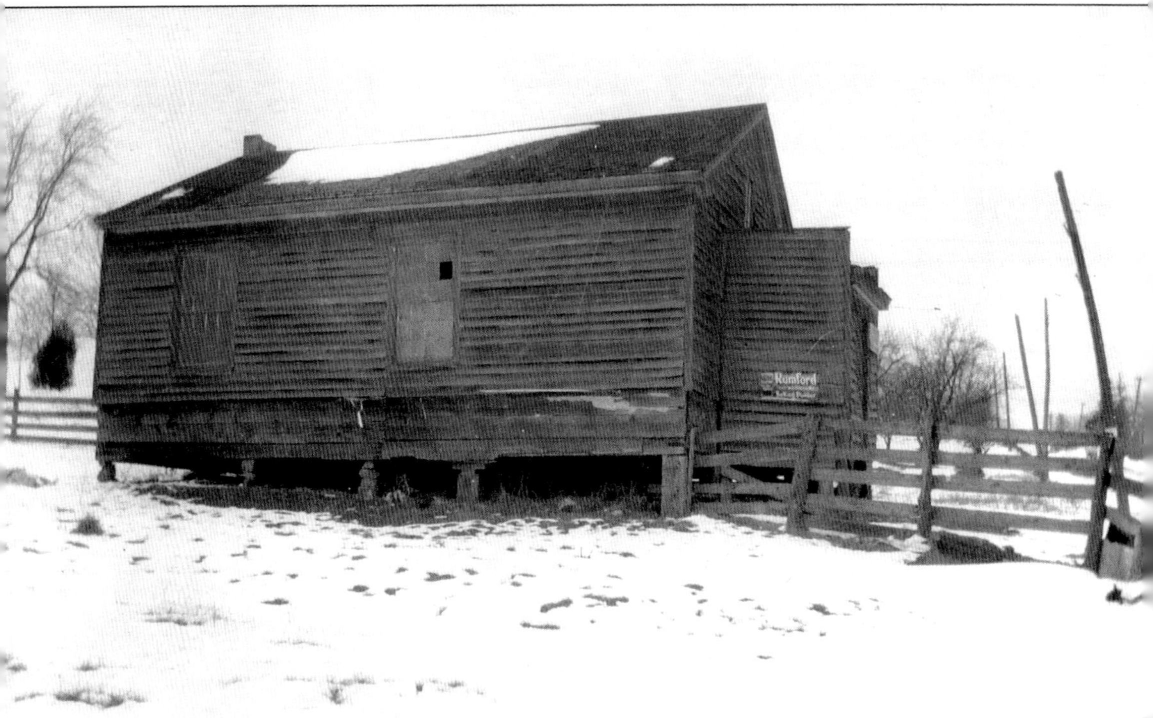

The Beginning of Education in Sheboygan Falls. The education of their children was a prime concern for the first Yankee settlers of Sheboygan Falls. Various dates have been put to the erection of the first school house dating anywhere from 1836 to 1845. The school house also served as a meeting place for the residents for socials, and on Sundays, for church services. It was also used as a voting place for elections and for conducting the business of the village. The building stood near the southwest corner of present-day Jefferson and Poplar Streets. It had a single room measuring 16 by 24 feet, and was open for free public education. The building was never painted, and after the second school house was built, was little used. It stood on the site for approximately 80 years until it was razed in the mid-1920s. One of the more famous teachers at this school was Horace Rublee, who was later appointed Minister to Switzerland by President Grant. For many years Rublee was also the editor of the *Milwaukee Sentinel*.

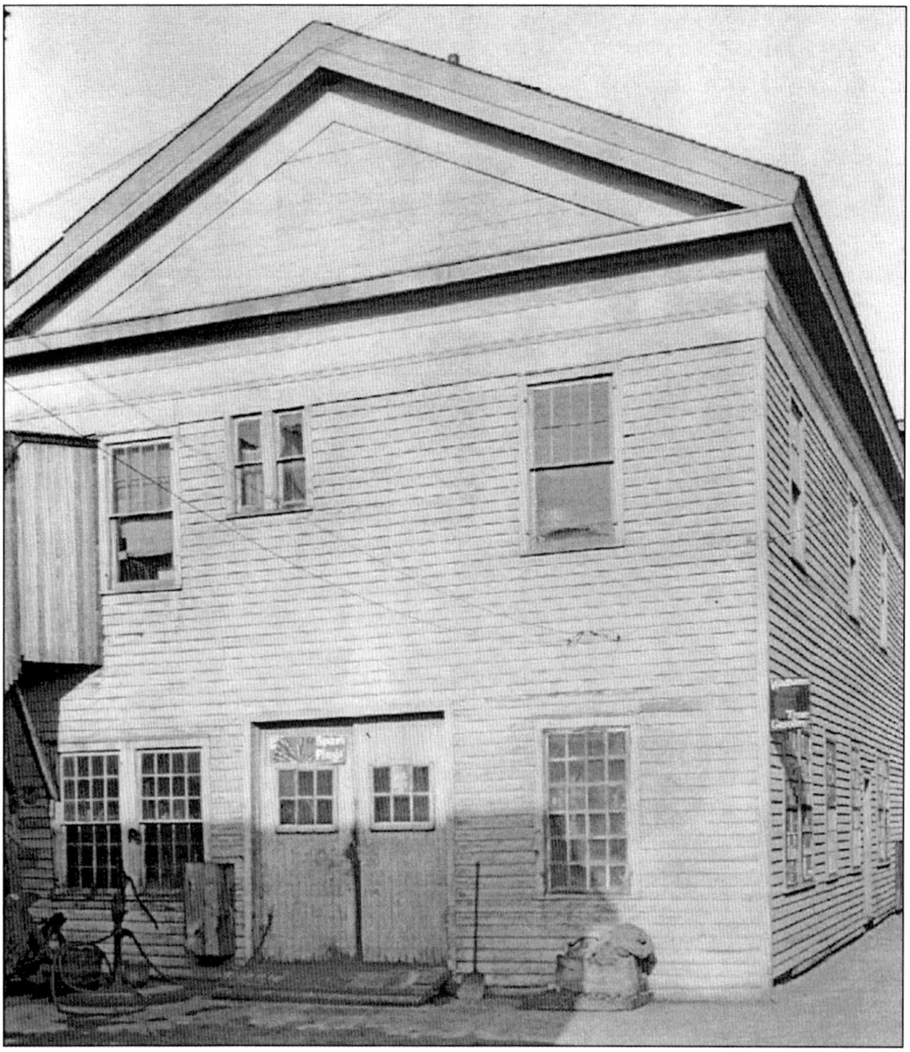

THE SECOND SCHOOL. The second school was located on Broadway across from the old Lutheran Church. It was built in 1856 and was a select school supported by subscription and taxes. The Greek Revival style building had two floors. The first consisted of two classrooms and a corridor and housed the primary and secondary grades. The second floor, reached by two winding stairways was divided into three classrooms on the west and an assembly room to the east. Three teachers were employed at the beginning, a primary, secondary, and principal. Their pay averaged $30 per month. Benches and desks were cut from white pine, again from the sawmill, and the school could accommodate 140 students. One of the first teachers here was William Kirkland, who had the local cooperage. This second school was abandoned in 1870. A disastrous fire in April 1867 ravaged a block of frame buildings on Broadway from Monroe Street (then Bridge Street) north. The fire destroyed seven buildings and left families homeless and without portions of their businesses. The two-story school building was put on rollers and moved down Broadway and situated where The Other Place tavern is now located. Many different businesses were located in this building until 1917, when it was moved again, directly across the street. The movers neglected to turn the building around, so that the back of the school became the front. Henry and Clarence Fricke used the building as a garage until 1973. Today the 'backward' school is a part of Fire House Pizza Restaurant and has been thoroughly renovated by owner, Dorothy Schueffner.

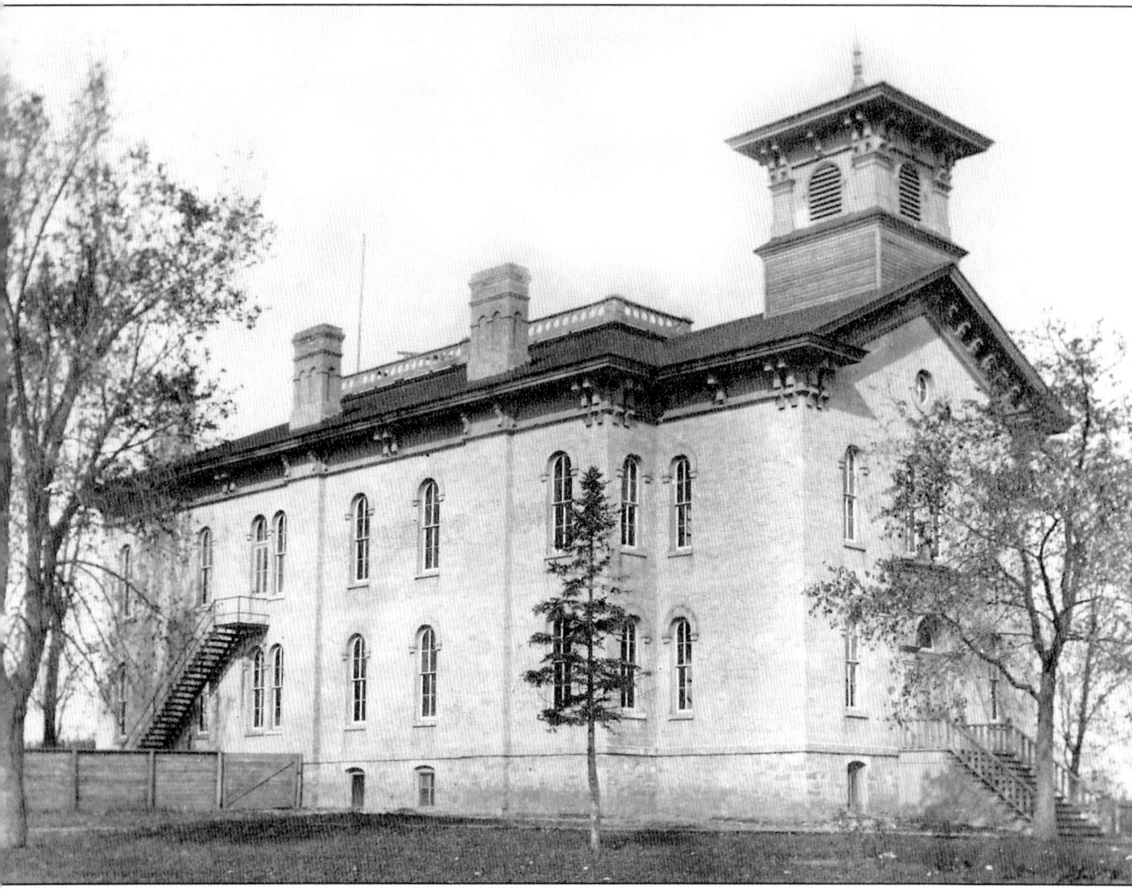

HIGH SCHOOL. The first high school was taught in the third school building. It was built in 1870 by William Galloway at a cost of $11,000 from bricks manufactured in the Whipple and Goodrich brickyard adjacent to the school. The two-story building had entrances on Detroit and Chicago Streets. The high school classes occupied the top floor and the grade school classes were on the first floor. Six chimneys were needed to heat the building until the installation of a central heating plant in the basement. The first high school class was graduated in 1875 with a class of 14 students. The principal was C.W. Clinton and the faculty were Mrs. Clinton and Emma Dean. Graduates were Carrie Richardson, Annie Shepard, Addie White, Martha Guyette, Sarah Meritt, Frances Walsh, Arthur Leighton, Charles Scott, Wallace Hanford, Dwight Jackson, Guy Shepard, Sylvester Palmer, Sumner Sprague, and Clara Evans. The building contained seven rooms and taught grades one through twelve. A kindergarten was added in 1912. Due to increasing enrollment a second building was constructed in 1906 to be used for a high school. With the completion of that building, the brick school house was used as an elementary school until 1963. It was razed in that year and the site is now used for a parking lot and a playground.

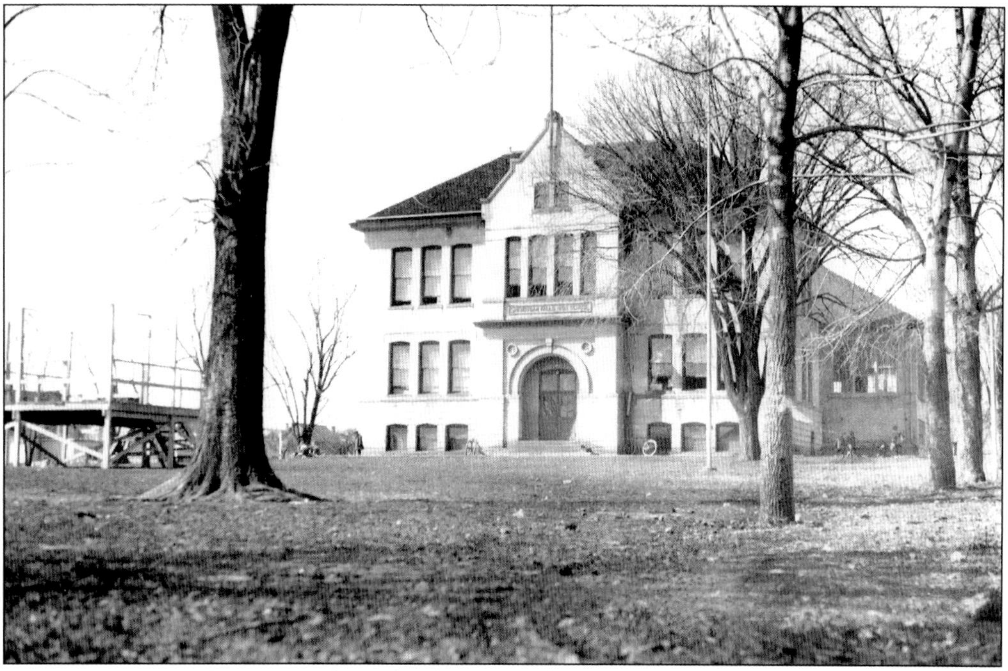

THE NEW HIGH SCHOOL. This school measured 47 by 65 feet and had two stories and a basement. It was built of West Bend sand-lime brick with sandstone trim. The mason contractor was William Guenther & Son of Sheboygan, and with the furnishings, it cost $12,000. An assembly room, library, principal's office, and teachers' cloakroom were on the second floor, while the first floor had four recitation rooms and pupils' cloakrooms. The first class to graduate from this building, in 1907, had eight members, one boy and seven girls. They were Myrle DeLong, Marcia George, Edna Houwers, Grace Goodwin, Andrew Pfeiffer, Mildred Sisson, Hazel TeSelle, and Nina Hobart. Basketball practice and games, class plays, and commencement exercises were held in the Woodman Opera House.

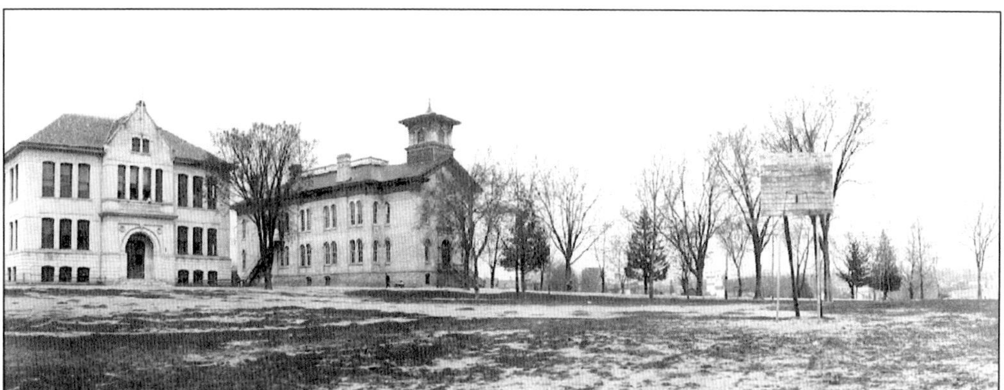

1907 SCHOOL CAMPUS. The Sheboygan Falls High School and Grade School with playground in front of both buildings are seen here c. 1907. A single basketball hoop was the extent of the playground equipment.

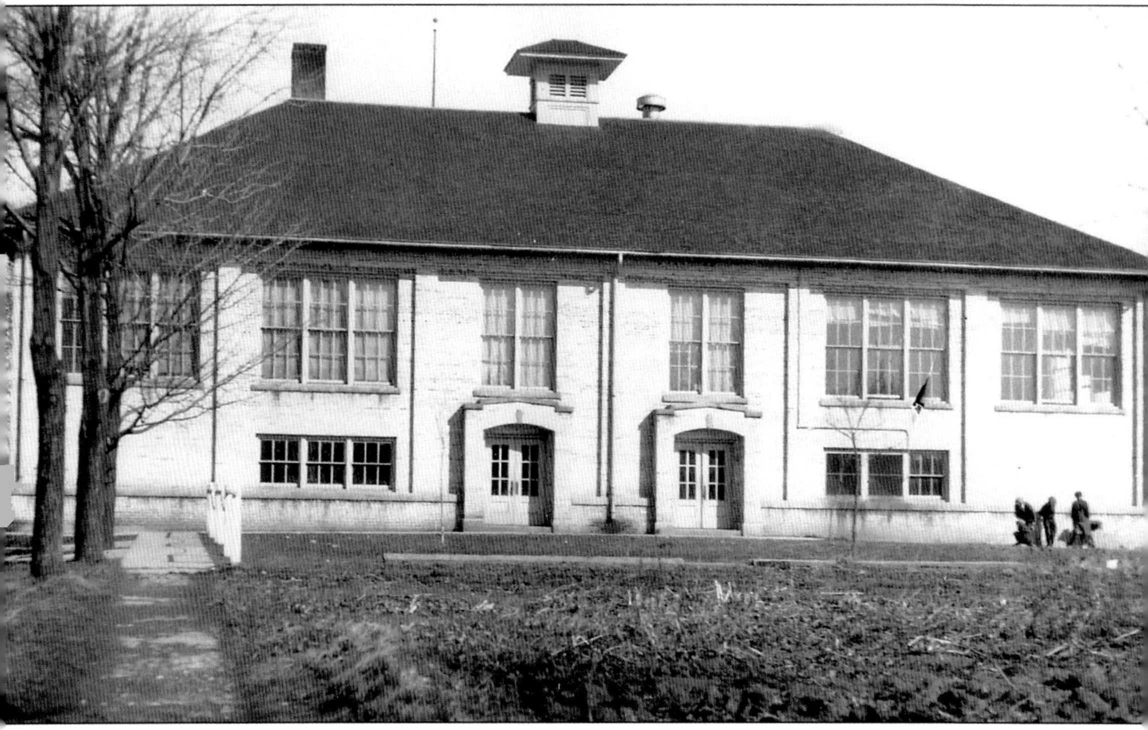

SCHOOL EXPANSION. Increasing enrollments, especially after World War I, made it necessary to add a third building to the school yard in 1921. This building also contained two floors with a science room and laboratory in the northern half of the first floor and lavatories in the south end. The second floor had a study hall and two classrooms. It was used temporarily as a junior high and then as a high school for a limited number of classes. The last class graduated from this building in 1928. There were 36 members, 13 boys and 23 girls. When a new high school was built in 1928, the inside walls were removed and the building became the gymnasium for the high school. The entire building was torn down in 1961 to made room for an addition to the high school.

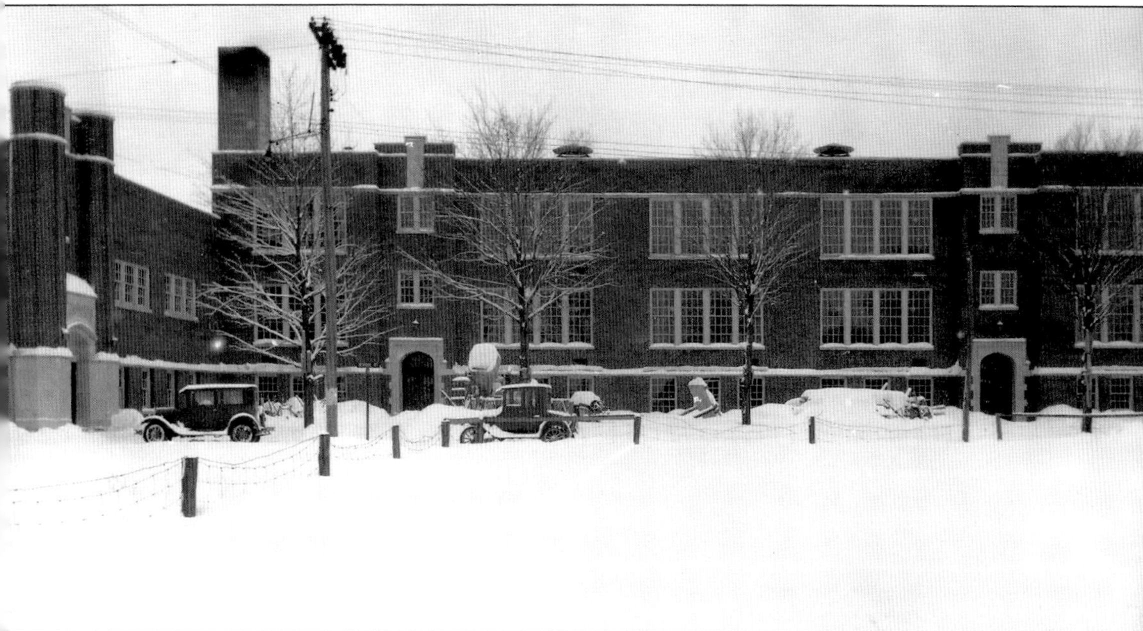

A NEW HIGH SCHOOL. In 1928 a new school was built on School Street, southwest and west of the other school buildings. The exterior was built of red-colored brick made of shale and fire clay. Much of the material was furnished by local firms. The three-story building had a main corridor which ran east to west, with stairways at each end. Two front entrances face School Street. An auditorium seated 500–550 people and was located on the first floor. The ground floor also had an art room, band and music room, biology and general science room, and two showcases containing athletic trophies. The second floor contained the school office, restrooms, six classrooms, and another display case for student's work. On the third floor was an entrance to the balcony of the auditorium (now converted into offices), large study hall, library, chemistry and physics lab, two classrooms, typing room, and two offices. There were also lavatories for boys and girls, lockers, drinking fountains, and bulletin boards on every floor. The high school remained in this building until 1970, when a new school was built on Amherst Avenue.

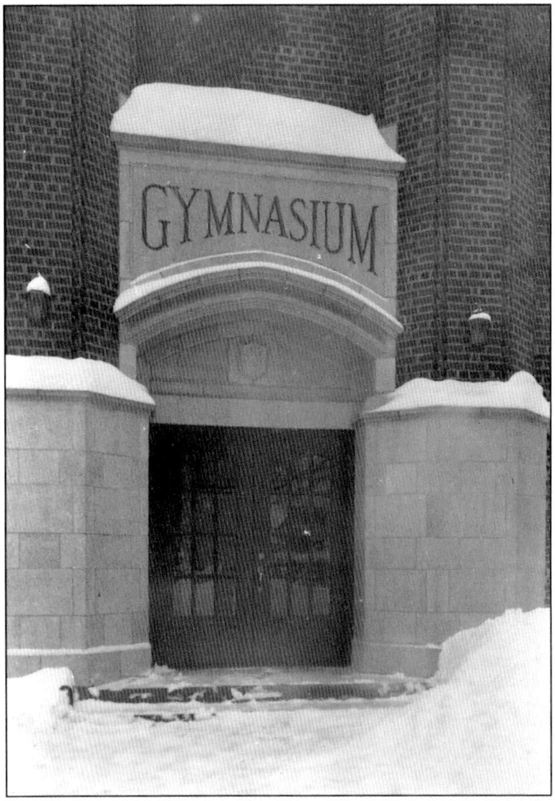

GYM ENTRANCE. This photo shows the entrance to the gymnasium of the new 1929 school. In 1962, a $500,000 addition to the high school was dedicated. This gymnasium was converted into additional classrooms and a new gym with shower facilities, locker rooms, offices, equipment room, and a first aid station were added.

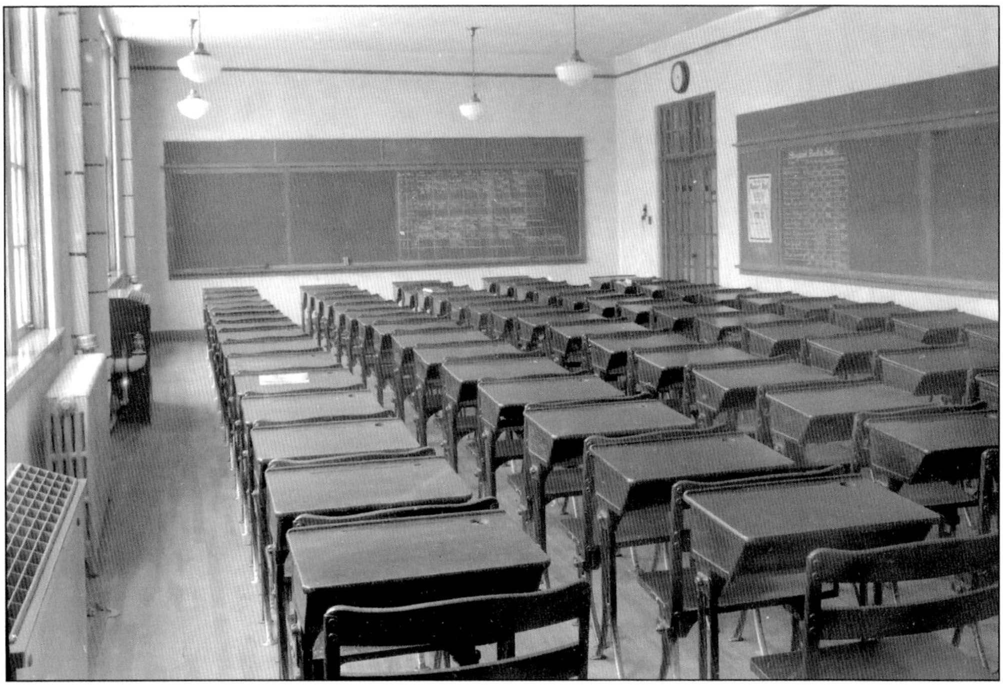

STUDY HALL VIEW. This interior shot highlights the modern study hall in the new high school.

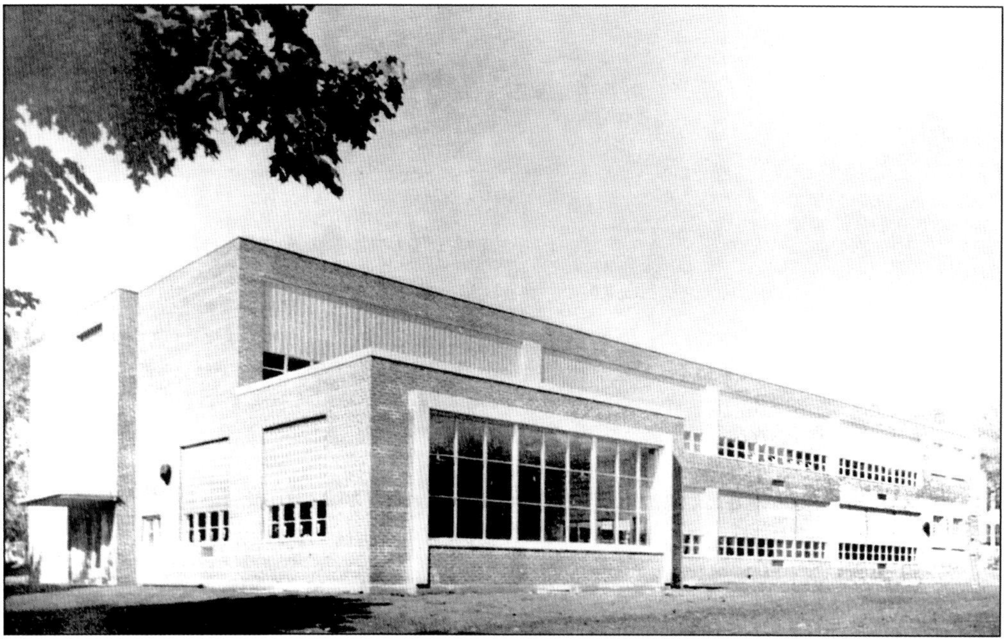

1948 ELEMENTARY SCHOOL. In February 1948, it was decided to replace the old elementary school. The old buildings, now more than 70 years old, were rated barely passable. They lacked space, were poorly arranged, had poor service systems, suffered from inadequate heating and ventilation, and there were fire hazards. The new two-story building was built of brick to match the high school. Sixteen classrooms, toilet facilities, and a remedial reading room were included. A kindergarten room, 32 by 40 feet, was the largest classroom. The school was completed in 1949 at a cost of $350,000.

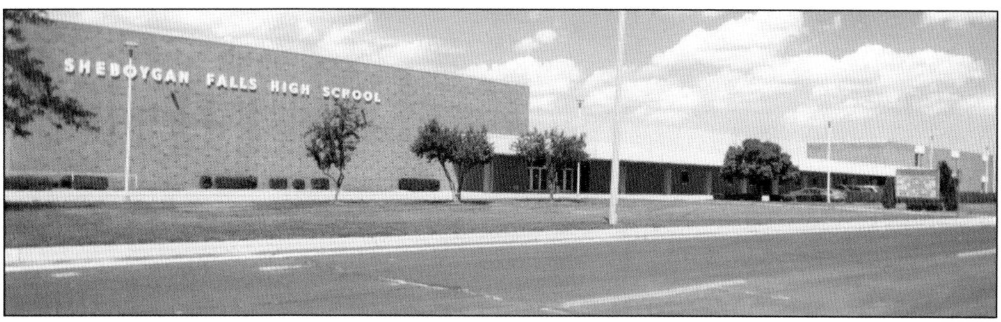

1970 HIGH SCHOOL. Planning was begun in 1966, but it was not until plans were modified that the voters approved the bond issue of $3,378,000 by a vote of 814 to 413. The complex was built on Amherst Avenue and dedicated July 12, 1970. Ground breaking for a new 24,000 square foot aquatic center at the high school began in August 2000. The $2,167,000 center was dedicated with an open house in March 2001. The focal point was an 88-foot water slide. The pool had been planned for 30 years before it came to fruition.

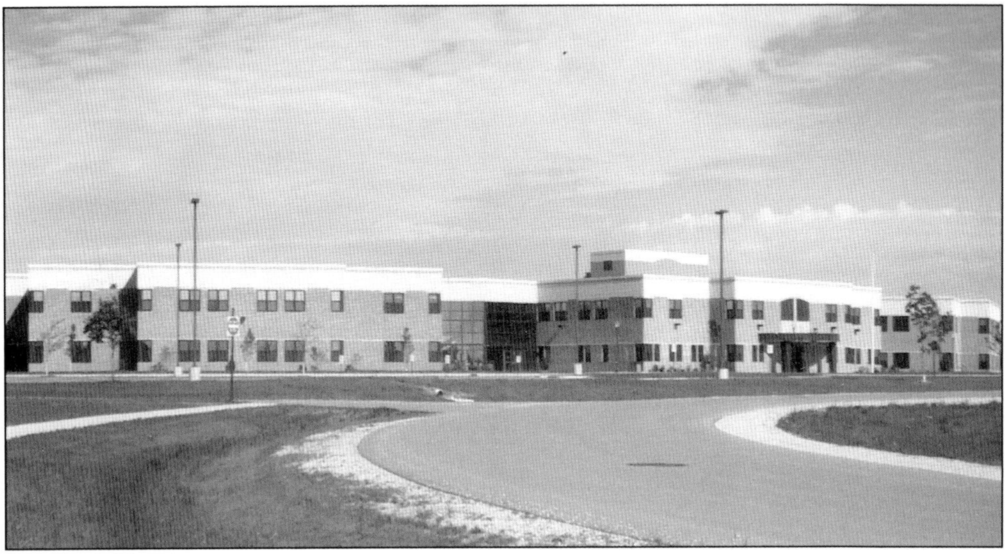

1999 ELEMENTARY SCHOOL. Ground for a new elementary school was broken June 1, 1999. The 100,000-square-foot facility was built on Alfred Miley Way on the city's northeast side, a departure from the school complexes on the southside. The facility was sorely needed, as kindergarten through second grade students were being educated at the Lightfoot School and grades three through eight were in the existing elementary school. With the completion of this K through fourth grade school, the elementary school now houses grades five through eight.

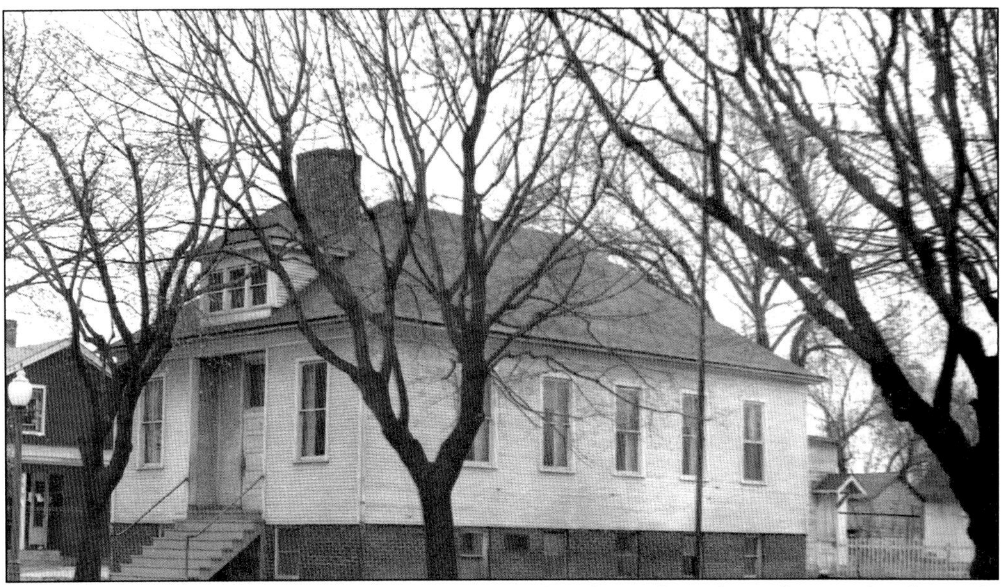

ST. PAUL LUTHERAN SCHOOL. St. Paul Lutheran Church conducted a Lutheran school as early as 1869 when the congregation built a combination parsonage and school house on the corner of Buffalo and Cedar Streets. Enrollment climbed and in 1907 a new school house was built at a cost of $1,600. In the early 1930s, enrollment began to decline as parish members sent their children to public schools. In 1943, the projected enrollment was so diminished, the teacher accepted a new position in Milwaukee, and the school was closed.

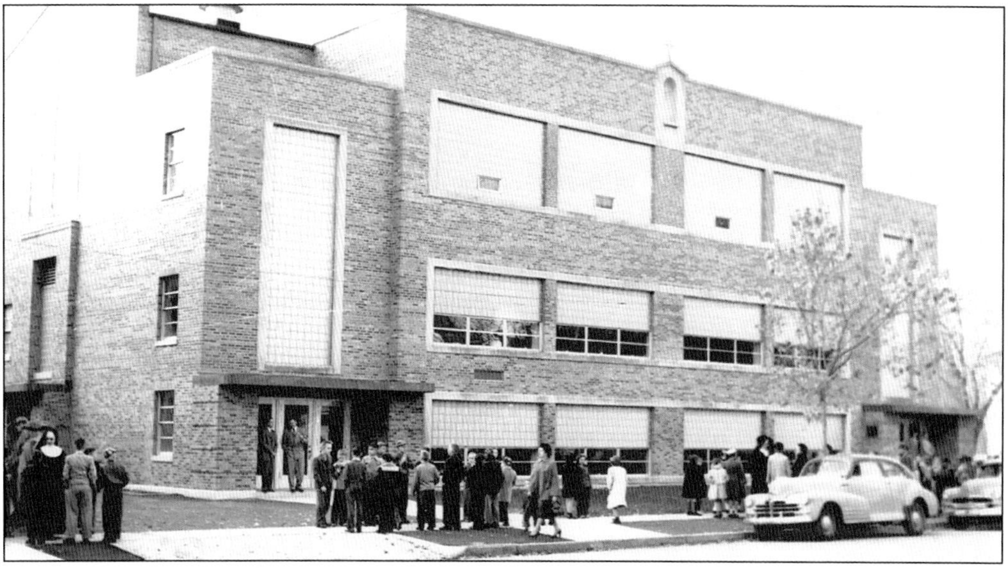

ST. MARY CATHOLIC SCHOOL. St. Mary Parochial School was many years in the planning but didn't get started until 1951. The $40,000 school's ground breaking took place in October 1949 and its dedication was held in October 1951. The teaching staff consisted of Sisters from the Order of St. Francis of Assisi in Milwaukee. Today the school has lay-teachers as teaching staff for pre-school, kindergarten, and grades one through six, and will add seventh and eighth grades during the next two years.

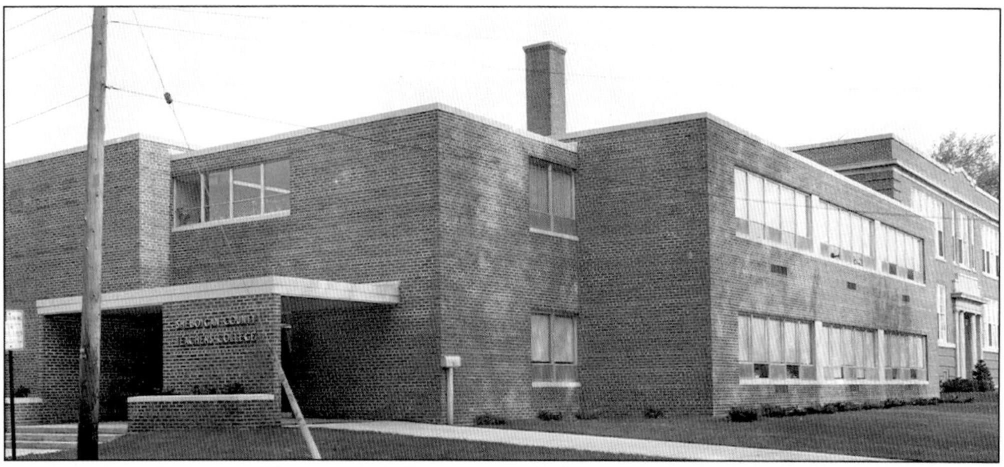

SHEBOYGAN COUNTY TEACHERS' COLLEGE. Sheboygan Falls had one more center for education. This was a teacher's college which was established in Plymouth in 1909. In 1923, the name was changed to County Rural Normal School and the school was moved to Sheboygan Falls in 1924 into a building fit for the needs of a teacher training school. Three years later the name was again changed to County Normal School. Until 1937, the school provided one year of training beyond high school. In 1937, it was changed to two years. In 1955, the school became the County Teachers' College. In April 1965, a disastrous fire gutted the brick building causing cancellation of all classes. The building, which had been extensively remodeled in 1959, was considered a total loss. By October, construction workers were dismantling the wreckage and preparing to rebuild the college. In September 1966, the Sheboygan County Education Center was dedicated and the Teachers' College was reopened.

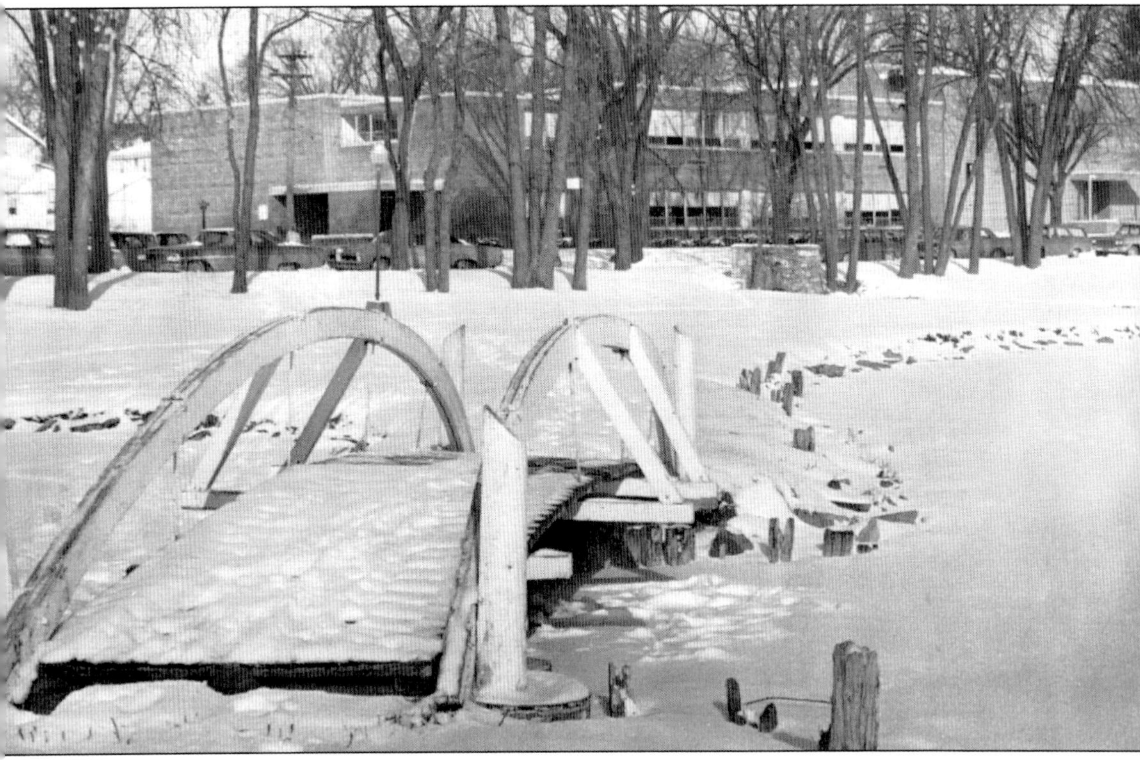

LIGHTFOOT SCHOOL. In 1972, the state required a four-year degree to become a teacher in Wisconsin. As a result of the ruling, the Sheboygan County Teachers' College was terminated. From 1918 until 1972, over 2000 students completed the course. The building continued to serve as an educational training facility for children with learning difficulties and exceptional needs. Adequate gymnasium facilities, a swimming pool, and a variety of shop programs were available at the school. The school was renamed Lightfoot School after Ray Lightfoot a long time Sheboygan County Superintendent of Schools. With the building of the new K–4 elementary school and the mainstreaming of children with exceptional needs, the Lightfoot School was closed and put up for sale. A developer has purchased the site for remodeling. He hopes to make apartments in the building. So far that has not happened, and the building remains vacant. This view looks at Lightfoot School over the footbridge in River Park.

Four

City and Government Services

For many years city and government services were non-existent. Road building was one of the first services managed by local government. But as the population grew, services were required. The year 1916 was a banner year for the City of Sheboygan Falls. The privately owned power and light plant, owned and operated by the Weisse Tannery, was purchased by the city. The plant was installed in 1898 and supplied the needs of the tannery and, additionally, citizens with light from dusk to 1 a.m. daily. Before this time, there was no electric street lighting system. Instead, a lamplighter went around at dusk to light the kerosene lamps hung on poles. A ladder was needed to reach the lamps. Later, when lights were extended over the streets suspended from tall poles, the lamp was lowered by means of a rope and pulley. This was known as carbon lighting. Also in 1916, the construction of a city waterworks system was approved. The first well was located in the city hall building on Maple Street. A total of five wells were drilled between 1916 and 1945. By 1949, the water supply was inadequate for the community and in July 1950, a contract was signed with the City of Sheboygan to provide water to Sheboygan Falls. A transmission line was completed in 1951. Other municipal services and activities are discussed in the following pages.

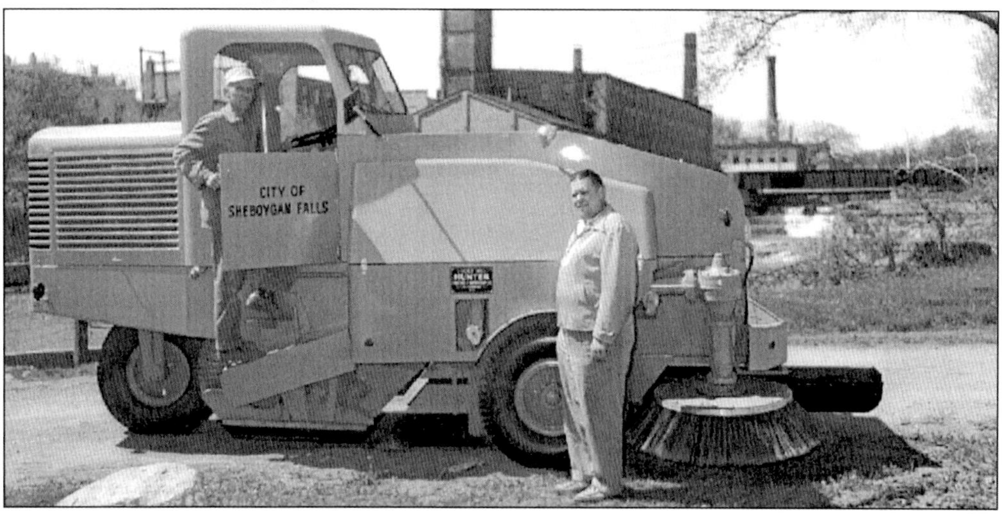

Street Sweeper. This photo, taken in May 5, 1959, shows the Sheboygan Falls Utilities newest convenience, its very first mechanical street sweeper.

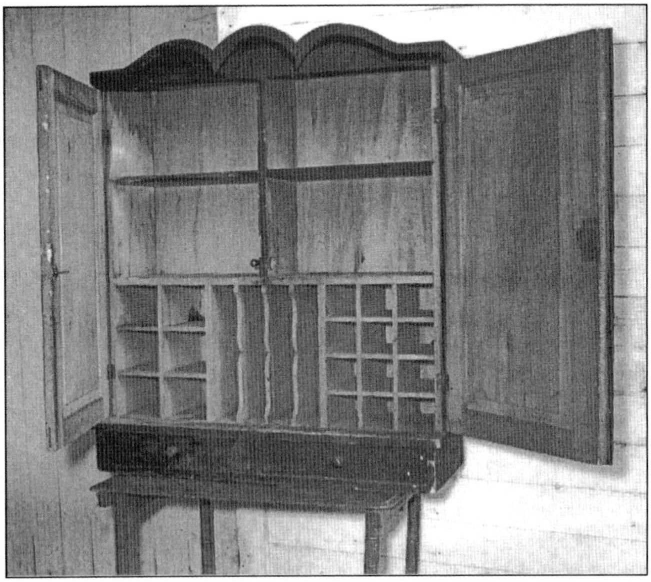

First Post Office. The earliest post office in Sheboygan County was built for Charles Cole, second postmaster of Sheboygan County from 1840 to 1845. When Cole was appointed there were 133 residents in the entire county. This small box-like affair met the needs of the entire county and handled postal supplies as well. The post office remained in Cole's store as it changed owners over the years. It was donated to the Sheboygan County Historical Research Center by a descendant of the Lumsden family, Elizabeth Matheson.

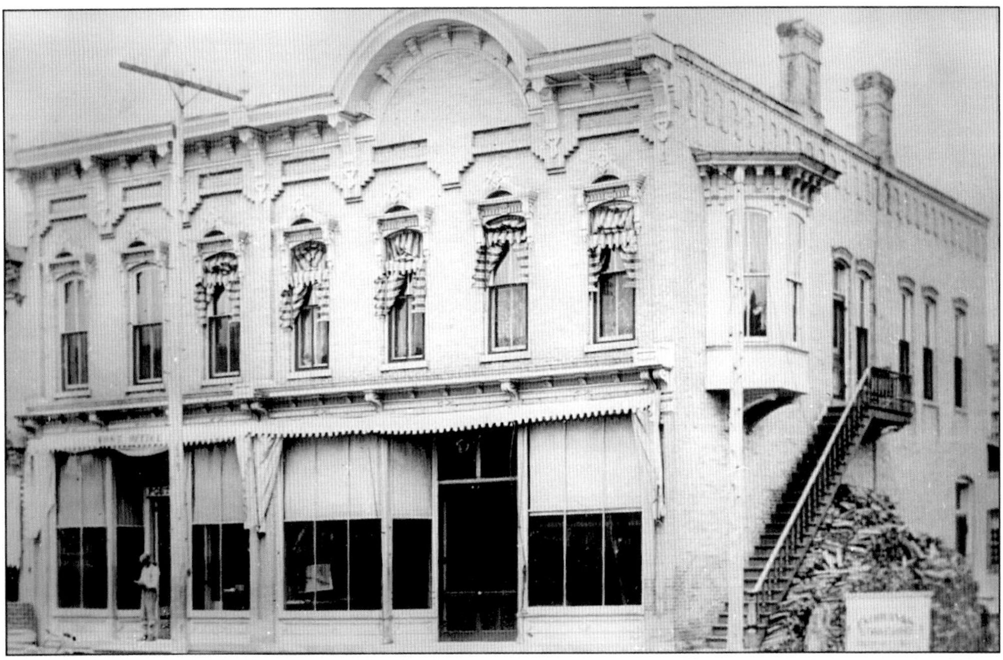

Second and Third Post Office. The second site of the post office was in the Payne building on the southwest corner of Pine and Buffalo. This building was razed. The third location was in the Smith building, beginning in 1892. The man in the picture is standing in the doorway of the post office on Broadway.

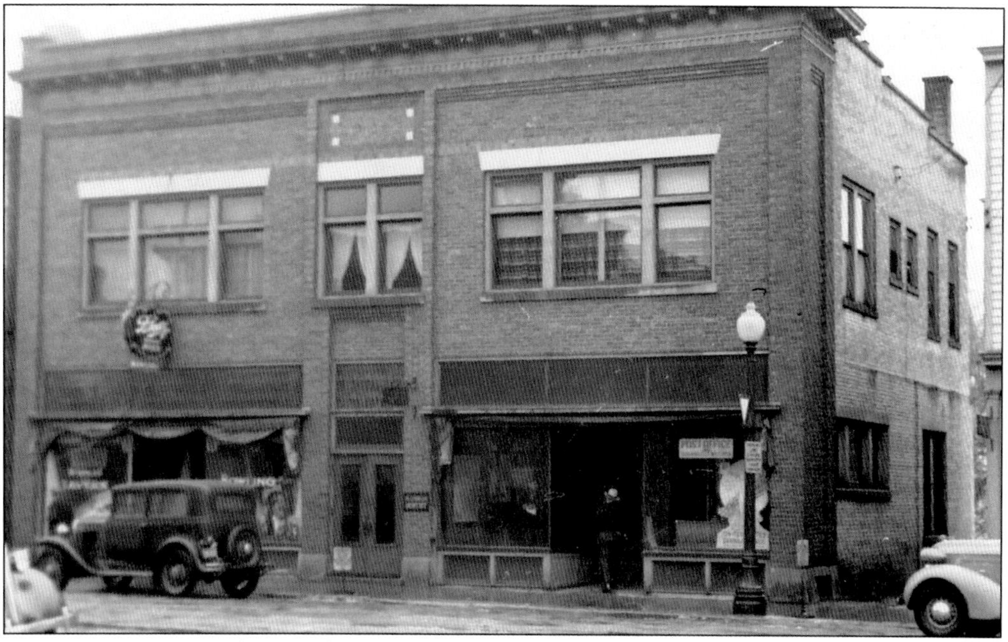

FOURTH LOCATION. The next location of the Post Office was in the Martin block on Broadway. The space occupied 1,180 square feet and soon grew too small for the office. In 1937, the U.S. Post Office was moved to the Schultz building, less than two blocks down the street.

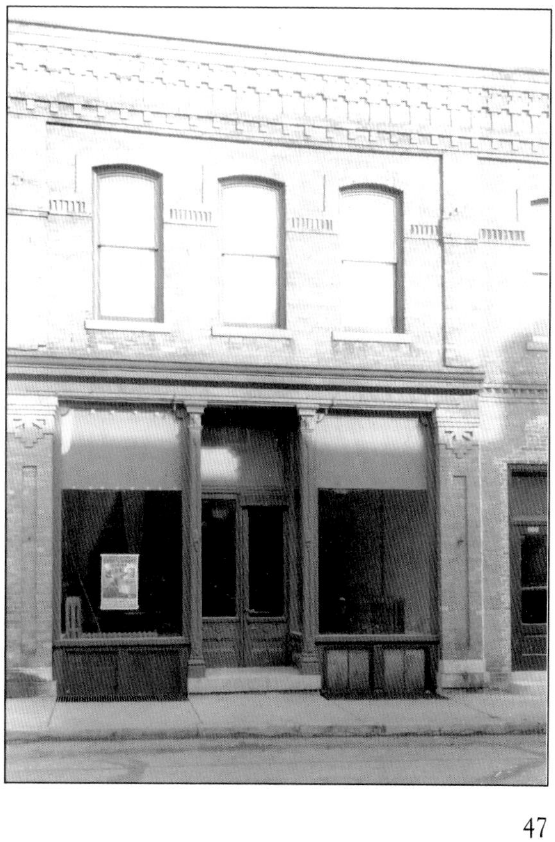

FIFTH LOCATION. From 1937 until 1962, when a new building was constructed, the post office remained in the Schultz building. The new office had 1,385 square feet of space and a large vault which was used to keep the stock of envelopes, stamps, bonds, and other items in good condition.

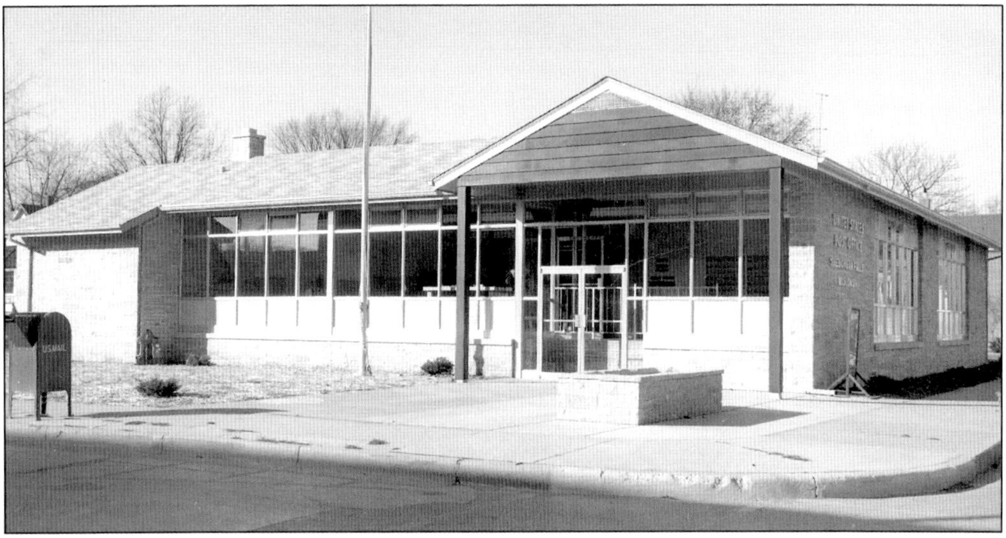

PRESENT POST OFFICE LOCATION. In 1962, after years of planning, a new building was erected to be used exclusively as a post office. This building on the corner of Maple and Broadway Streets is the sixth home of the Sheboygan Falls Post Office. Today the building is too small and lacks sufficient parking for mail trucks to maneuver. Plans are being made to construct a new building, probably out of the downtown area. Postmaster Daniel Guell has served the Sheboygan Falls office since 1980.

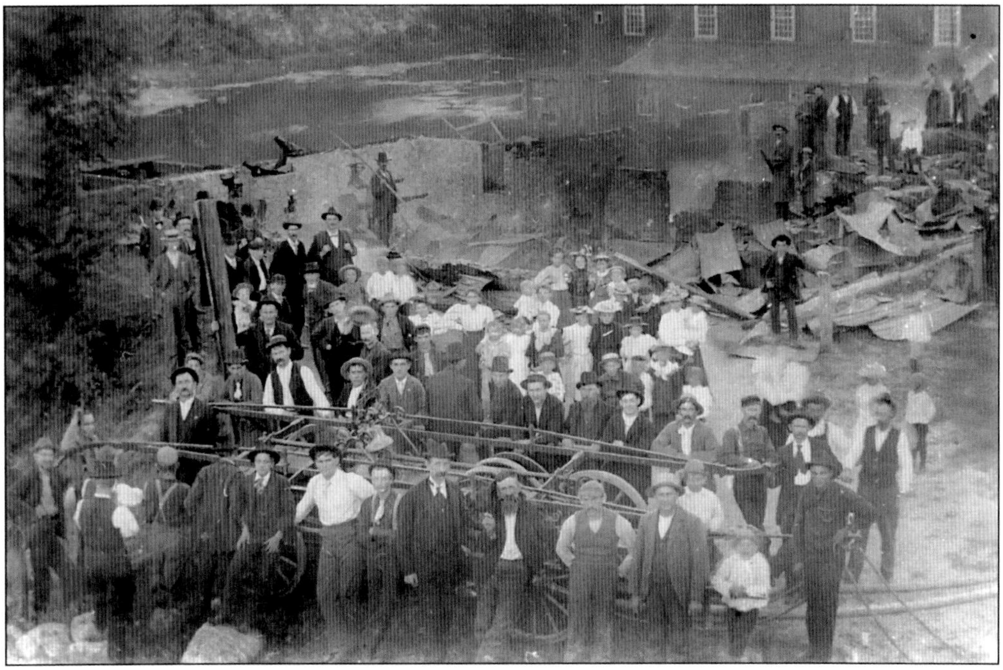

FIRST FIRE COMPANY. The first fire company was organized in 1863 and named the Germania Engine Co. No. 1. In 1866 the trustees of the village authorized a call for discussing the purchase of fire fighting equipment. But it was not until 1869 that the sum of $300 was approved to purchase the R.A. Williams Engine. It was a hand-drawn truck which took a dozen men to pull. This 1890 picture shows the R.A. Williams hand-pumper at the Rock Roller Mills fire.

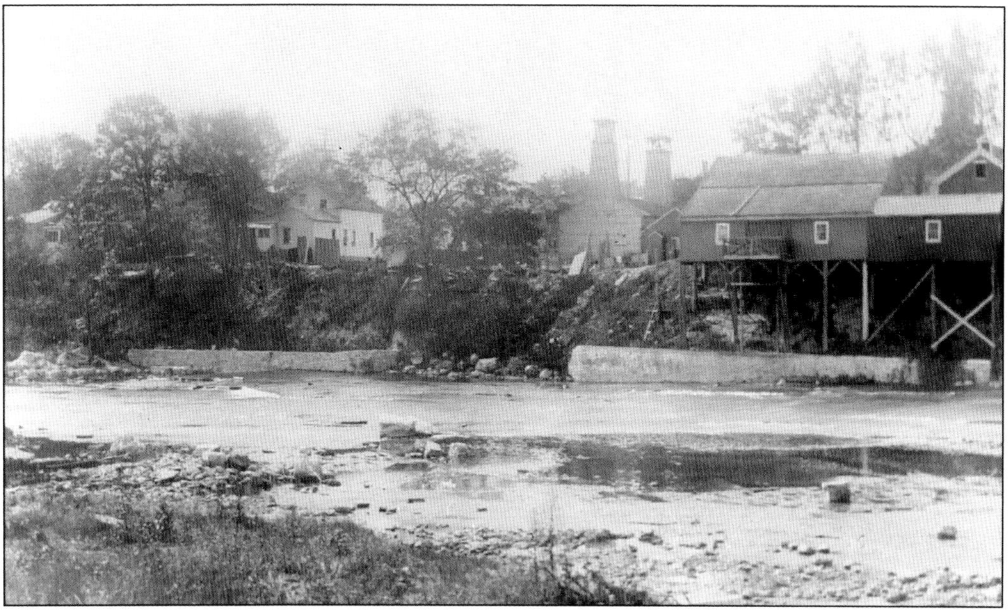

First Fire House. The fire house was located at 628 Broadway. This building was also used as city hall and as the voting place. There was a bell on top of the building which was used for sounding fire alarms. The fire house is located in the middle of this undated picture. It shows the back of the building and you can make out the bell tower at the front. When the department moved into new quarters in 1909 the building was moved and became a part of the Falls Co-op building on Buffalo Street.

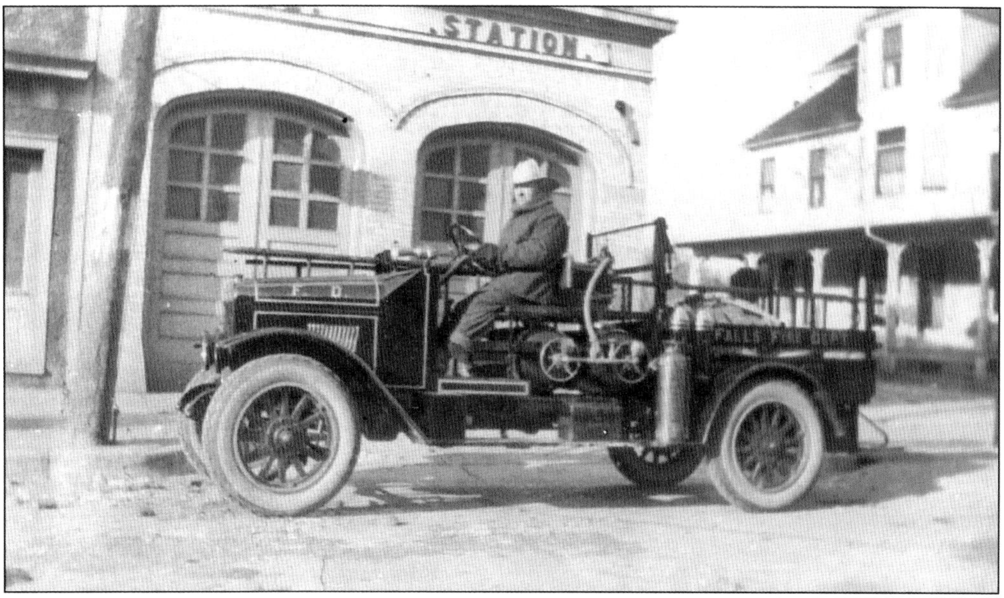

First Fire Truck. In 1929, a contract was awarded to the Peter Pirsch & Sons Company of Kenosha for a new fire truck with a booster tank. The truck had a 500 gallon capacity and the cost was $6,400. This picture shows Joseph Schneider at the wheel of the truck in front of the fire station with the City Hotel in the background.

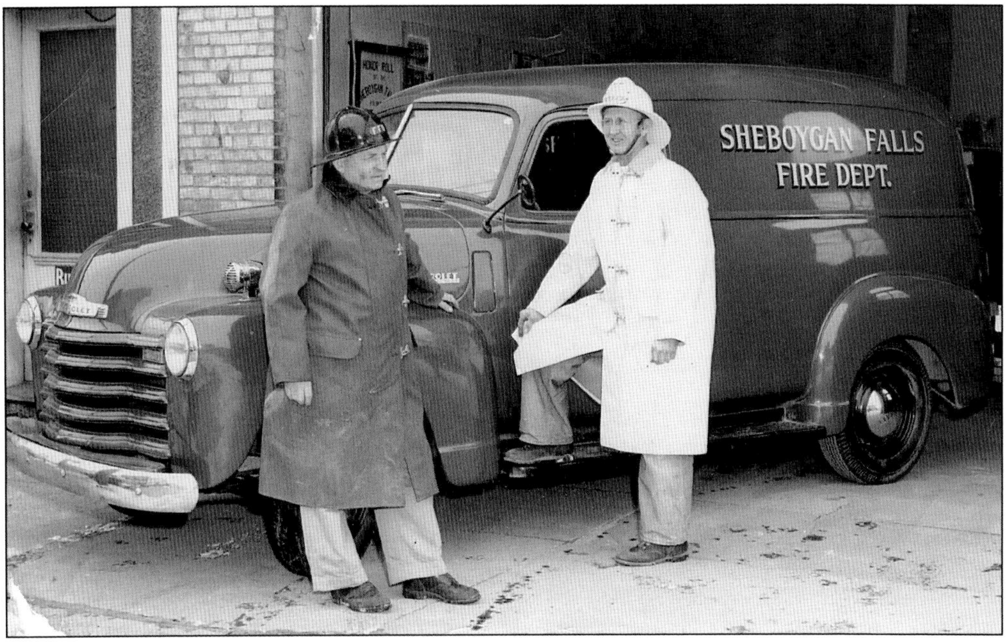

1940s Fire Officials. During the 1940s, the fire chief was Ed Kriplean (left) and Henry Kennedy was the assistant chief. Since 1958, when the Municipal building was constructed, the fire department has been housed in the south part of the building. The fire department is made up of volunteer firemen today.

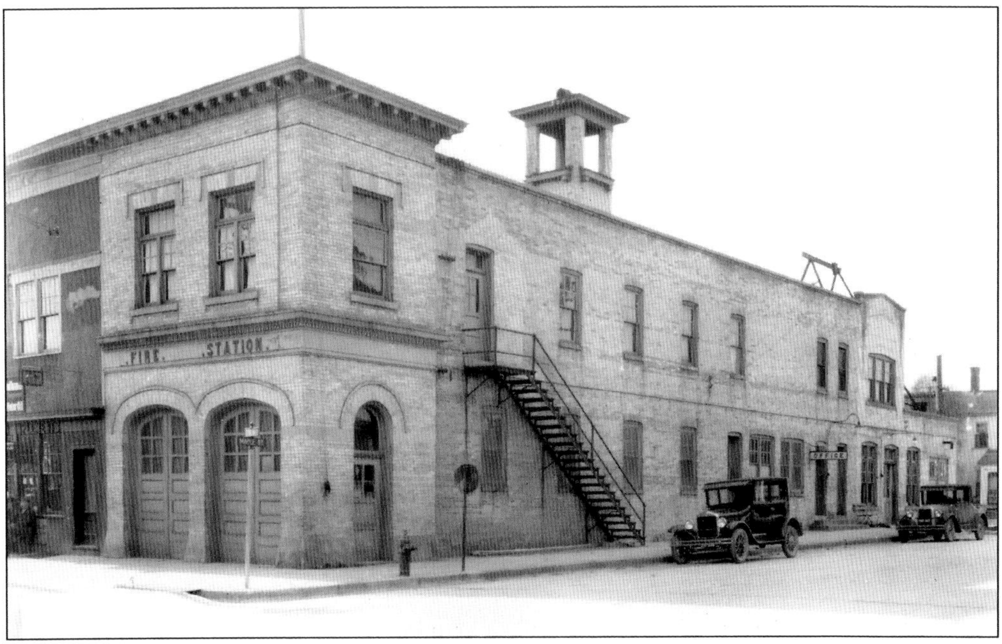

Early City Hall and Fire Department. This photo of the combination city hall and fire department was taken in 1927. The old William Servis carriage shop was purchased by the city in 1909 for $7,000. The property at the corner of Broadway and Maple Streets was built in 1854, and from 1909 until 1958 it would house the city offices, fire and police stations, and the utility offices.

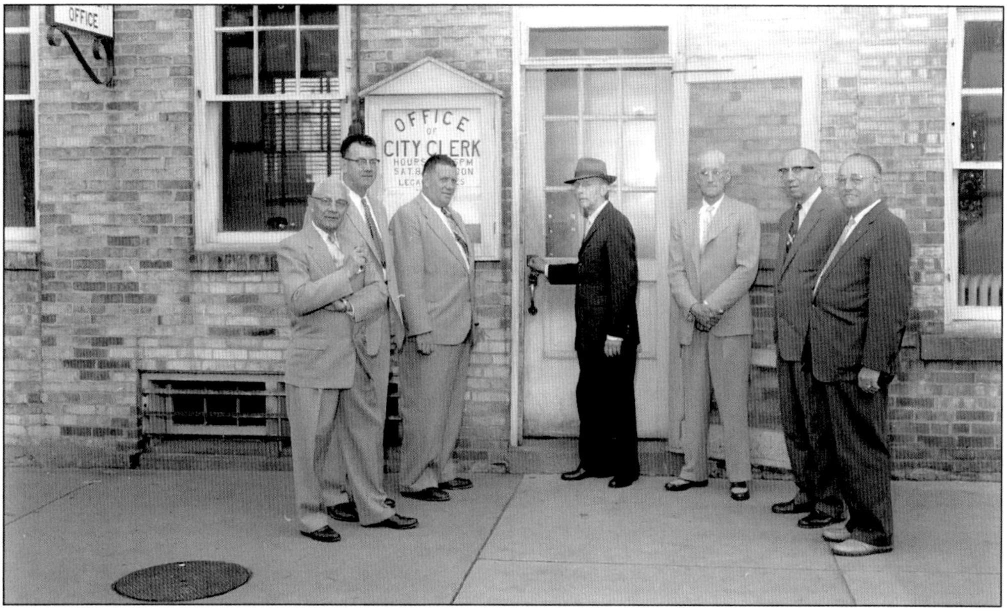

End of An Era. On June 25, 1958, Asher Leavens, city clerk, turned the key, locking the door of the old city hall building. Watching the action from left to right were aldermen Rufus Busch, Russell Heidenreiter, Mayor Andrew Kohlhagen, city clerk Leavens, alderman George Loofbourow, and city attorney Lester Weisse.

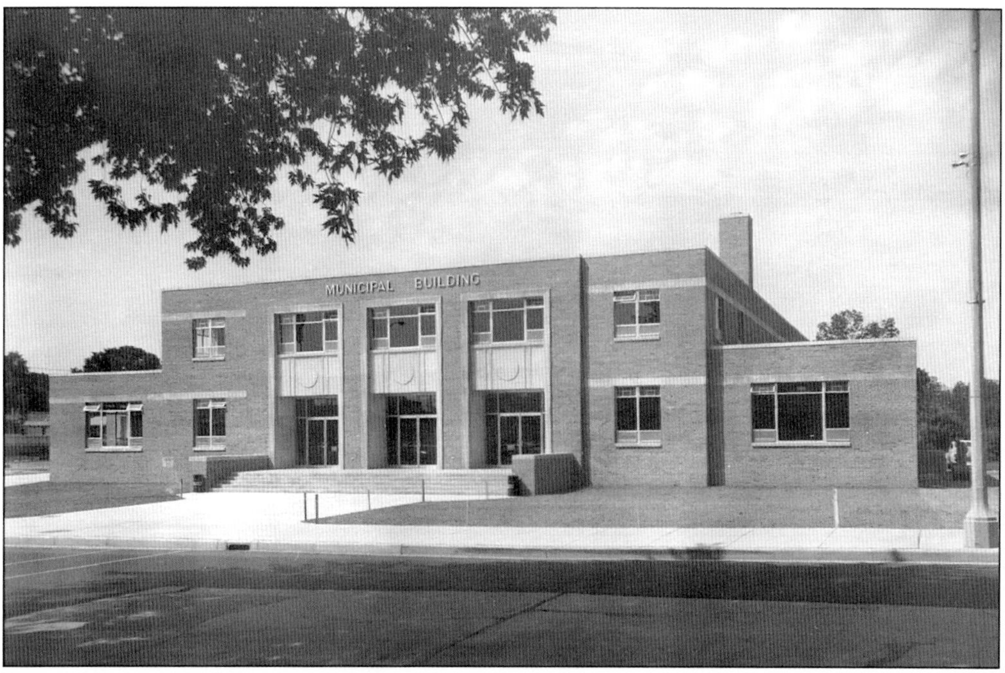

Falls Municipal Building. After 15 years of planning, the Sheboygan Falls Municipal Building and Auditorium was finally realized in 1958. A four-day celebration and dedication was held June 18-21, 1958. This third home of the city offices is still in use today and houses all of the city offices and departments.

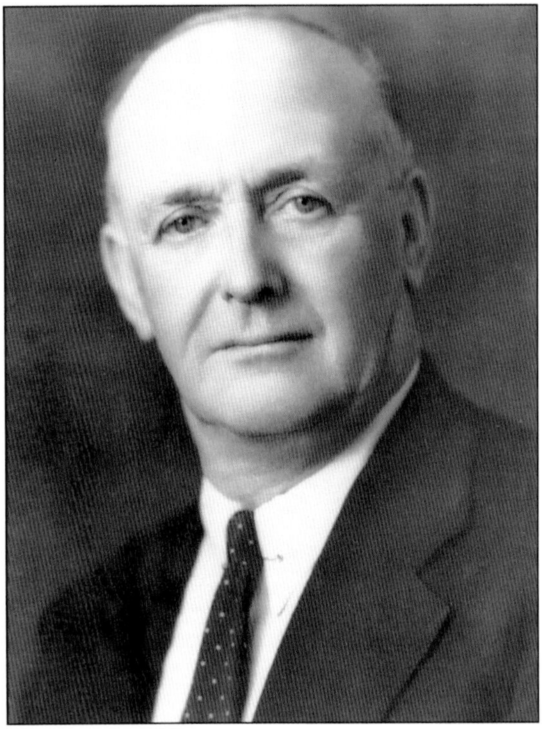

POLICE DEPARTMENT. Edgar A. George was appointed village marshall in 1911, following a long line of men who held this position since 1854. In 1913, Sheboygan Falls became a city and George was named the first police chief serving until 1934. George was the only police chief who was involved in a battle with thieves. In 1917 burglars attempted to blow up the safe at the Eastern Wisconsin Electric Station. Alerted to their night-time activities, George confronted two men. In the ensuing gun battle, the chief wounded one, and barely escaped being shot when a bullet ripped through his coat. The wounded bandit was apprehended, but refused to identify his partner.

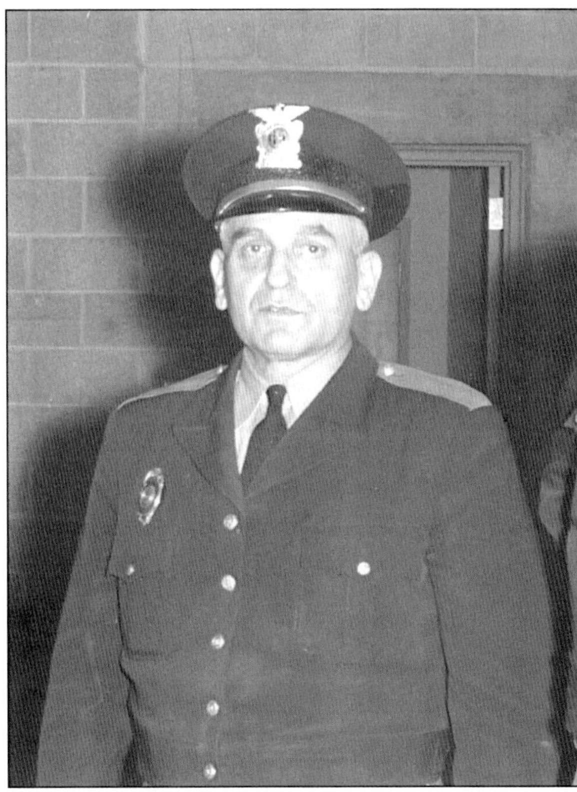

HENRY BILLMANN. In 1934 a two-man police force was created, Fred Brown, chief, and Joseph Widder, officer. Brown resigned after three months, and on September 3, 1935, Henry Billmann was appointed chief and Widder remained as officer. Billmann remained chief until his retirement in 1967 after serving for 32 years. During his tenure, the first patrol car was purchased (1939). Until that time it was mostly foot patrol, and when a vehicle was needed, they used their own cars. The lengthy Kohler strike was probably the touchiest period of his tenure.

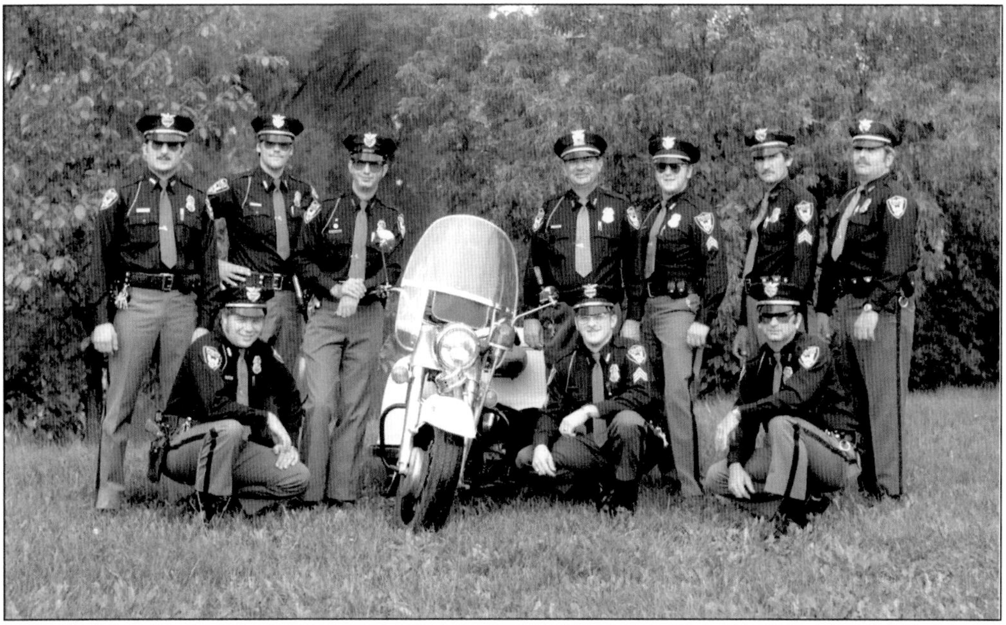

SHEBOYGAN FALLS POLICE DEPARTMENT. By 1980, the police force had risen to ten including Chief Jacob Hermann. Standing, from left to right, are: Mark La Pean, Scott Jurk, David Liedtke, Chief Hermann, Sgt. Dennis Walosz, Sgt. Robert Ploeckelman, and Ted Hahn. Kneeling in front are: Robert Hildebrand, Sgt. James Sloma, and Dewey Glancey. In 2000, the police department, located in the Municipal Building, underwent a $368,000 renovation and expansion. The department gained about 1,000 square feet. The department now consists of 12 officers and two confidential secretaries.

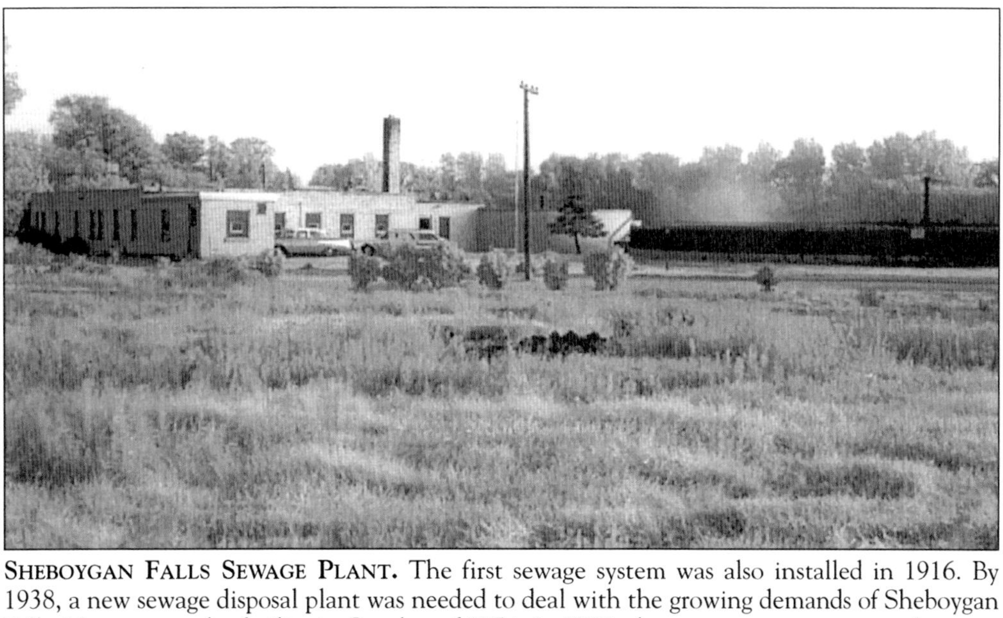

SHEBOYGAN FALLS SEWAGE PLANT. The first sewage system was also installed in 1916. By 1938, a new sewage disposal plant was needed to deal with the growing demands of Sheboygan Falls. Here we see the facility in October of 1954. In 1980, the wastewater treatment plant was closed due to the inadequate size. A force main was installed and all effluent is now pumped to the Sheboygan Waste Water Facility.

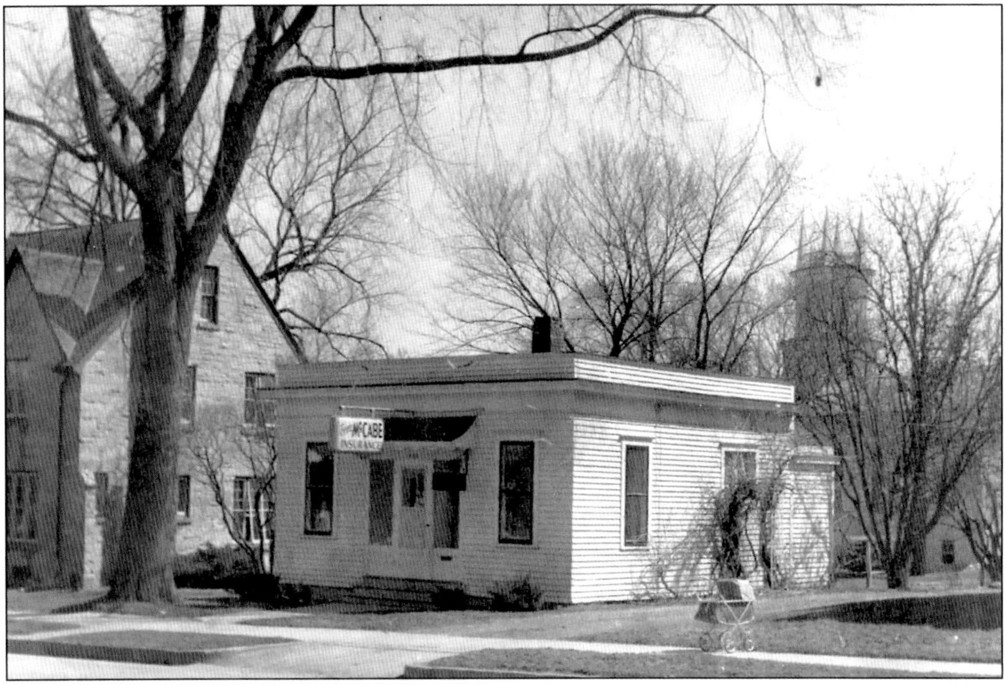

FALLS' FIRST LIBRARY. This building was originally the office of Dr. Robert Nichols. In March 1925, it became the first home of the library in its own building. There had been a social library from 1867 to 1896, and in 1924, a one-room library in a private home was established. In 1955, the building housed McCabe's Insurance Company, and by 1956 Attorney Arnold Langner also hung his shingle there.

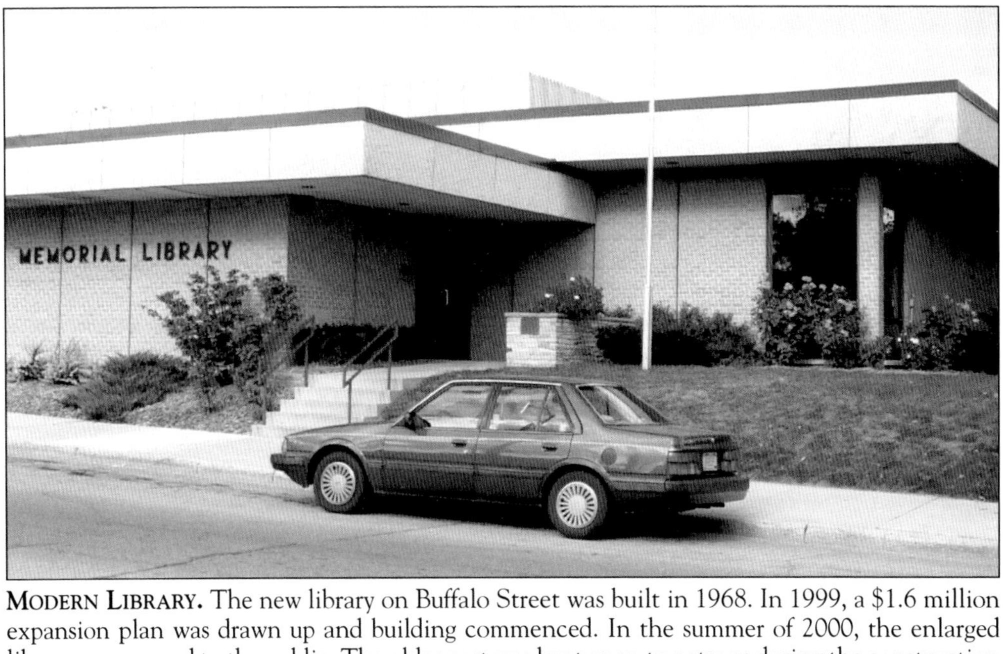

MODERN LIBRARY. The new library on Buffalo Street was built in 1968. In 1999, a $1.6 million expansion plan was drawn up and building commenced. In the summer of 2000, the enlarged library was opened to the public. The older part was kept open to patrons during the construction period. This photo was taken in 1995.

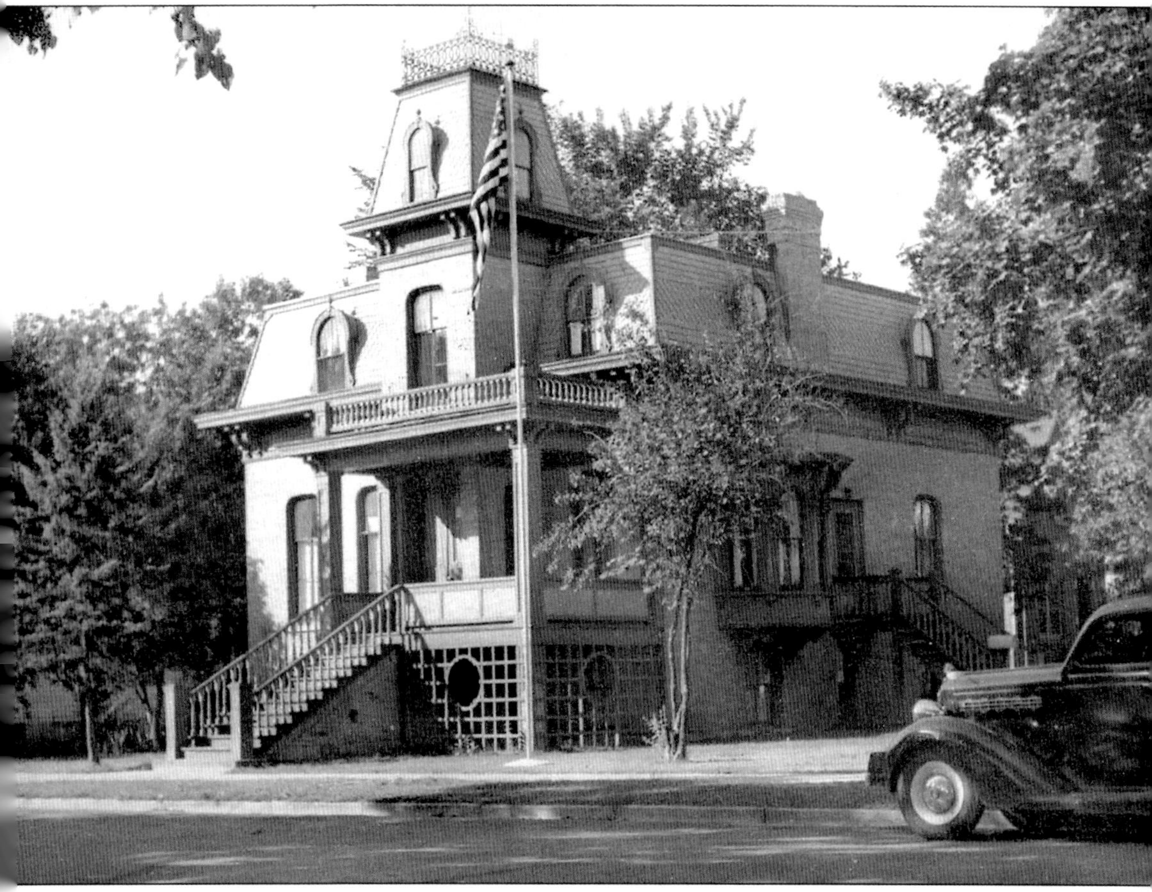

SECOND EMPIRE BEAUTY. Located at 613 Detroit Street, this imposing Second Empire-style house with a mansard roof was the home of William Prentice. The structure was built in 1870 for the founder of the Prentice Woolen Mills, the predecessor of the Brickner Mill. The Prentices hailed from New York where this style of architecture was very popular. At the time it was built, there was a concerted effort to use only the best materials: marble for fireplaces, etched glass for the doors, cherry and mahogany woods for interiors. The house became a showplace and social center during the last part of the 19th century. It is one of a handful of the style in the county. In June 1943, Otto Weisse deeded this home to the city for a library. Some 13,000 books were housed on the first floor during the 25 years it served as a library. The second floor was made into an apartment. It was named Sheboygan Falls Memorial Library in memory of all who had helped in establishing the library. The building was sold to a private party when a new library was constructed in 1968. This photo was taken in 1953. The home was designated a historical landmark in October of 1976.

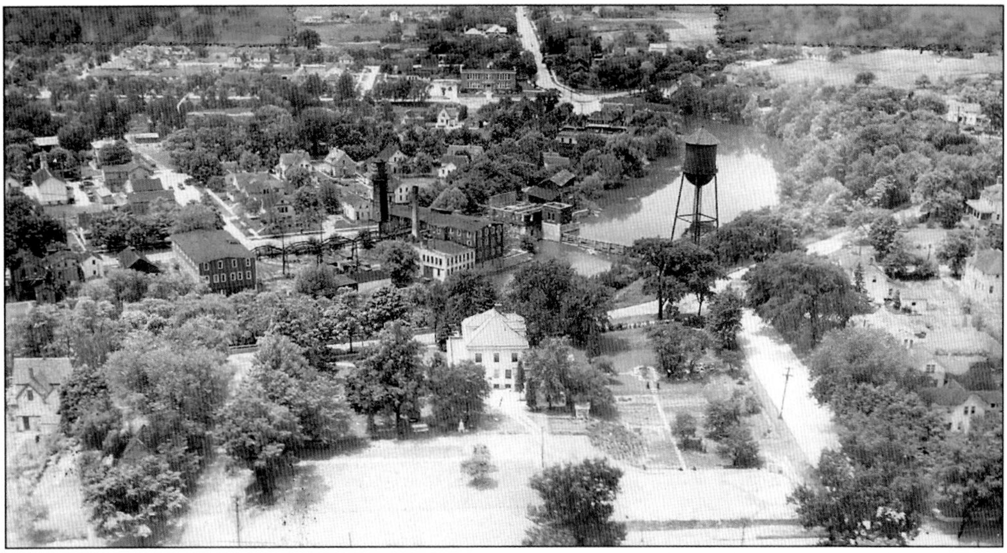

WATER SUPPLY. Sheboygan Falls' original spring was known as the Cole Springs and located just off Adams and Water Streets on the site of the old Falls' utility building. It was the site of a Native American encampment for centuries. This first water source bubbled to the surface of the ground, providing clean cooking and drinking water for the earliest residents. Over time the city has had numerous water storage systems. This aerial view of the river overlooking Water Street and the upper dam shows an early water tower located on top of Peck's Hill. The house situated in the center was owned at one time by the Peck, Dornbush, Schlichting, and Schmitt families.

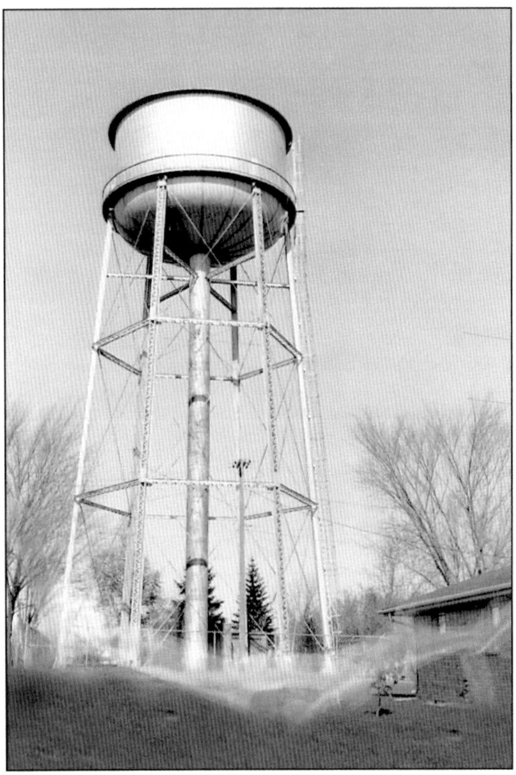

INCREASED WATER NEEDS. In 1966, a new water tower was constructed on Fond du Lac Avenue. The tower, shown here, was a 200,000 gallon tower, 105 feet high, with the name "Sheboygan Falls" lettered on the side of the tower. Another water tower was built off Western Avenue on the city's west side in 1976. This tower with a capacity of 2 million gallons cost $482,000.

Five

ENTERTAINMENT

Sheboygan Falls has always been a lively place, and music was a great part of the entertainment. The first piano was purchased by John E. Thomas in 1850, and the first pipe organ was found in the home of Deacon William Trowbridge in the 1870s. The first brass band was organized in 1850. Members were John Beckman Cole, director, Amos Cole, George Cole, William Cole, Henry Payne, Dr. M.L. Marsh, Sam Hotchkiss, and John Thomas. No picture was taken of this band, and it probably disbanded about the time of the Civil War. The Hills Brothers' Fife and Drum Corps was organized by the G.A.R. in 1868, and played music for their parades. In the 1880s, a cigar-maker who was a tuba player, organized a few local men and they called themselves the Star Cornet Band. They played July 4th concerts and weekly concerts during the summer in a park north of the Louis Ballschmider store on Broadway. Later on the Boy Scout Fife, Drum and Bugle Corps was formed to serenade the returning veterans of World War I. Small bands and orchestras provided entertainment at picnics, parties and celebrations decade after decade. Card clubs, social and study clubs, and theater groups added to local entertainment.

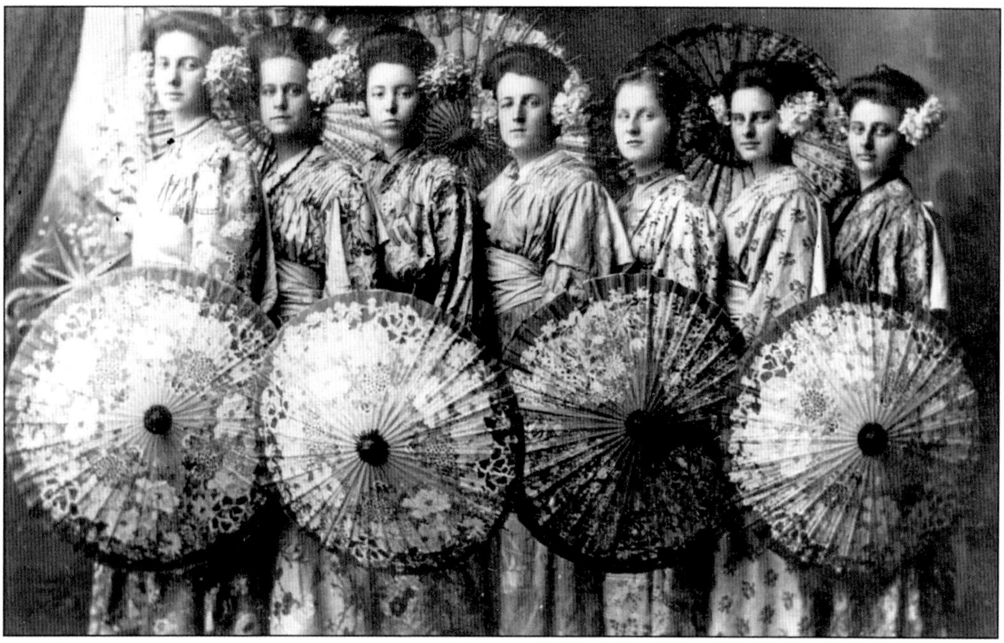

COSTUMED LADIES. These young ladies from Sheboygan Falls took part in one of the many amateur theater productions directed by and starred in by local actors and actresses.

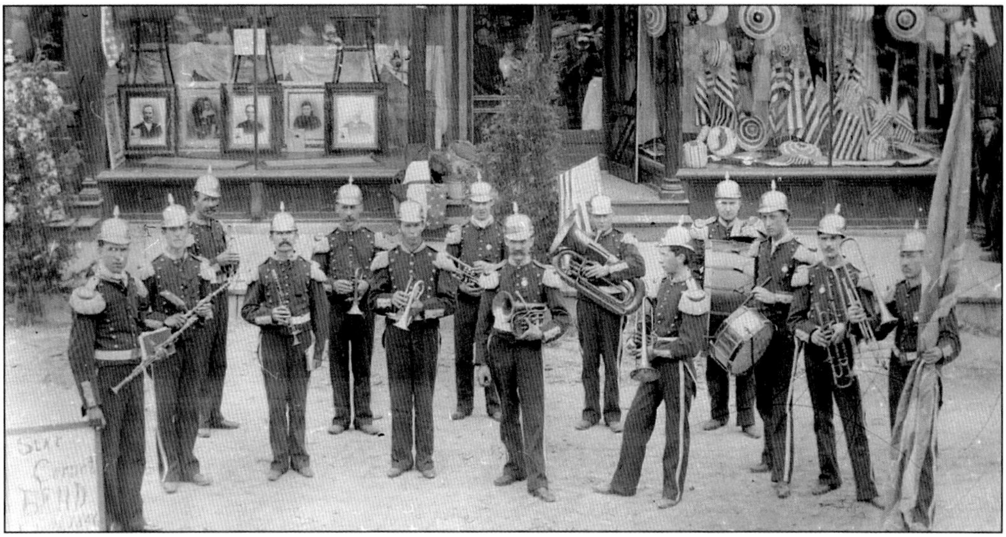

Star Cornet Band. This 1896 picture of the second Star Cornet Band is taken in front of the Schlichting store (now Richardson Emporium) on Pine Street. This band was formed in 1892. The band continued through the 1920s. Members were, from left to right, Oscar Hertzberg, Frank, Kehl, Charles Meyer, Charles Wachter, Henry Heide, Ed McKinnon, Christ Never, Art Schlichting, Charles Heald, George Thierman, Willie Heide, Louis Dicke, and Arthur Hertzberg.

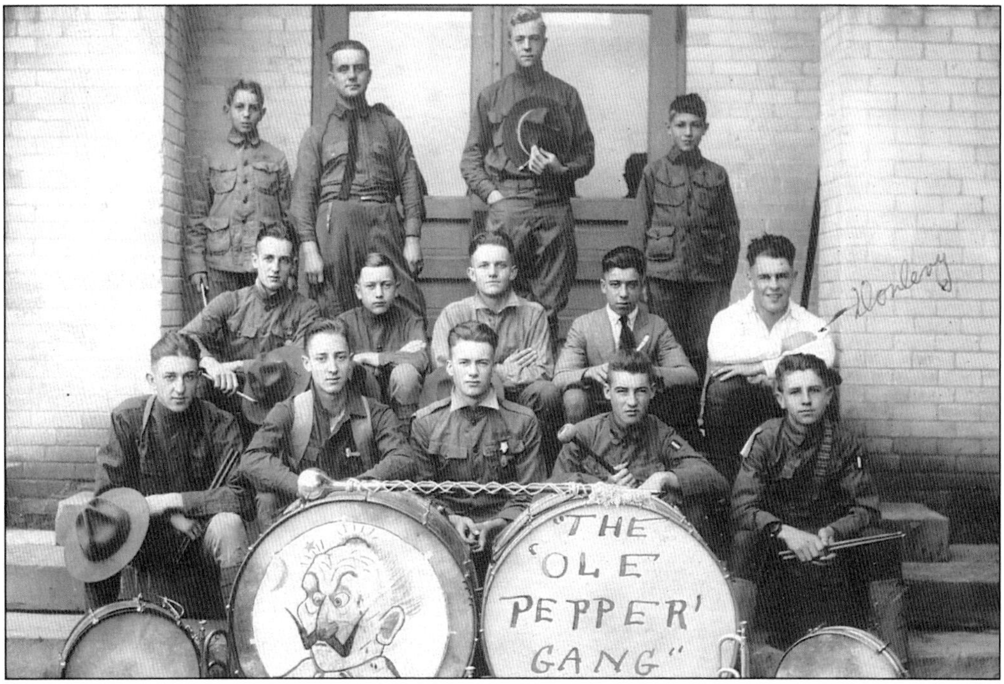

Boy Scout Fife, Drum and Bugle Corps. The Boy Scout Fife, Drum and Bugle Corps was organized in 1917, the first of its kind in the state. Robert Pfeiffer painted a picture of Kaiser Wilhelm on his drum, and during parades would hit the Kaiser on the nose. Pictured here, from left to right, are: (first row) Henry Boldt, Victor Kutzback, Abner Heald, William Schneider, and Reuben Pfeifer; (middle row) Elmo Nelson, Thomas Hertzberg, Henry Schlichting, and Brian Donlevy; and (top row) Milford Wachter, Robert Pfeifer, Volney Leister, Albert Phalen, and Alex Kolb.

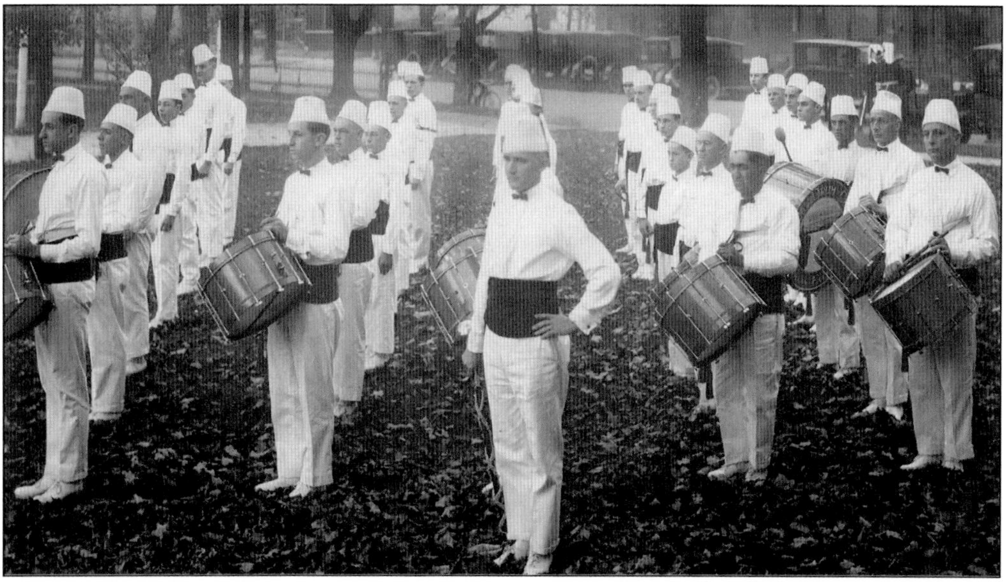

FALLS FIFE DRUM AND BUGLE CORPS. The Falls Fife and Drum Corps was prominent during the 1920s and 30s. This picture shows the group in 1923. The drum major with hand on hip in front was Lester Schleider. Other members were (no order is known): Ruben Schroeder, James Stroub, Hank Boldt, Bill Schneider, Norbert Never, Carlos Schlichting, Otis Burich, Bill Rietz, Jim Deeley, Hertz Hertzberg, Hank Kennedy, Marty Kraus, Jack Van Ouwerkerk, Hank Boldt, Al Burich, Bill Brinkmann, Harvey Dittes, Red Hein, Remo Lindner, Fritz Kirtchen, Fritz Kraus, Milford Wachter, Len Kalk, Ernie Kohlhagen, Al Phalen, and Ray Wachter.

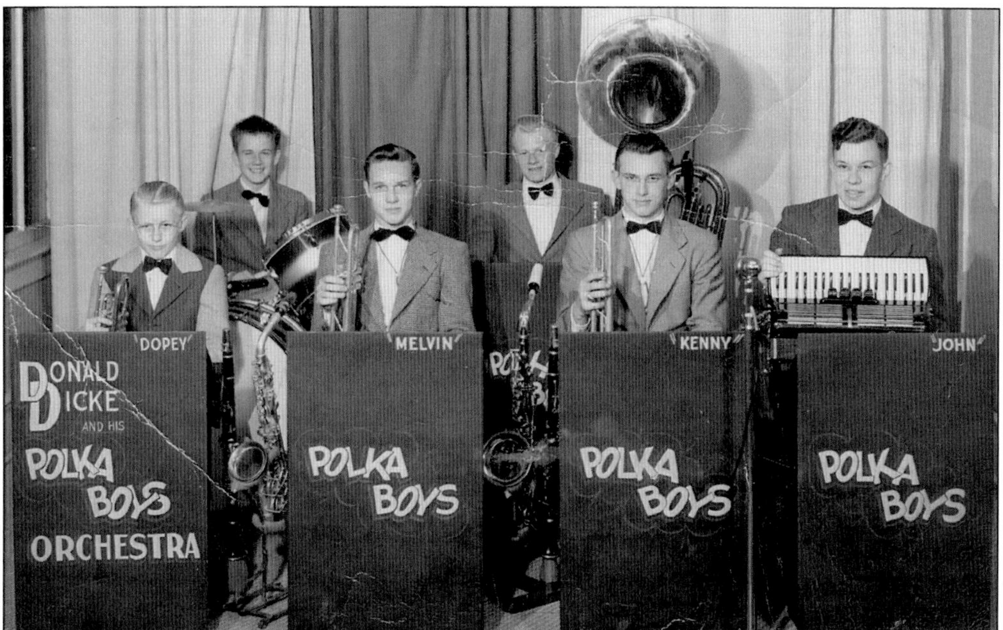

POLKA BOYS ORCHESTRA. The Donald Dicke Polka Boys Orchestra is shown in 1947. The boys began playing together in high school. They are, from left to right: Delbert Dickie, Paul Baumgartner, Melvin Nelson, Donald Dicke, Kenneth Mauer, and John Federwisch.

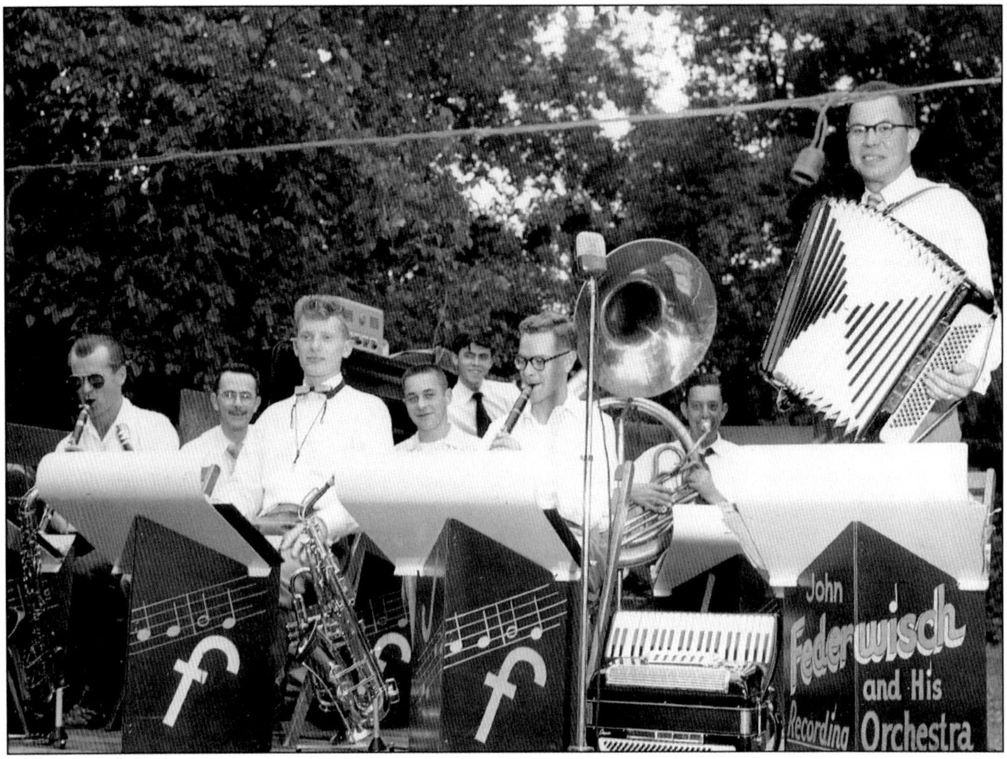

FEDERWISCH ORCHESTRA. John Federwisch organized his own orchestra in the 1950s. They are, from left to right, front: Bob Kronen, Warren Ketz, Gus Bortz, and John Federwisch. Besides music, there were many other types of entertainment.

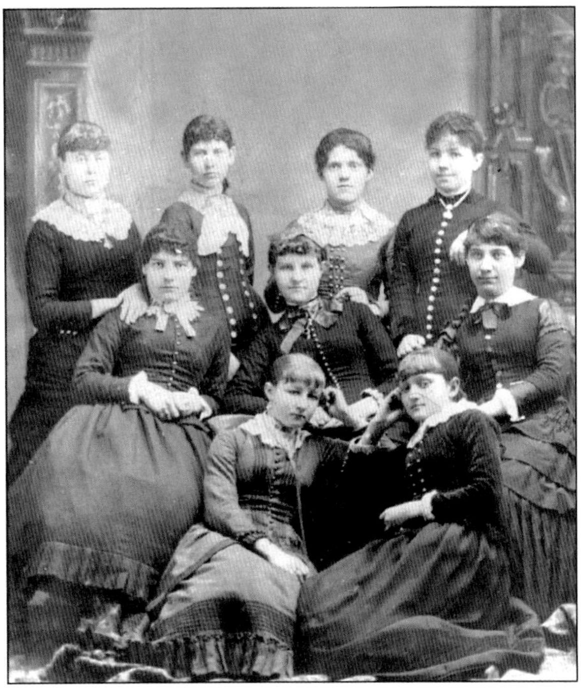

E.M. CLUB. The E.M. Club of 1886 included the following women: (standing) Lola Stewart, Emily Adriance, Jesse Dennet, and Clara Bode; (second row) Inez Ashcroft, Jennie Dixon, and Hattie DeLong; and (front row) Jennie Ballschmider and Clara Smith.

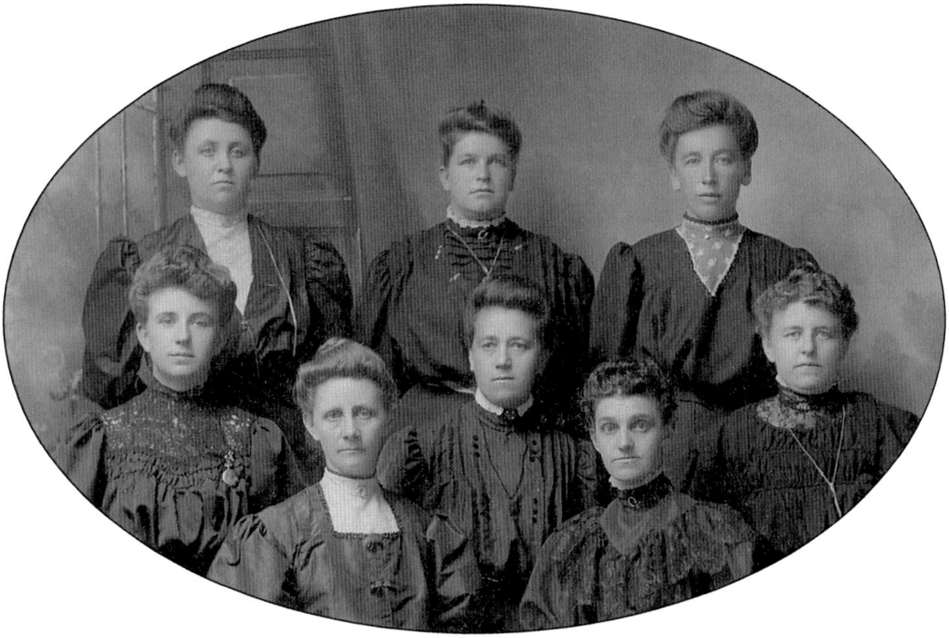

FALLS CARD CLUB. Card playing was a popular pass time in 1911 when this picture of the Sheboygan Falls Card Club was taken. The women in the picture are Laura Wachter, Minnie Rohle, Leana Kehl, Ella Schneiderwent, Minnie Mandle, Anna Vick, and Anna Bart.

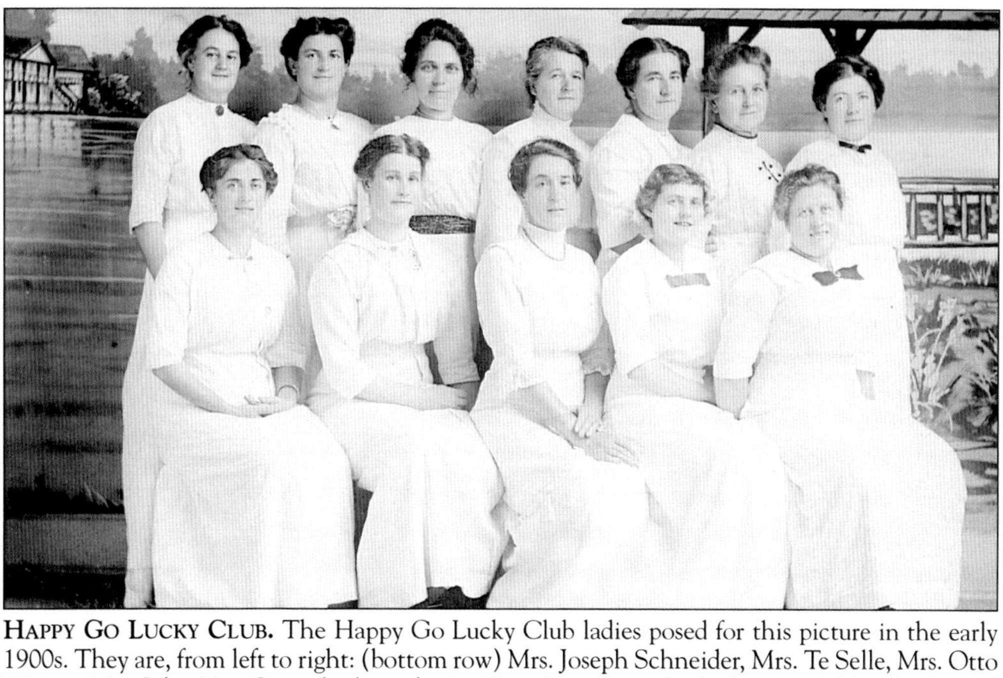

HAPPY GO LUCKY CLUB. The Happy Go Lucky Club ladies posed for this picture in the early 1900s. They are, from left to right: (bottom row) Mrs. Joseph Schneider, Mrs. Te Selle, Mrs. Otto Weisse, Mrs. John Van Ouwerkerk, and Mrs. Tony Van Ouwerkerk; (top row) Mrs. Anderson, Mrs. Herman Boldt, Mrs. Never, Mrs. William Habighorst, Mrs Louis Weisse, Mrs. Bauernfiend, and Mrs. O.J. Matthias.

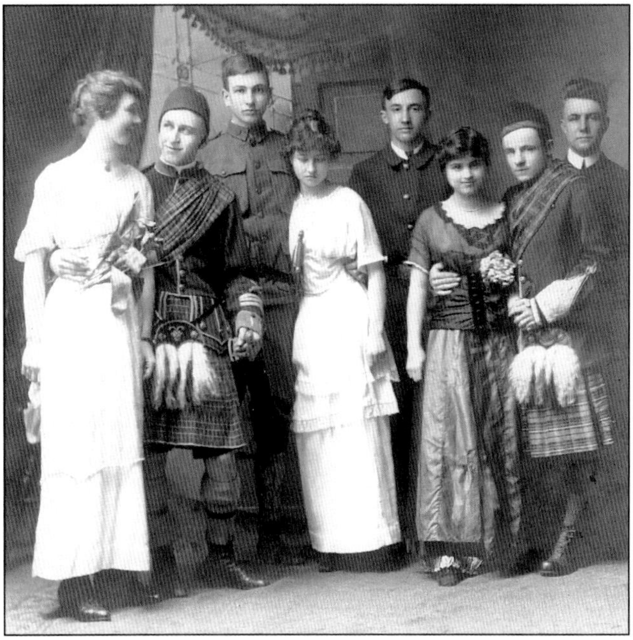

BUSY LIAR. The play *A Busy Liar* was presented at the Woodman Opera House in 1915. From left to right are: Elizabeth Phalen, Philip George, Oliver Pfeifer, Virginia Meyer, Burton Leavens, Marjory Van Ouwerkerk, Edward Barry, and H.D. Leister (director).

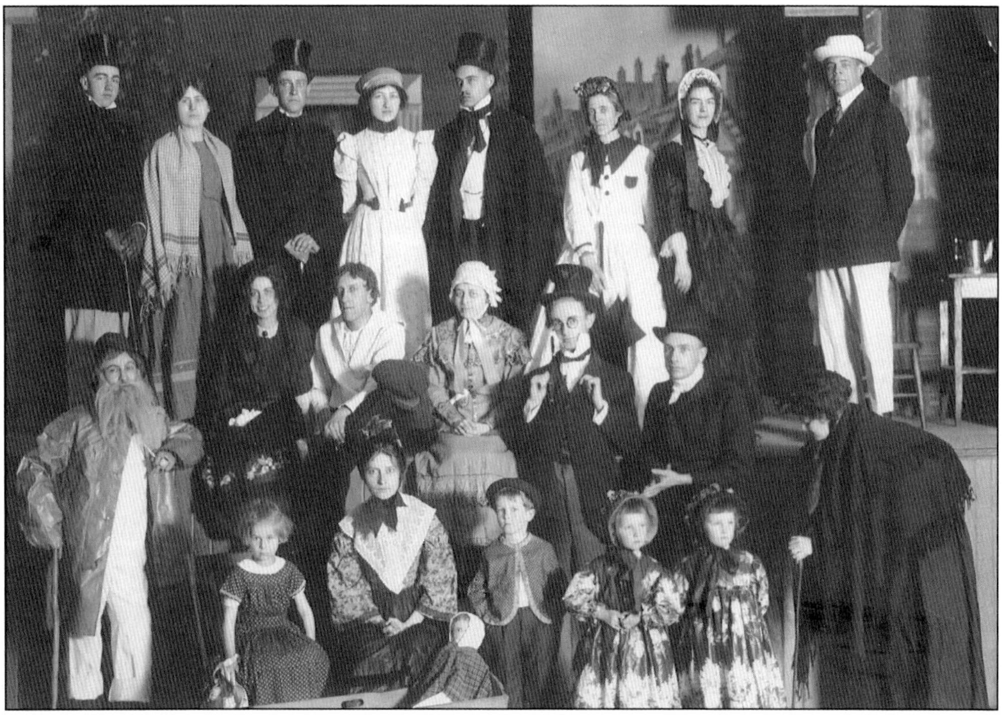

WOMAN'S STUDY CLUB. Another play, *David Copperfield*, was presented at the opera house in 1915 by the Sheboygan Falls Woman's Study Club. Participants are: (seated, in the foreground) Adell Hartenberger, Esther Nichols, Henry Whitson, and Ethel and Edith Fricke; (standing, bottom row) Maurice Kalk, Perle Goude, Paul Schlichting, Hazel Sanford, Harold Theobald, Asher Leavens, and Adelle Le Lano; and (top row) Theodore Phalen, Lillian Froggaet, Herbert Wildemuth, Rose Towrogg, Robert Richardson, Neil Cashman, Bertha Riedel, and Gilbert Kohlhagen.

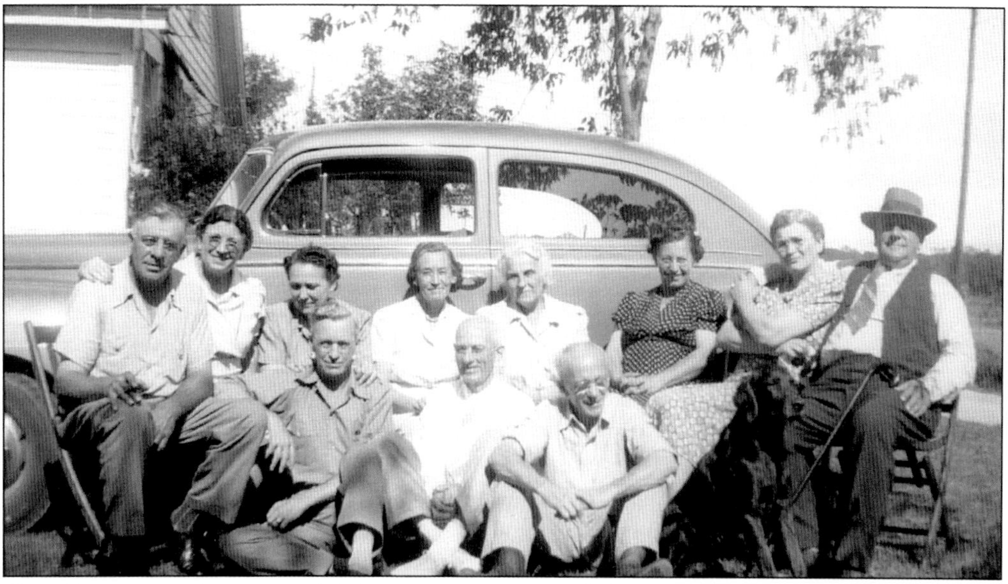

THE GANG. Another card club featuring women and their spouses was called "The Gang" and played in the 1930s. Pictured are: (front row) Joseph Kohlhagen, Tim McKinnon, Hugo Reichert, and Albert Schneiderwent; and (back row) Ella Schneidewent, Erma McKinnon, Margaret Reichert, Emma Blust, Myrl Kohlhagen, and Edward Blust.

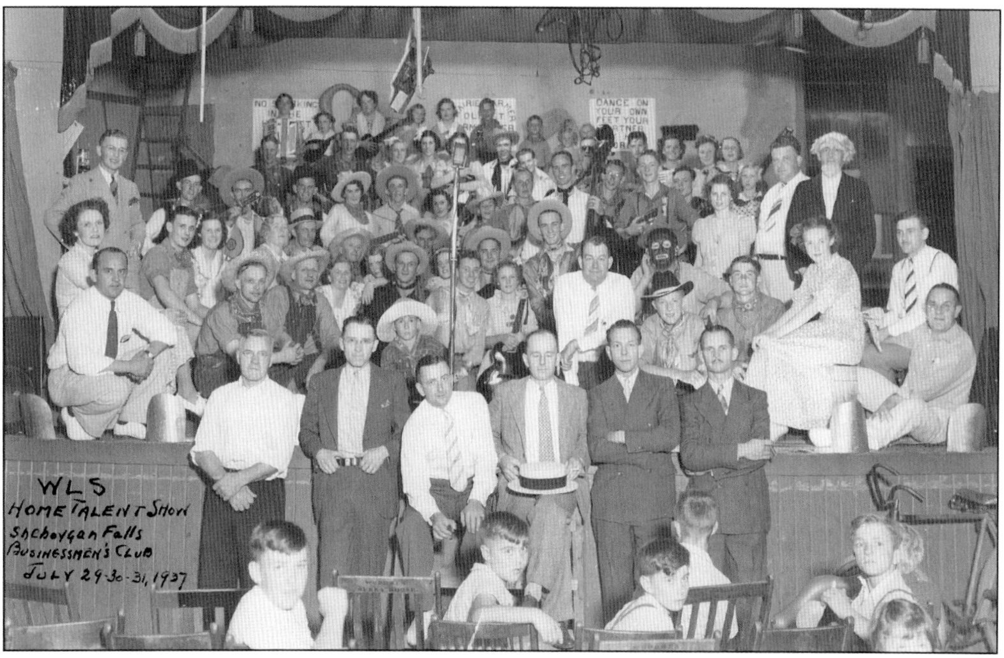

FALLS BUSINESSMEN'S CLUB. The Sheboygan Falls Businessmen's Club sponsored a Home Talent Show in connection with radio station WLS July 29-31, 1937. Pictured, from left to right, are: Elmer Gerber (kneeling on stage); Joseph Schneider, Larry Pierce, Henry Rath, Willard Erdman, Carlos Schlichting, and Bert Fowler (standing in front of stage); Al Koepke and John Claerbout (sitting on right of stage and standing behind them); and Joe Sanford and Paul Ebbers. Luke Zumbro is in the center.

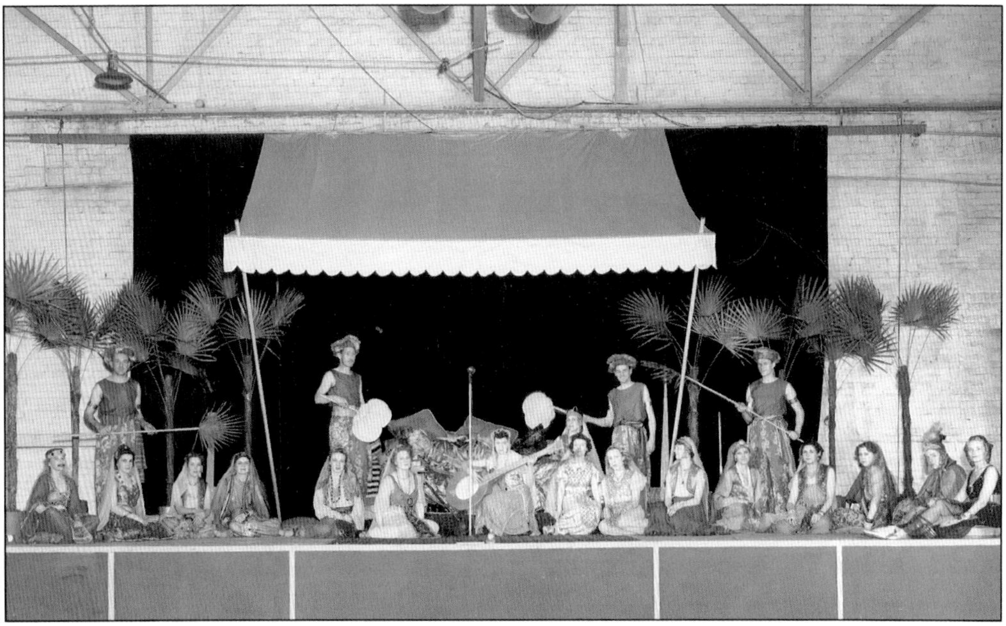

Streets of Baghdad. During World War II an ambitious production entitled *Streets of Baghdad* was held in the Market Hall of the Curt G. Joa plant. It was the climax of the community's Fourth War Loan Drive in February 1944. It was the most successful war bond drive in the county. The Market Hall was transformed into a Persian market where costumed musicians, fortune tellers, and vendors strolled through the crowds of people attending. J.A. Sampson, Sheboygan manufacturer, was the Sultan, and his harem were "sold" at auction. More than $300,000 in war bonds were sold.

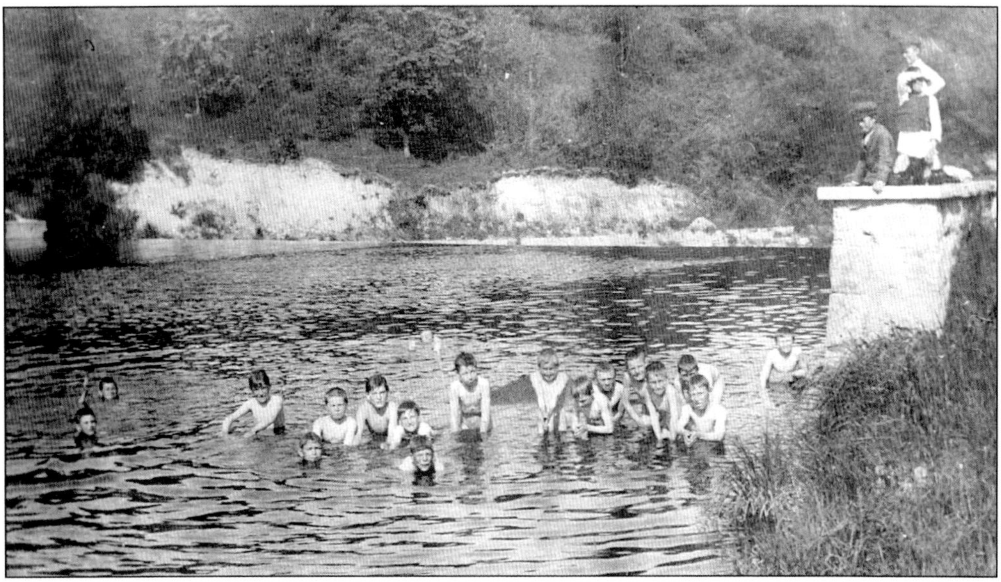

Swimmers. The Sheboygan River provided all types of entertainment for children and adults alike: fishing, boating, swimming, and, in winter, ice skating. These young boys found a place to swim above the upper dam in 1908. The upper dam is located off what is now Settlers' Park on Broadway Street.

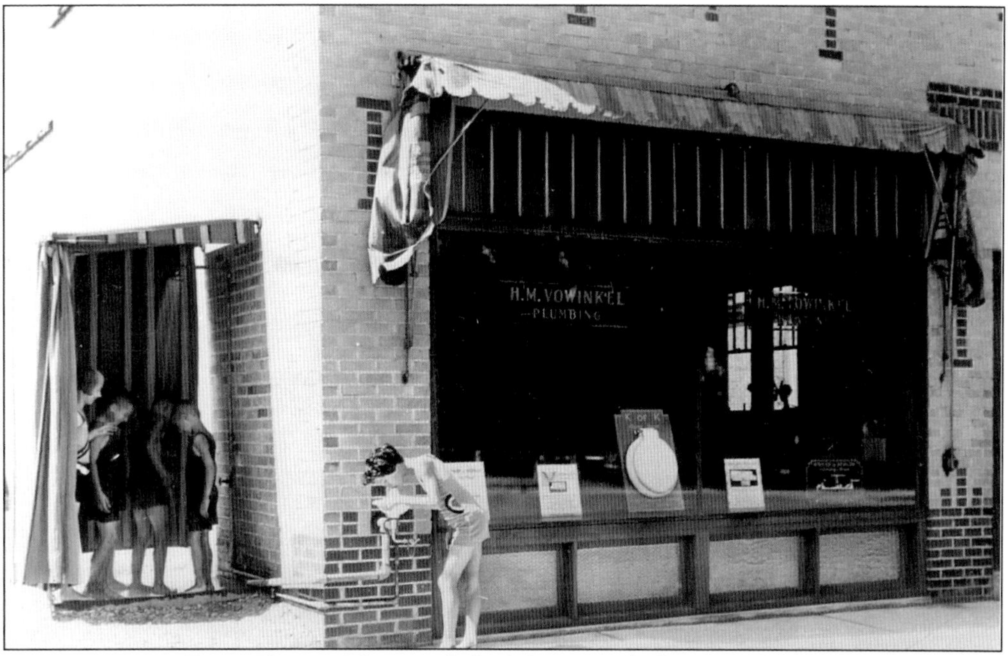

NEIGHBORHOOD BATH HOUSE. This simple bath house with shower and drinking fountain was provided for swimmers by Vowinkel Plumbing. Swimmers from the nearby local swimming hole in the Sheboygan River were able to stop and shower off before going home, and get a cold drink from the water fountain attached to the building.

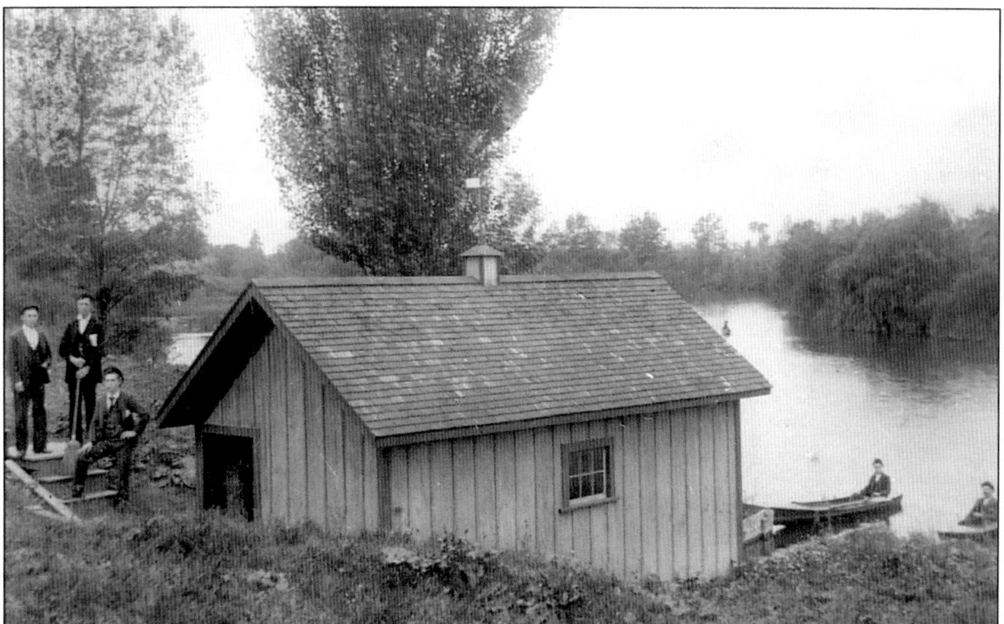

SERVIS BOAT HOUSE. The Servis boat house safely stored boats to be used on the Sheboygan River. This picture from October 1892 shows the following young men on shore beside the boat house: Fred Hauenstein, Les Servis, and William Hempschmeyer. The swinging bridge now begins at this spot on Monroe Street, just to the east of the Bemis Manufacturing Company.

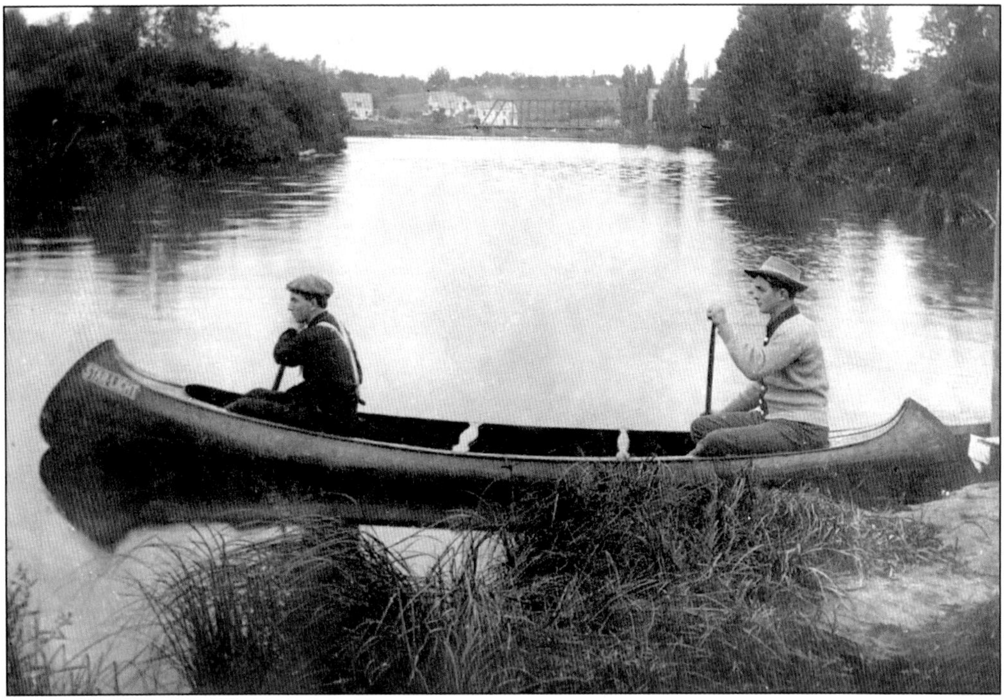

CANOEING ON THE SHEBOYGAN RIVER. Will Lumsden and Fred Gardner canoe what was known as "Baptist Bay" in 1905. They kept their canoes in the boat house in back of the Franklin House on the River. Teenagers, when allowed to date, took canoe rides up the river, especially on moonlit nights.

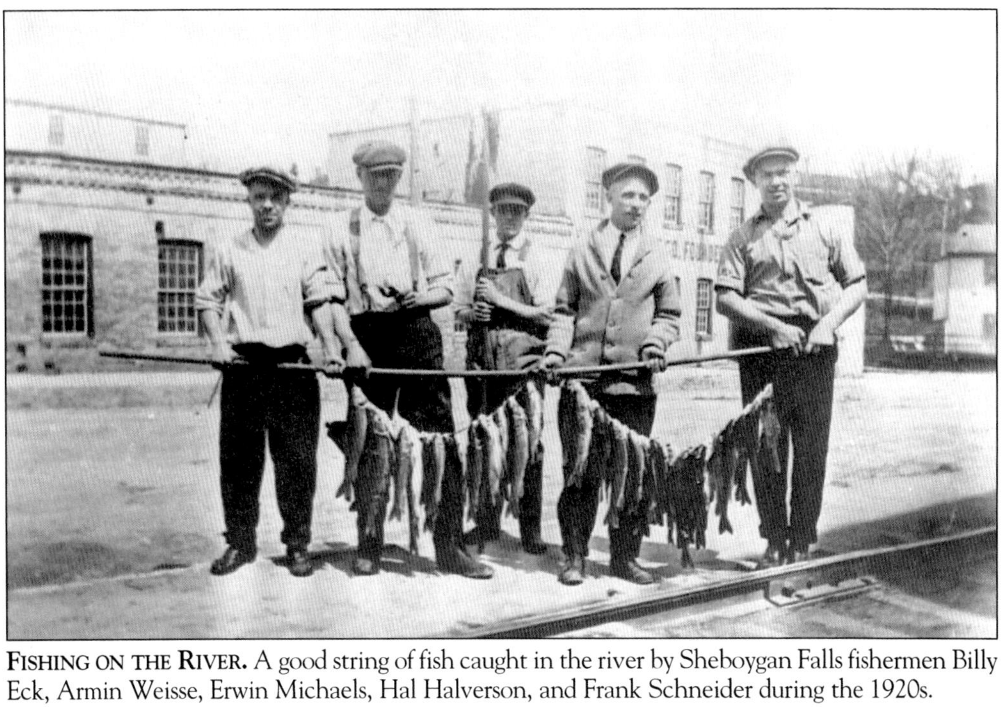

FISHING ON THE RIVER. A good string of fish caught in the river by Sheboygan Falls fishermen Billy Eck, Armin Weisse, Erwin Michaels, Hal Halverson, and Frank Schneider during the 1920s.

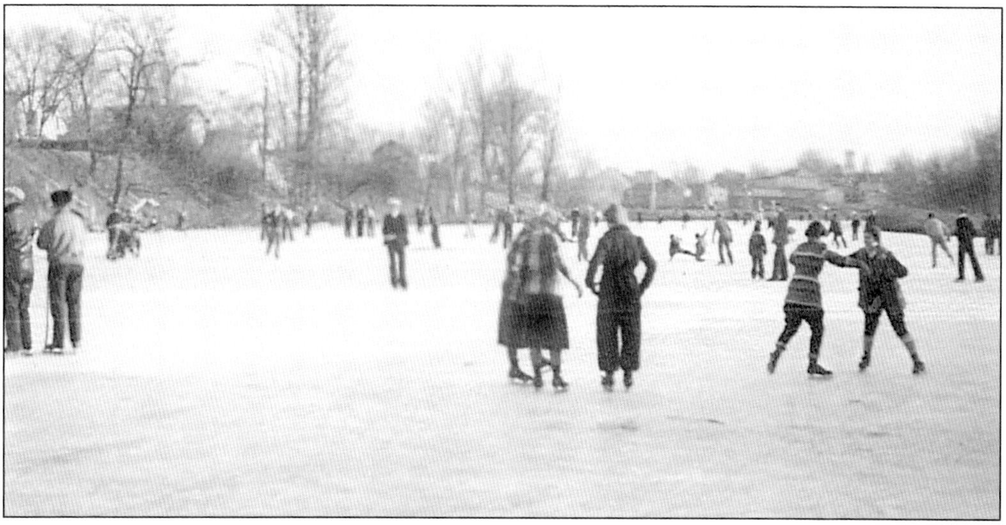

SKATING ON THE RIVER. Skating in winter was a popular pastime on the river from the swinging bridge to the Leavens Avenue Bridge. Children and adults alike took part in the fun. Today, the lagoon is a popular place for hockey games, crack-the-whip, and racing.

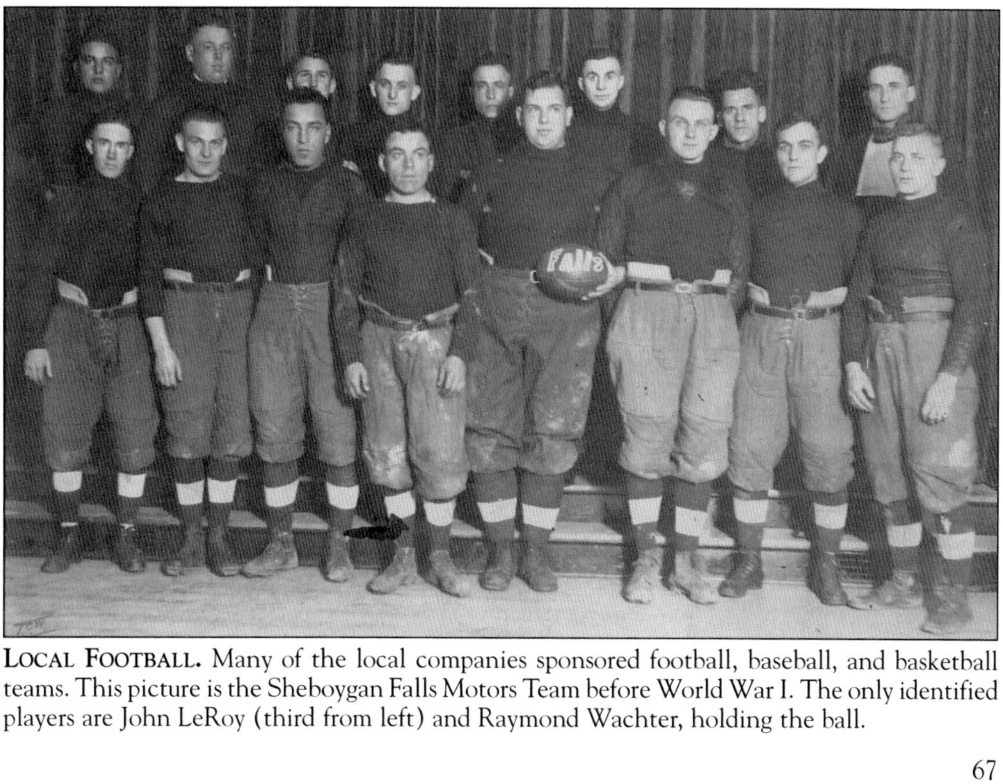

LOCAL FOOTBALL. Many of the local companies sponsored football, baseball, and basketball teams. This picture is the Sheboygan Falls Motors Team before World War I. The only identified players are John LeRoy (third from left) and Raymond Wachter, holding the ball.

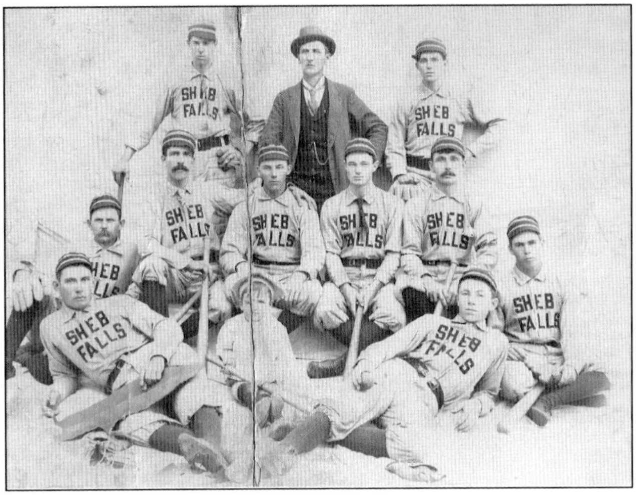

FALLS BASEBALL. The following men, pictured here from left to right, played for an early baseball team, c. 1898: (first row) Edwin Wolf, George Ogle, and Art Hertzberg; (second row) Henry Schlichting, Otto Bassuener, John Delevan, Michael Deeley; and (third row) Louis Granold, Frank Gutheil, Paul Shenkelberger, Charles Visser, and Edward McKinnon.

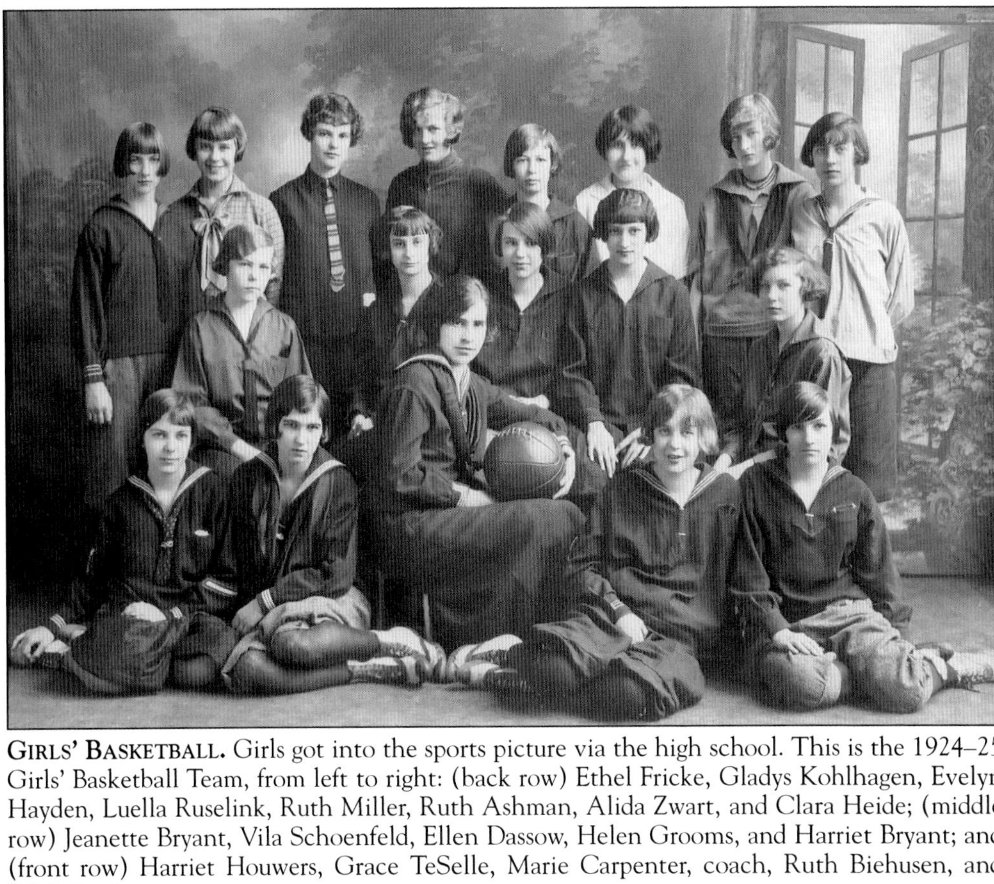

GIRLS' BASKETBALL. Girls got into the sports picture via the high school. This is the 1924–25 Girls' Basketball Team, from left to right: (back row) Ethel Fricke, Gladys Kohlhagen, Evelyn Hayden, Luella Ruselink, Ruth Miller, Ruth Ashman, Alida Zwart, and Clara Heide; (middle row) Jeanette Bryant, Vila Schoenfeld, Ellen Dassow, Helen Grooms, and Harriet Bryant; and (front row) Harriet Houwers, Grace TeSelle, Marie Carpenter, coach, Ruth Biehusen, and Edith Fricke.

Six

DISASTERS

Fires and floods are an exciting part of the history of Sheboygan Falls. In the early days, all buildings were wooden structures. Fire-fighting equipment was limited, and once a fire began, buildings were easily destroyed. On the east side of Broadway, extending north one block from the railroad tracks, were several frame buildings, all of which were destroyed in 1868 by one of the most disastrous fires in the history of Sheboygan Falls. The city has also suffered two damaging floods. The first occurred in 1883. Accounts state that, "a portion of the river branched off the upper pond—probably where the municipal parking lot is now—and went over the banks" The water was one to two feet deep along the railroad tracks. The wayward stream went along Buffalo Street to the railroad tracks and then traveled back to the river entering it just above the lower dam. The 1905 flood was accompanied by torrential rains which washed out many of the same areas. Leaf tobacco stored in the basement of Kehl Cigar Factory was damaged and found floating in the street. Water was four feet deep in the Richardson Mill, and up to the window sills of the County News building.

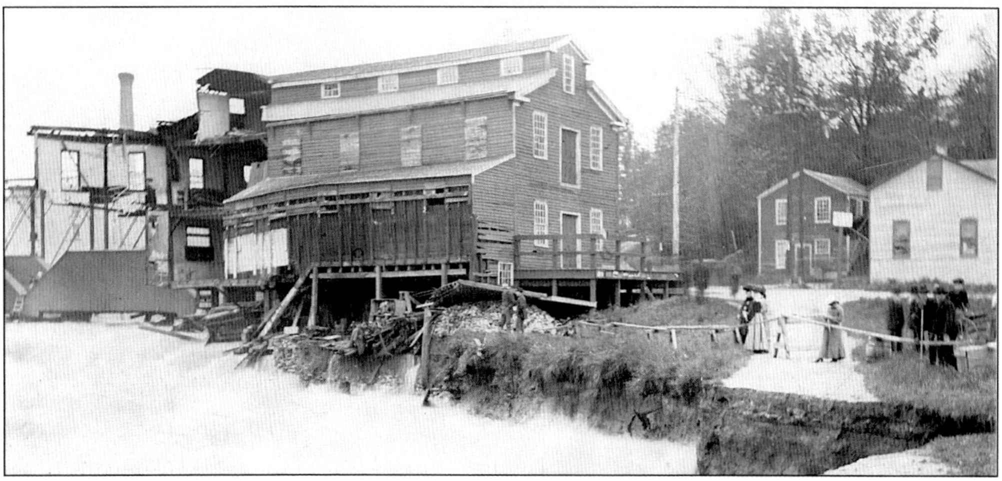

FALLS FLOOD DAMAGE. Situated and built around the meanderings of the Sheboygan River, Sheboygan Falls had its share of flooding during its history. The worst flood occurred in July 1883, when the old Stedman mill, the oldest standing landmark in the village, was swept away by the force of the water. In June 1905, an almost identical flood swept away a part of the Brickner Woolen mill warehouse, which had been built on the site of the Stedman mill. This image looks north towards the Kirkland Cooperage.

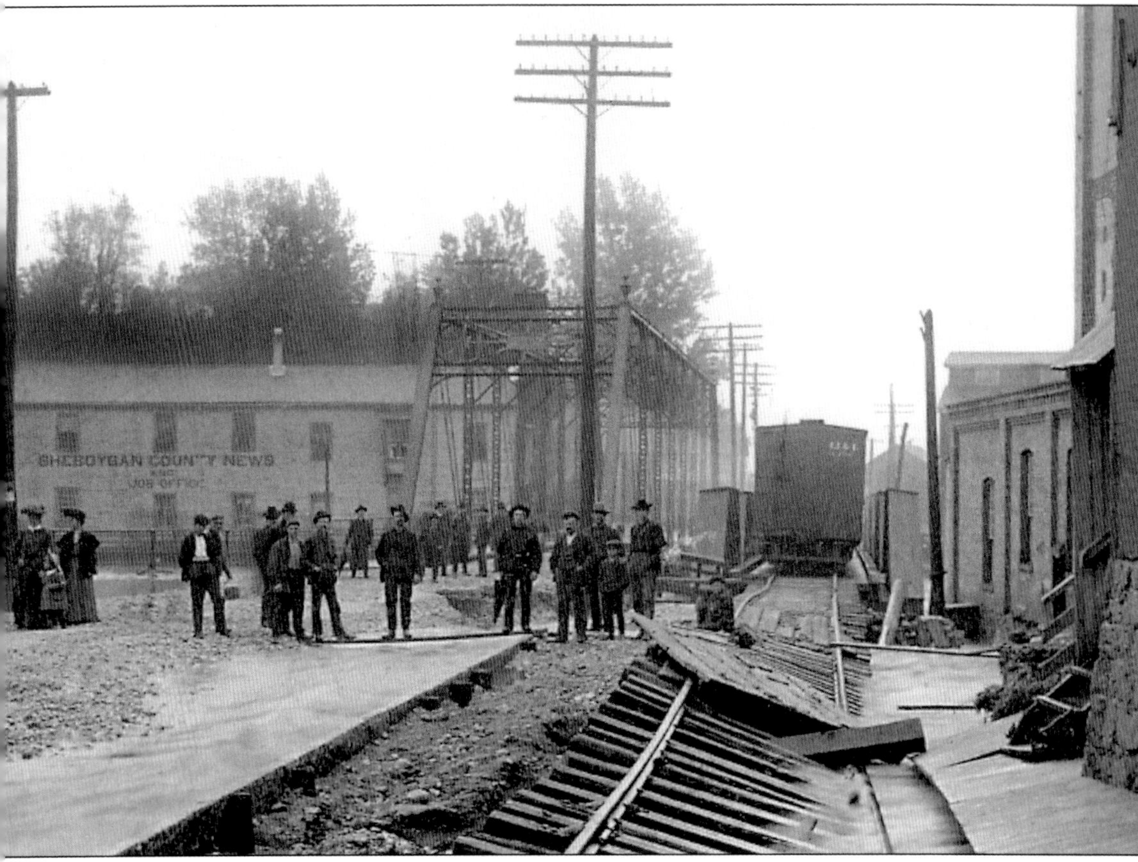

Historic Floods. Looking east on Monroe from Broadway, this photo shows more of the damage caused by the June of 1905 flood. Area residents gathered to view the terrible destruction. Throughout the village rail tracks were undercut by flood waters. It would be many weeks before train travel resumed. Loaded Chicago and Northwestern railroad cars were moved to the railway bridge over the Sheboygan River to hold it down as the flood waters raced underneath. This photo was taken by early Falls' photographer A.M. Bertram. The Sheboygan County News building is seen in the background at left. What is left of the Brickner Woolen Mills warehouse is seen at far right.

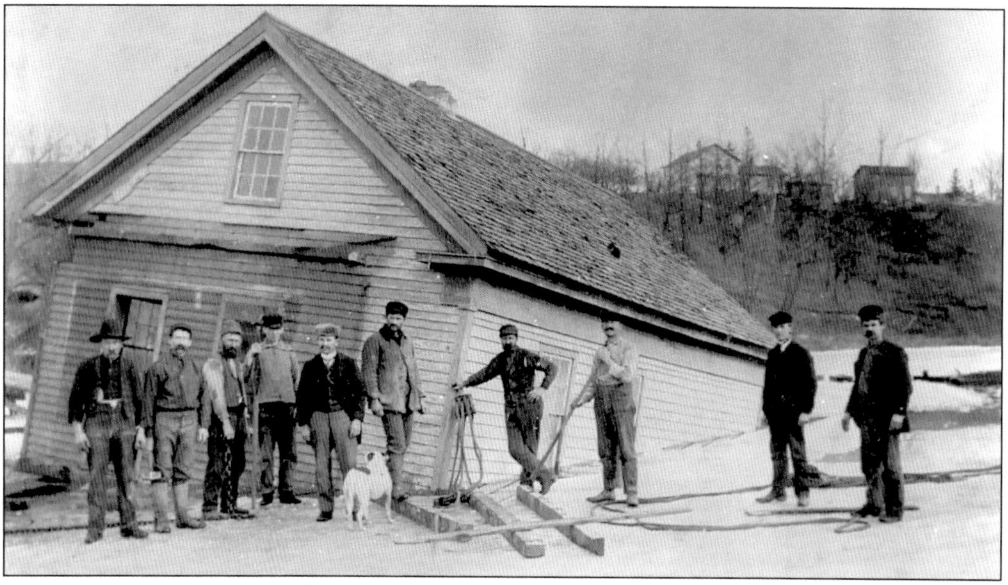

RIVER TRANSPORTATION. The river has always played an important role in the life of the community. In a day and age when it was commonplace to move buildings from one site to another (January of 1900), Otto Rickmeier and his crew attempted to move a building across the ice just above the upper dam. This one story building originally stood next to Henry's Creamery on Buffalo Street. It was bound for a site across the river, when the rear end of the building broke through the ice. Rickmeier and crew managed to get the building to the opposite shore in one piece without much damage.

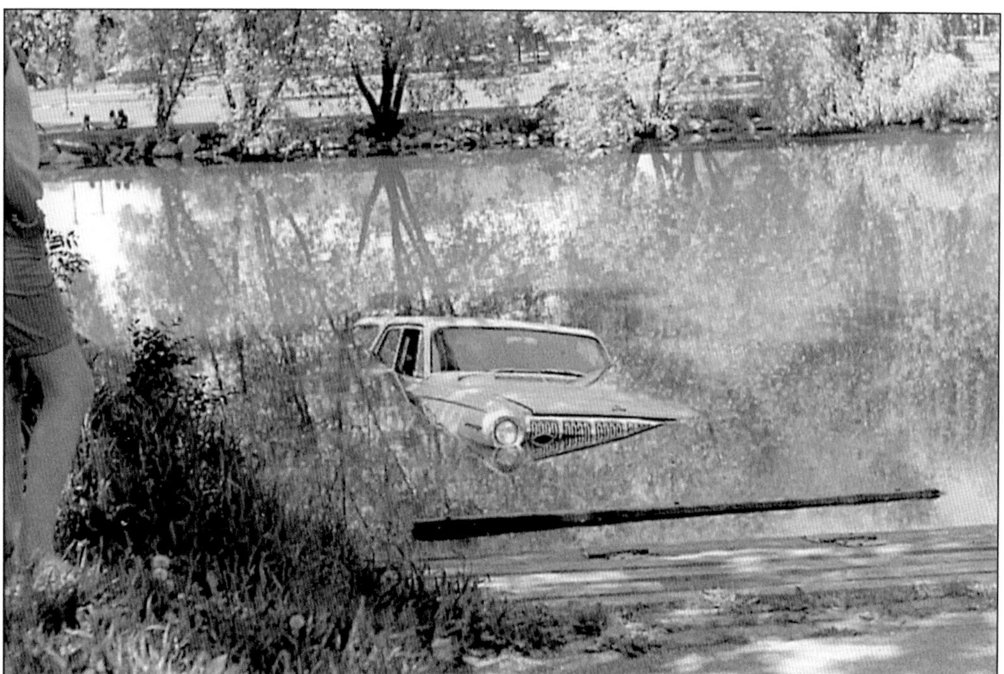

WRONG TURN. In a more modern day, the river attempted to swallow a car near Riverview Park. It was rescued by the B. & B. Ford wrecker.

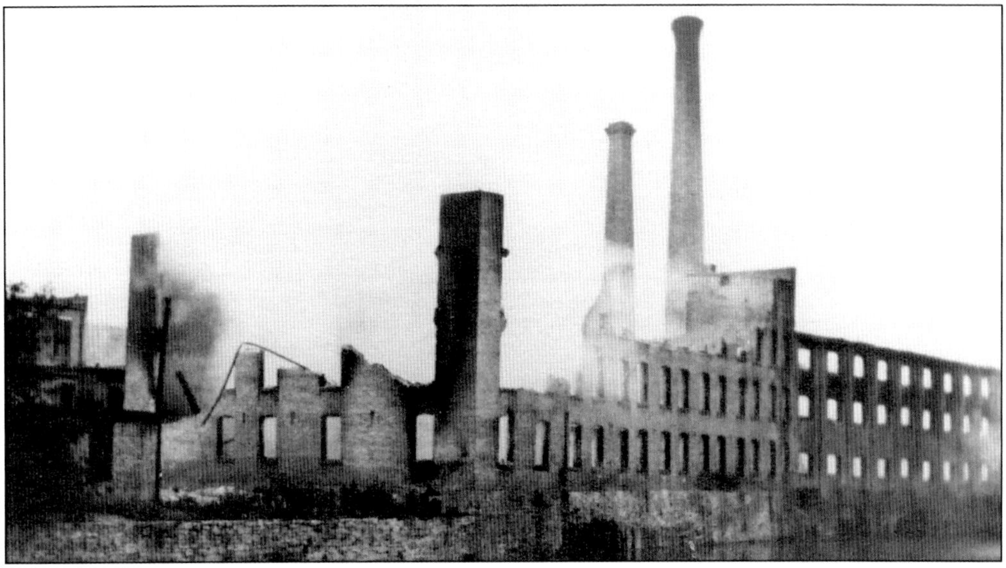

FIRE DISASTERS. Fire has always been a destructive force especially in buildings constructed of wood. One of the worst fires in Sheboygan Falls' history occurred in April 1867. An entire block of wooden buildings on Broadway north of Monroe was destroyed, and the block became known as the 'burnt district.' Probably the worst fire in monetary damages was that in the Weisse Tannery September 28, 1919. The tannery was a complete loss, with damages estimated at $160,000.

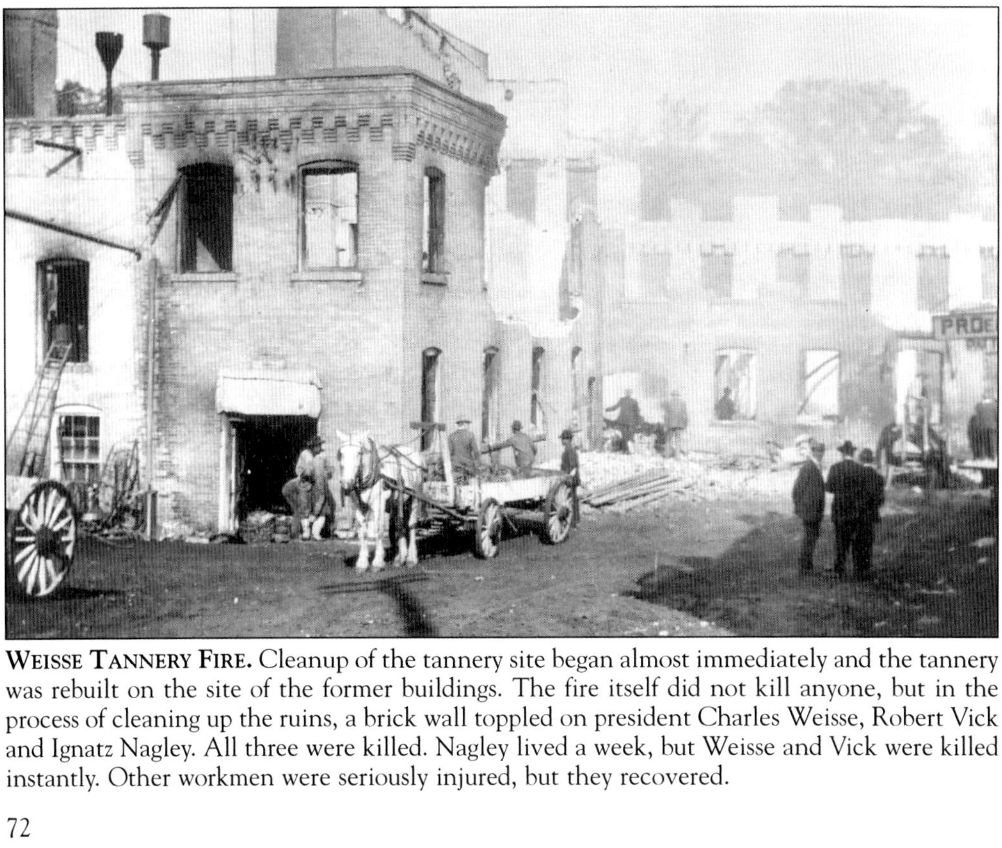

WEISSE TANNERY FIRE. Cleanup of the tannery site began almost immediately and the tannery was rebuilt on the site of the former buildings. The fire itself did not kill anyone, but in the process of cleaning up the ruins, a brick wall toppled on president Charles Weisse, Robert Vick and Ignatz Nagley. All three were killed. Nagley lived a week, but Weisse and Vick were killed instantly. Other workmen were seriously injured, but they recovered.

CITY HOTEL. Built by Louis Ballschmider in 1892 at a cost of $10,000, the City Hotel was a showplace for Sheboygan Falls. This three-story structure had a bar, 25 rooms for rent, and a ballroom on the third floor where many dances, political meetings, and banquets were held. The hotel stood on the northwest corner of Broadway and Maple Streets. The Schreiners succeeded the Ballschmiders as owners. They were known for their hospitality, and, especially, their chili.

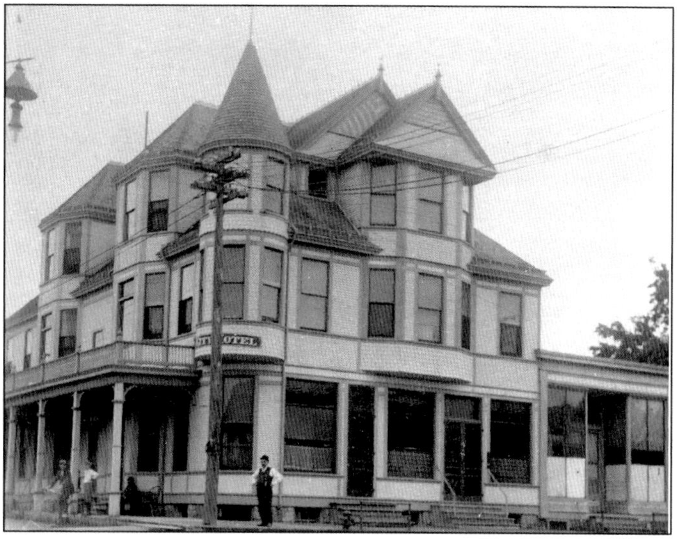

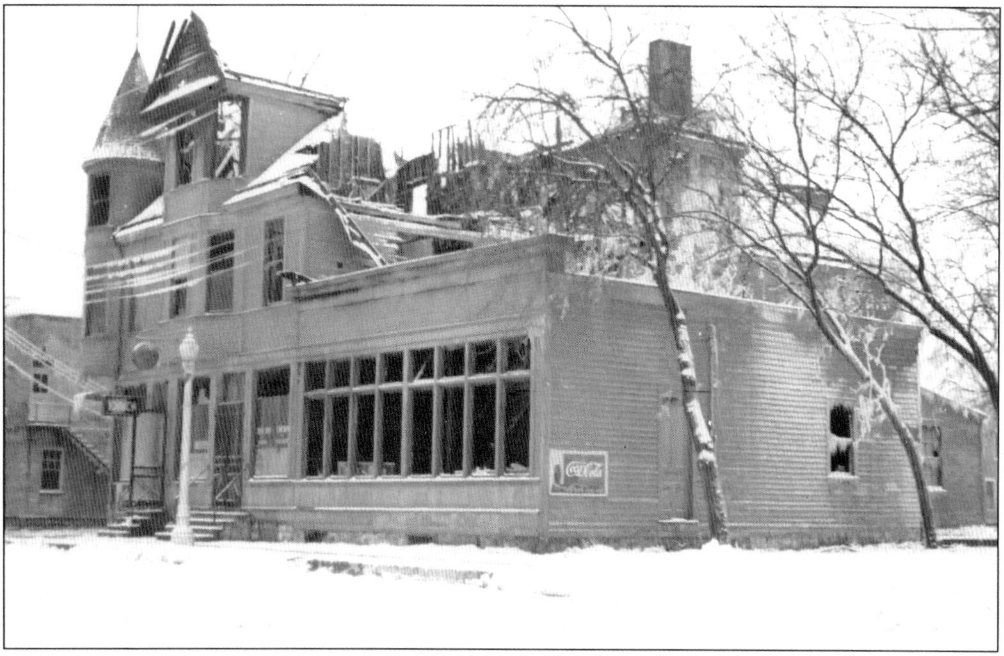

CITY HOTEL FIRE. The hotel had a history of fire. In 1908, the roof of the hotel caught fire. The fire department used such a heavy pressure hose that it knocked firefighter, Herman Boldt, from the peak of the building. He slid down the length of the roof, and, luckily, his clothing caught on the eaves, saving him. Another fire broke out at about 3 a.m. on December 19, 1937. When it was all over, the City Hotel was a charred ruin. Water was poured on the blaze at a rate of 1300 gallons per minute by 10 hose lines. Water froze on all surrounding wires, and formed a solid sheet of ice on the ground. Two men were fined $4.51 each for driving their cars across the fire hoses on Broadway during the fire emergency.

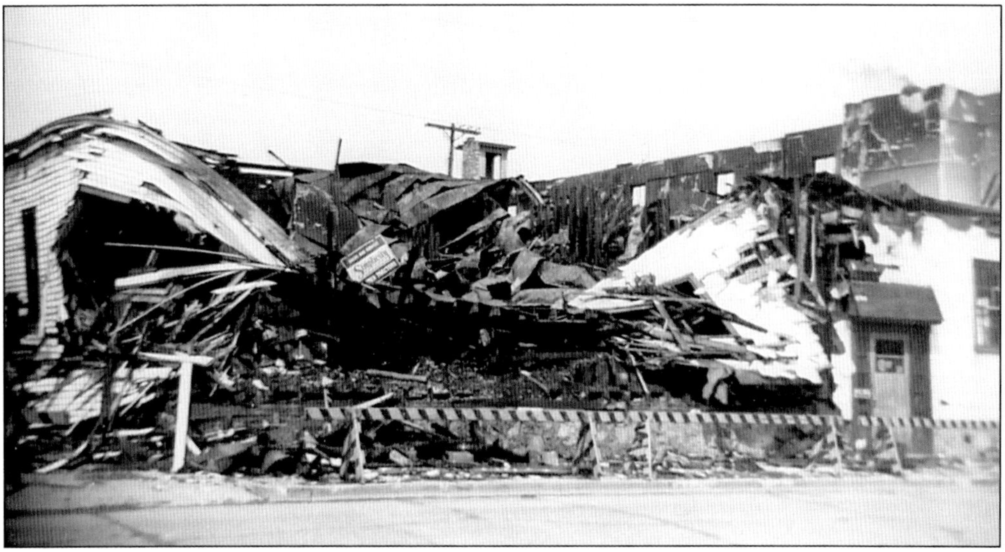

OPERA HOUSE FIRE. Fire struck the Opera House on August 22, 1955. Built in 1885 by Moses Guyett as a hall in conjunction with his hotel, the Guyett House, the Opera House went through many owners in its long life. Its last owner, Paul Ebbers, used it as a warehouse for his hardware store. The fire cost the life of Frank "Boots" Thierman, who was killed by the explosion and resulting fire.

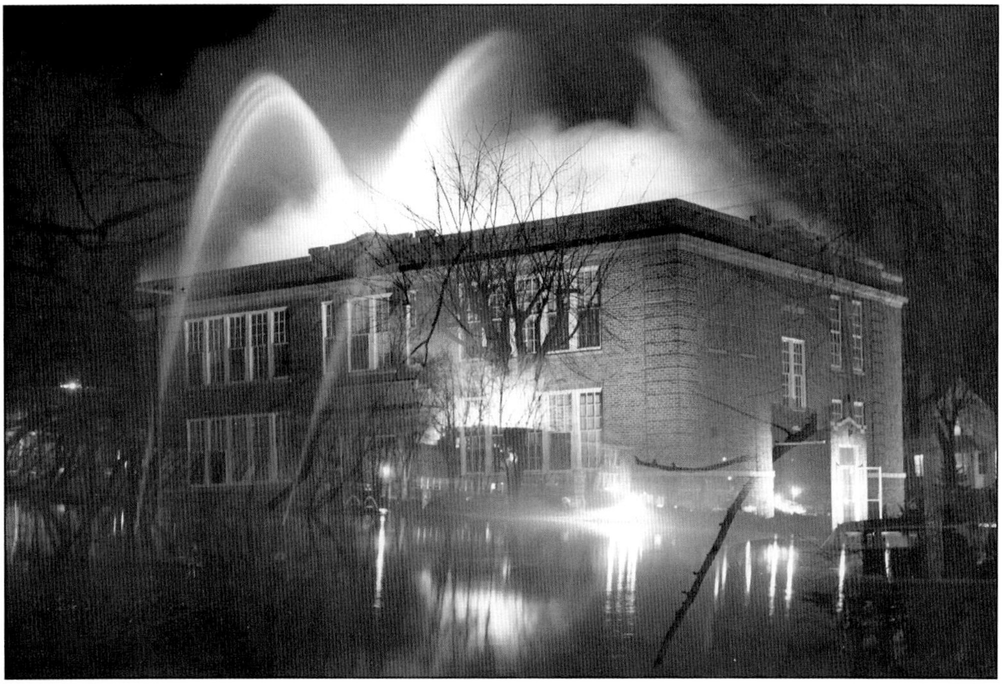

SHEBOYGAN COUNTY TEACHERS' COLLEGE FIRE. Another spectacular fire occurred in April 1965, when the older portion of the Teachers' College burned with a loss of $300,000. Built in 1924, and extensively remodeled in 1959, the night-time fire lit up the sky and brought spectators from all over the city. It took 12 hours to bring the flames under control. The school was rebuilt in a similar style.

Seven

Bridges and the River

So much of the lives of residents of Sheboygan Falls was spent, and is still spent, around the moods of the Sheboygan River. The Sheboygan River grows much larger in the immediate Sheboygan Falls area. The Mullet River joins the Sheboygan River just west of the city near the Richardson Brothers' plant. The Onion River joins the Sheboygan River downstream of the lower falls on its way to Kohler. This chapter will show photos of life around the river, including views of the river, upper dam, and lower falls, all manner of bridges crossing the river and the ravine, and the railroad tracks. Over time, the city has constructed nearly two dozen bridges, ranging from rickety swinging bridges that created shortcuts for residents, to the sturdy iron railroad bridges and concrete auto bridges spanning the water.

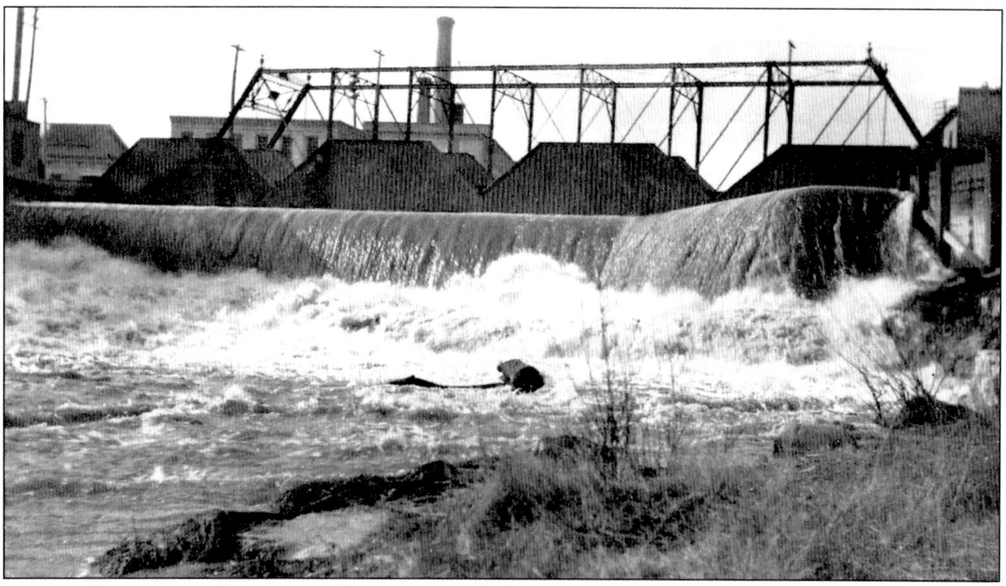

Lower Falls and Railroad Bridge. In Sheboygan Falls, the river is said to have an upper and lower falls, but what it really has is an upper dam and lower falls. Originally, the river had a 20-foot drop over a relatively short span making it ideal for producing power. But over time it has been physically altered by blasting and stone removal, making it far less imposing. Today, what is left of the falls is directly under the Monroe Street railroad and automobile bridges. Tourists who wish to see the city's namesake must look hard from the couple of vantage points south along the river to view the once impressive natural wonder. The tannery buildings are seen behind the bridge.

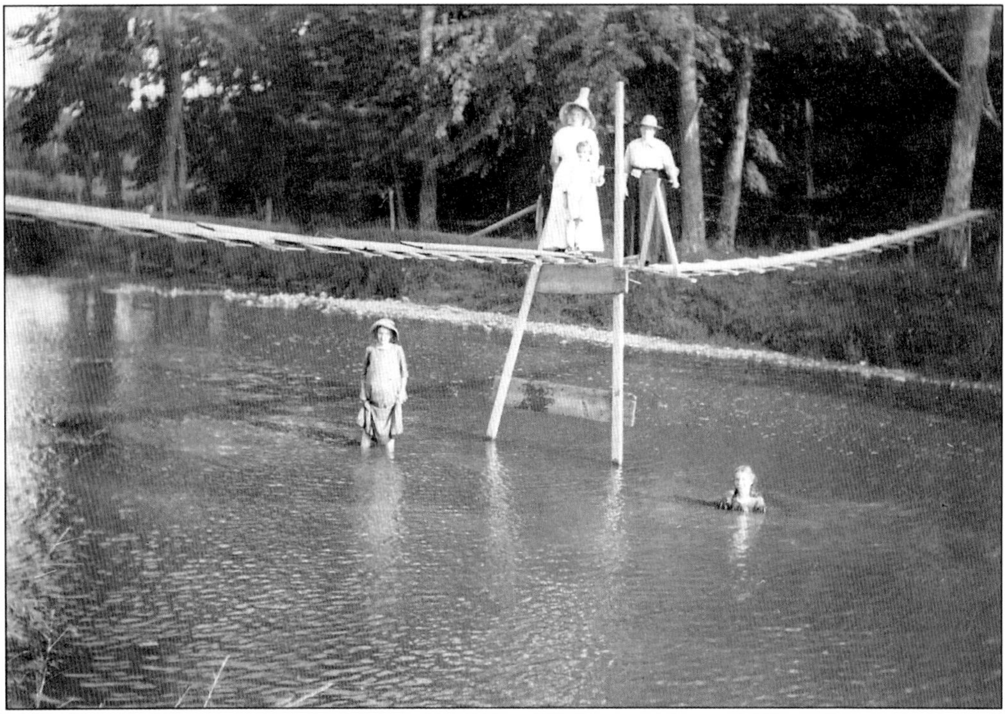

SWINGING BRIDGE. This is a very early view of the "Swinging Bridge" which provided transport across the Sheboygan River from Monore Street, north into River Park, giving access to the north side of the city.

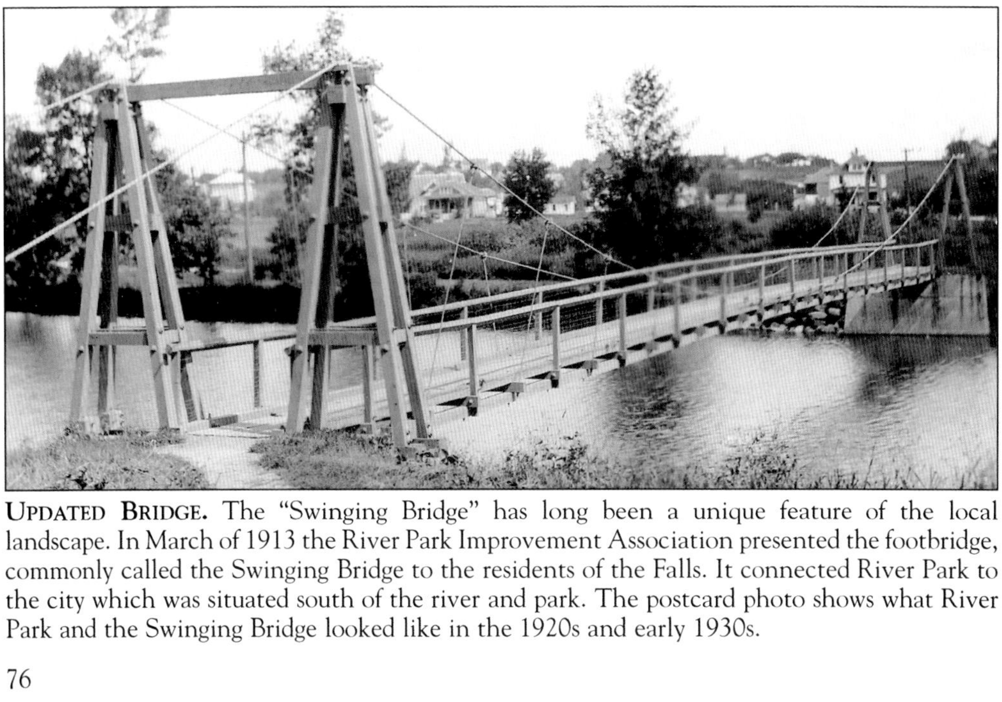

UPDATED BRIDGE. The "Swinging Bridge" has long been a unique feature of the local landscape. In March of 1913 the River Park Improvement Association presented the footbridge, commonly called the Swinging Bridge to the residents of the Falls. It connected River Park to the city which was situated south of the river and park. The postcard photo shows what River Park and the Swinging Bridge looked like in the 1920s and early 1930s.

SUSPENSION SHORTCUT. Here we see a rickety suspension bridge crossing the river at Simpson's Woods. It was used by Richardson employees to get to their jobs at the mill and furniture factory. Asher Leavens is standing on the bridge. The photo is dated 1910.

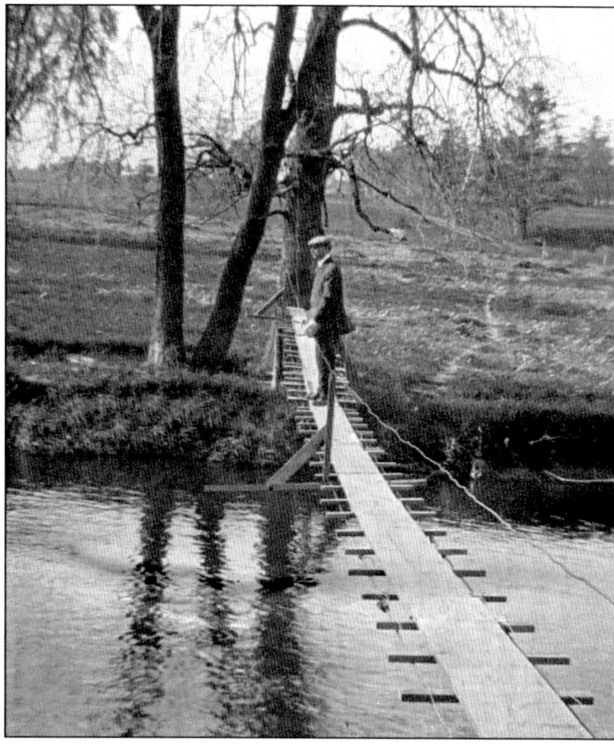

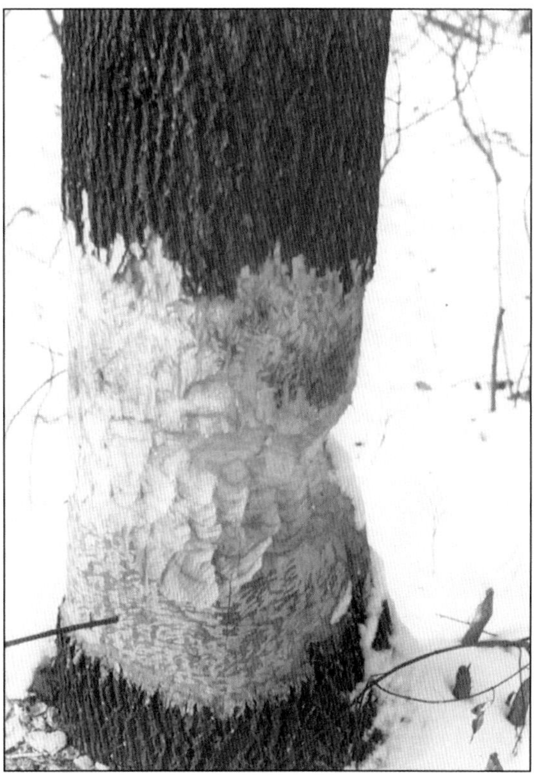

NEIGHBORHOOD RESIDENTS. Damage done by local beavers is shown here in this 1950s photo by Burton Leavens. Wildlife still inhabits the parks in town in large numbers because of the ready supply of water available year around. The Canadian geese that were novelties in the 1960s have become overly populous pests.

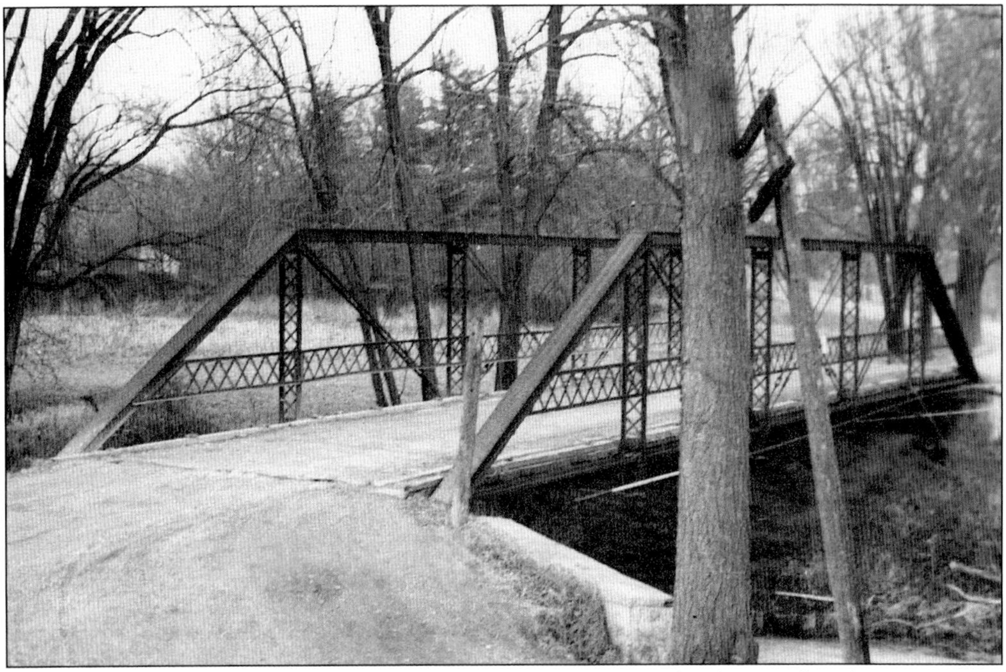

Metal Bridge. This old metal bridge on Highway PP near Richardson Mill is shown in 1898. Will Bryant is the young man looking at river.

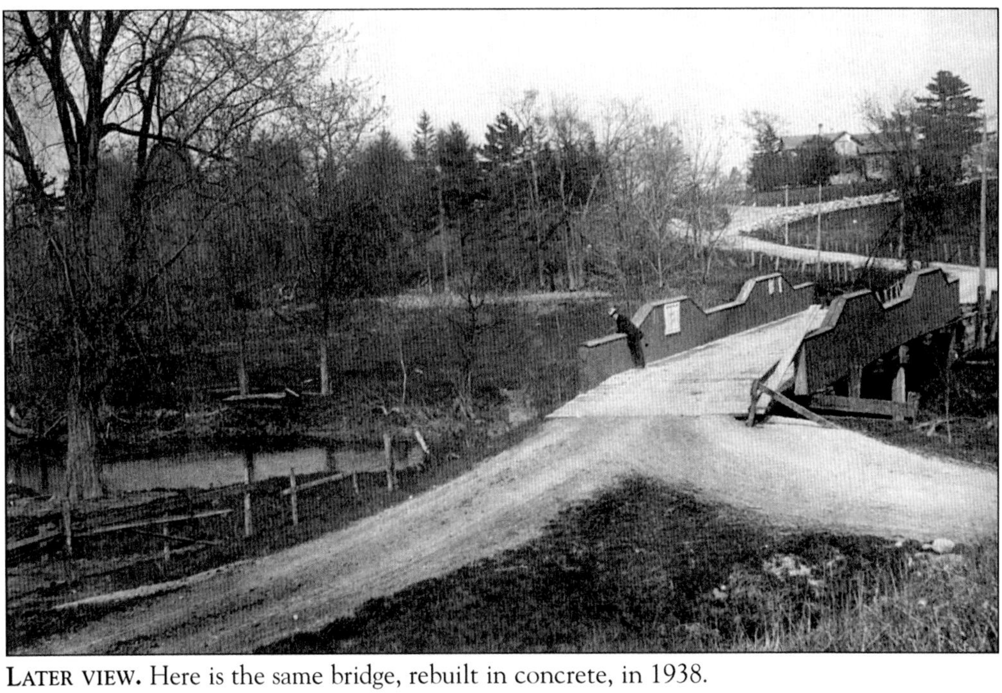

Later view. Here is the same bridge, rebuilt in concrete, in 1938.

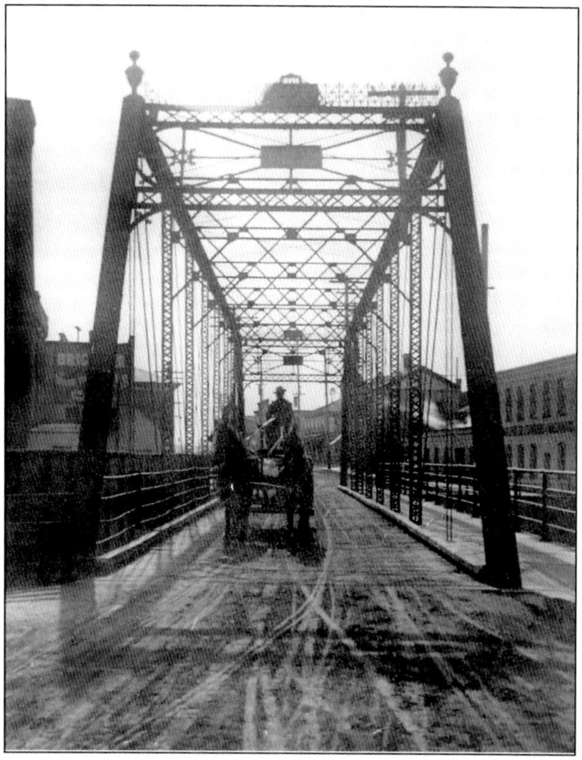

LOWER BRIDGE STREET. This view of the Bridge Street or Lower Bridge is looking west on Bridge or Monroe Street. As seen in the days of the horse and cart, there are no paved streets. Brickner Woolen Mills is on the left and Phoenix Iron Works are on the right. The date of this photo is *c.* 1910. The bridge was built in 1888 by the Milwaukee Bridge and Iron Works Company.

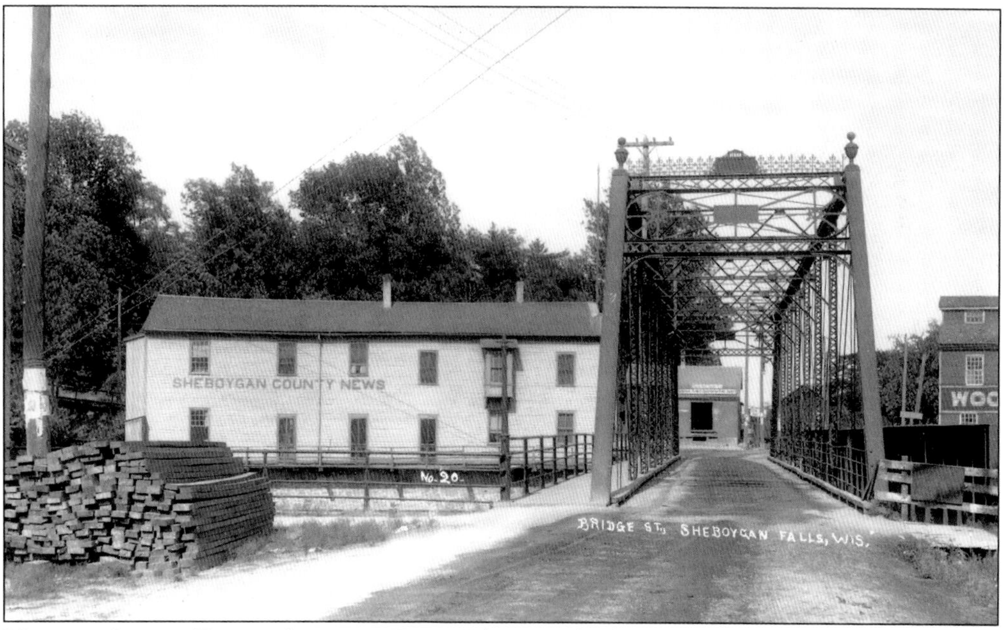

MONROE STREET BRIDGE LOOKING EAST. The same bridge is seen here looking east past the Sheboygan County News Building, on the left, with Brickner Woolen Mills Warehouse seen in the background on the right. This postcard still labels Monroe Street as Bridge Street. The river here was first spanned in 1847 to connect the two parts of the village: Rochester and Sheboygan at the Falls. This photo is *c.* 1905.

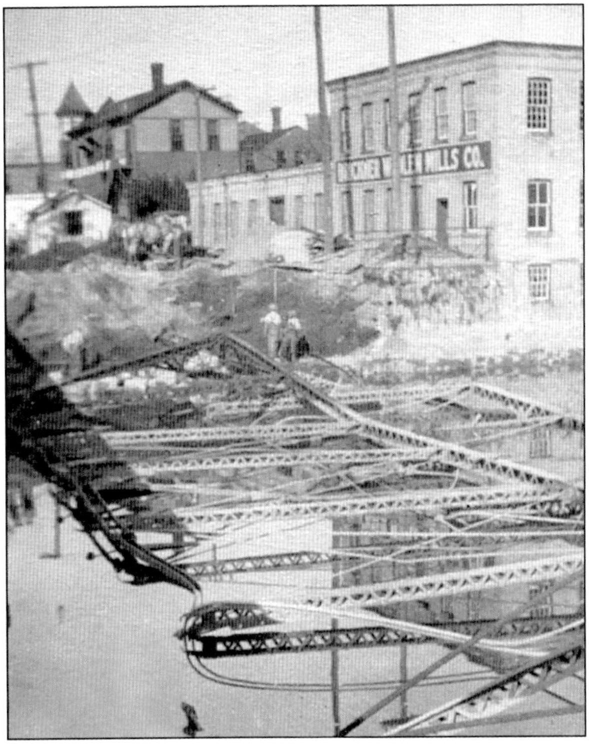

MONROE STREET BRIDGE DEMOLITION. On August 12, 1926, workmen weakened the old iron bridge, constructed in 1888 by cutting the supports. Cables were attached to it, and then with a tractor, workers pulled the structure clear of its moorings and away from the Chicago and Northwestern Railroad Bridge. The bridge tumbled into the river. News accounts mentioned that a large turnout of residents were on hand to witness the big splash.

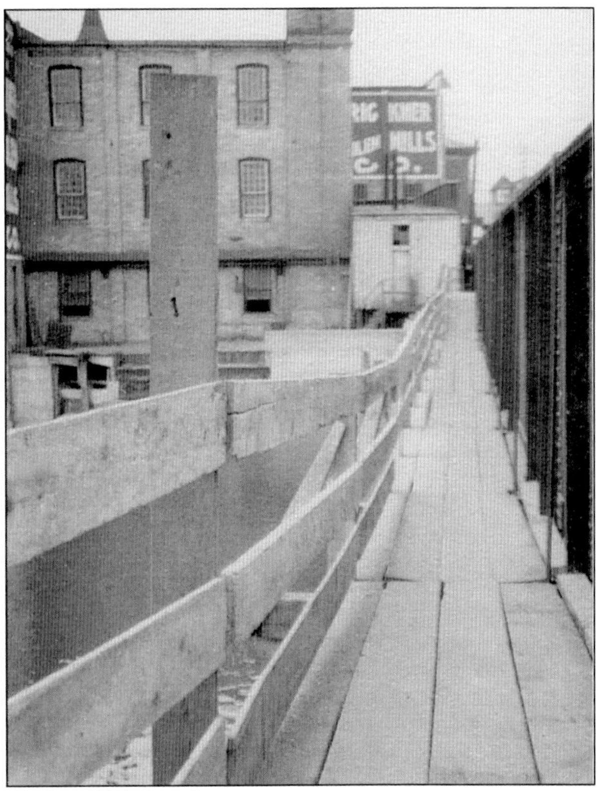

CAT WALK. Pedestrians used this footbridge constructed along the south side of the railroad bridge until the new concrete bridge on Monroe Street was completed. Planks from the old bridge were used in the construction of the new footbridge. Automobile traffic was directed north up the Water Street Hill, west over old Highway 23 (today's Fond du Lac Avenue), down Main Street (Broadway), and back into the city.

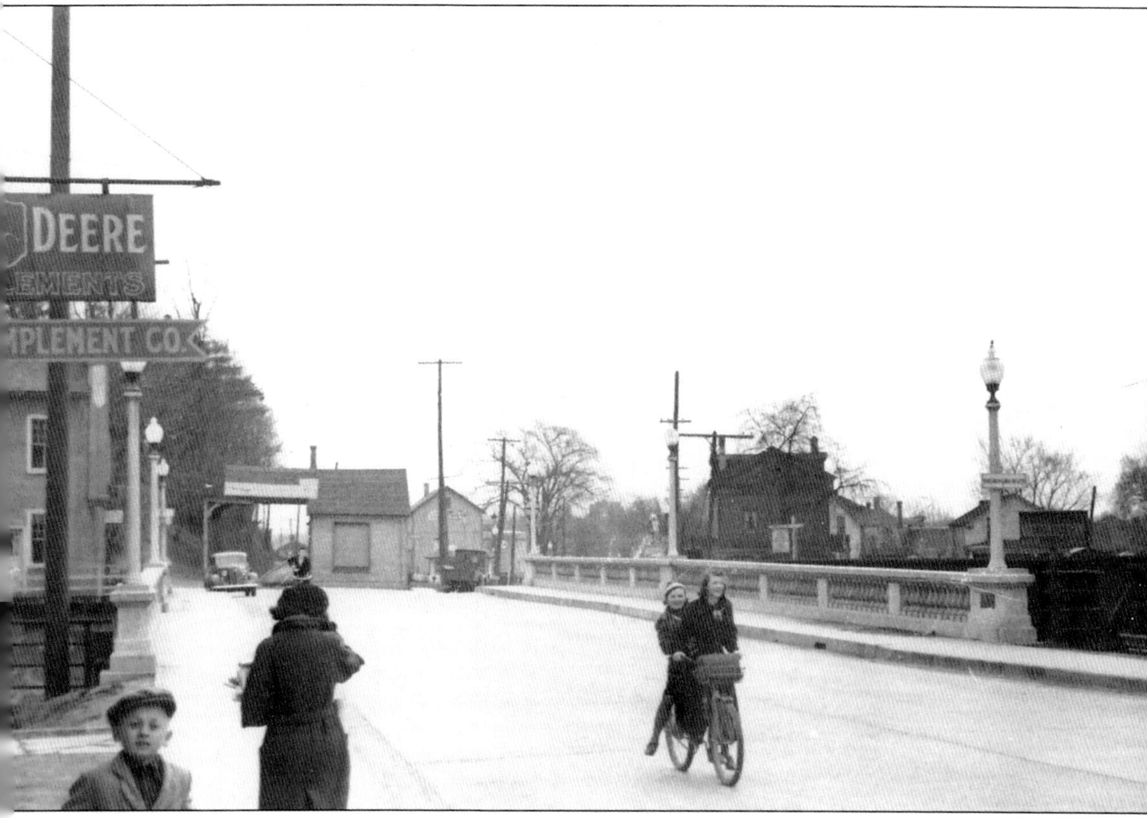

NEW CONCRETE BRIDGE. This photo, taken in 1938, shows the relatively new and very wide Monroe Street concrete bridge. At the rear of the photo is the streetcar depot and old bandage factory, now the Rochester Inn. Jacqueline Achtenhagen is riding a bicycle. This first concrete bridge opened to traffic on November 11, 1926. Ed Kohlhagen was the first to drive across the new structure, followed shortly by John Kohlhagen with a coal wagon. Within half an hour, a continual stream of traffic was moving both ways over the concrete. The bridge cost $12,862.77.

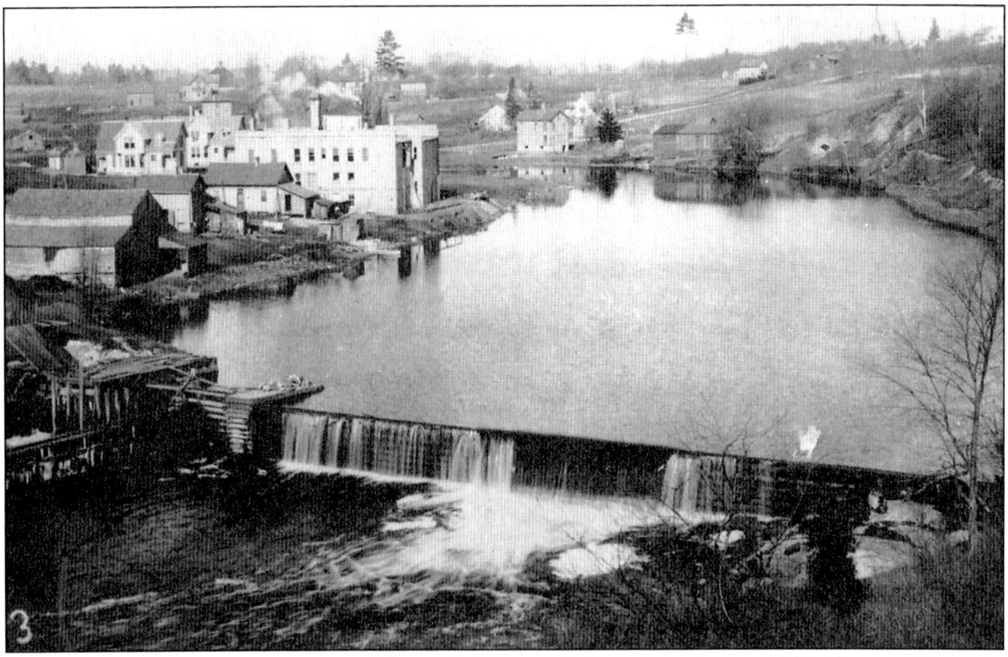

Upper Dam from Peck's Hill. This 1898 view of the upper dam and Sheboygan River is taken from Peck's Hill looking northeast. The dark cave just east of ice house in the upper right side of the photo is all that remains of Dicke Brewery. The brewery started by some of the first German settlers burned in 1879, never to be rebuilt.

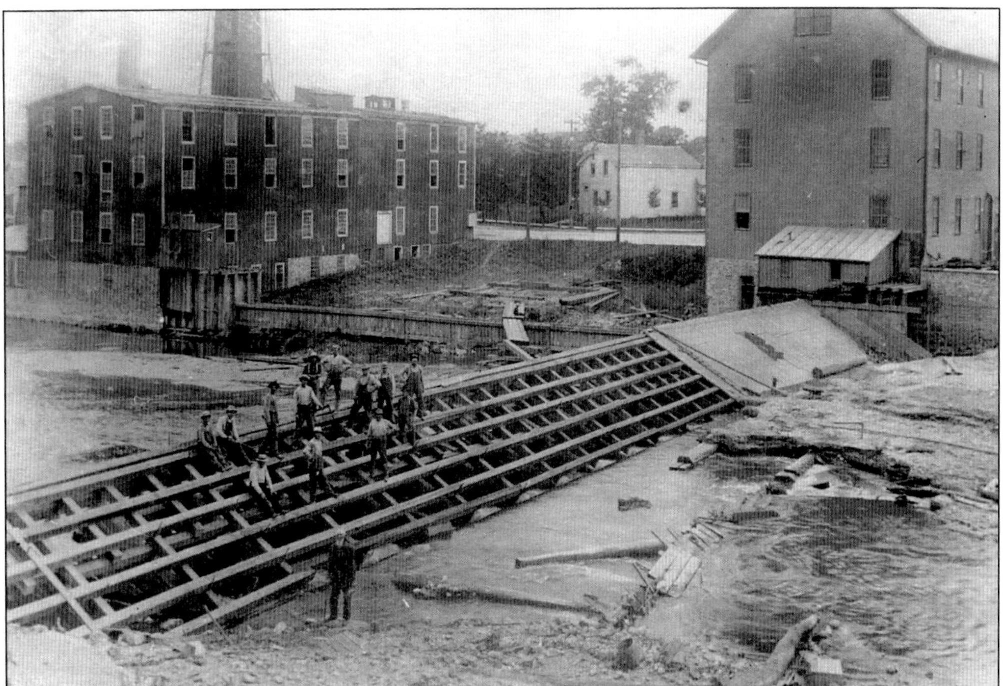

Upper Dam Repair. Even dams need repair. Standing in the foreground is George Spratt. At the rear are Rock Mills and White Wagon Works.

Peck's Hill Stairs. The steep grade of Peck's Hill or North Water Street was made easier with stairs. This 1910 view shows that they were located just east of the river, close to today's Jaycee River Walk path.

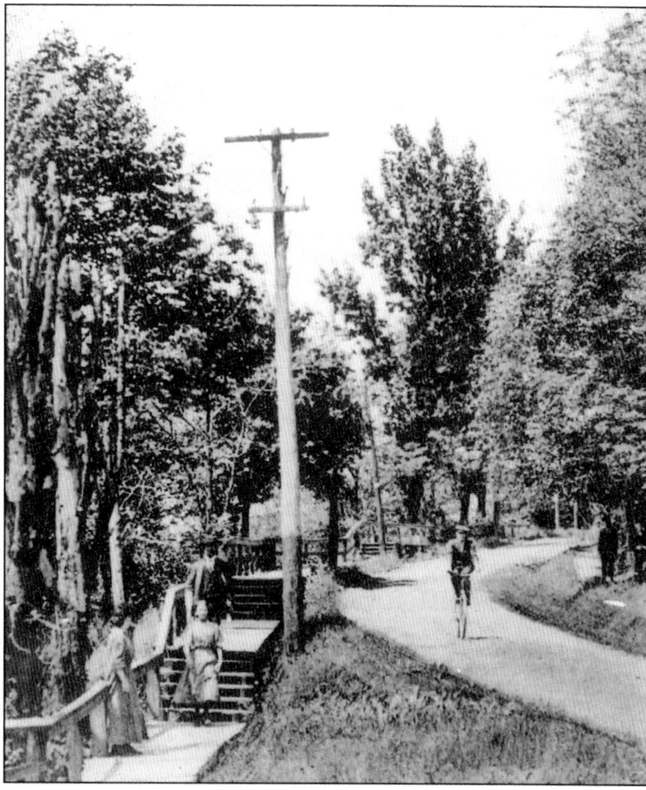

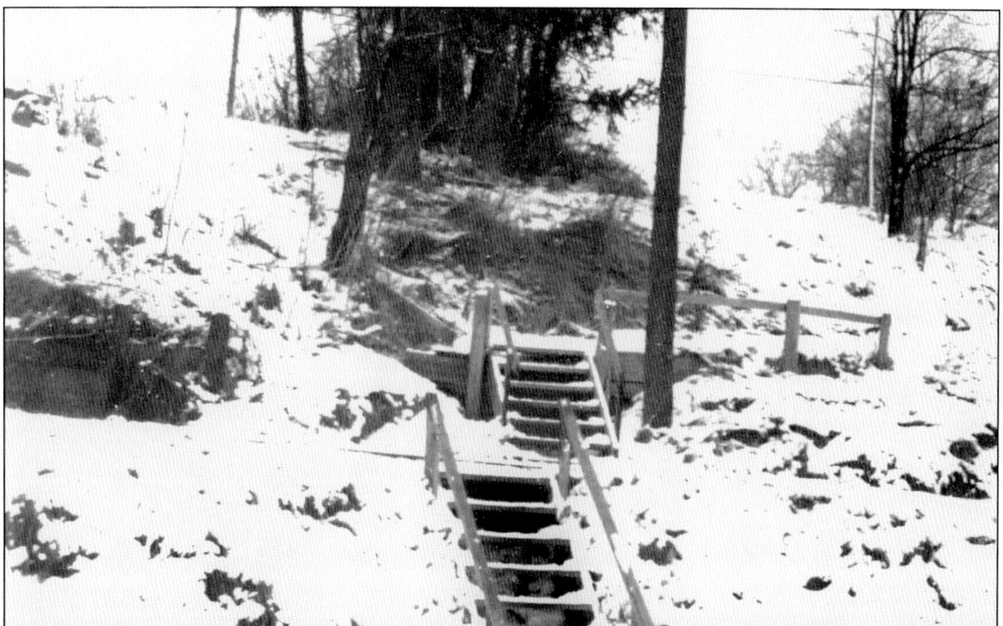

Steps over Streetcar Tracks. This snow-covered scene, taken in 1938, shows the steps that once helped walkers clear the railroad tracks east of the river. The stairs were accessed from the top of Peck's hill, just east of old Free Hall.

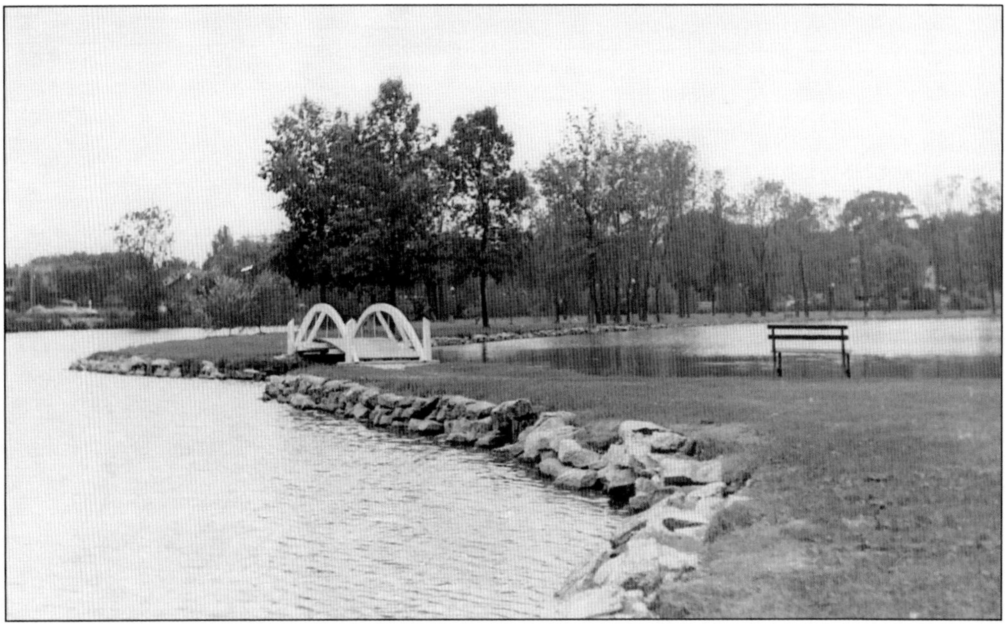

RIVER PARK FOOT BRIDGE. The River Park foot bridge spans the connection between the main channel of the Sheboygan River and the lagoon in River Park. This picturesque bridge frequently finds itself flooded during the spring thaw or a heavy summer rain.

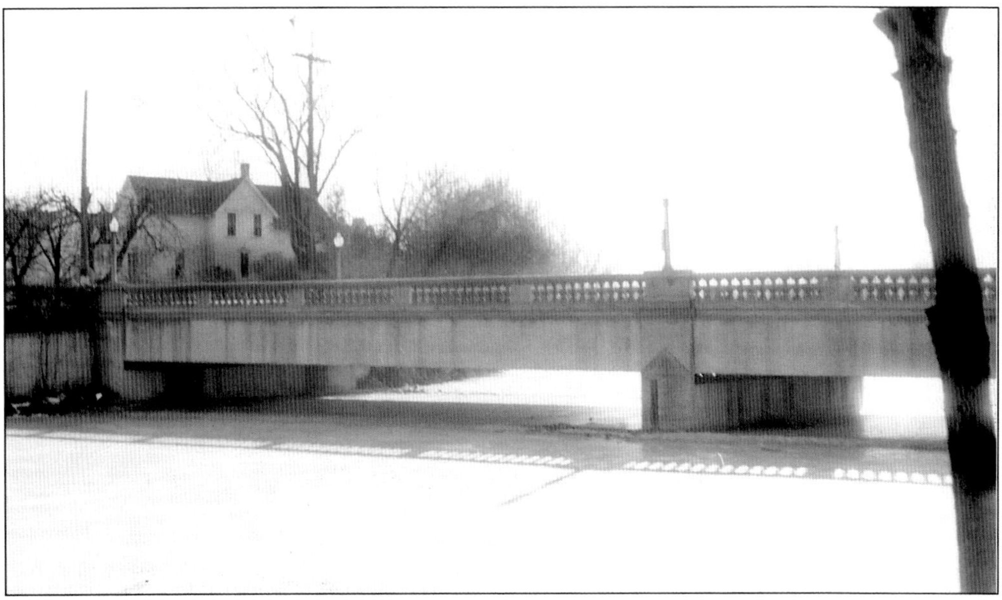

OLD LEAVENS STREET CONCRETE BRIDGE. One last bridge in town is the Leavens Street Bridge. This is the old concrete bridge, before it was replaced with the current bridge in the 1960s.

Eight

TRANSPORTATION

Transportation has changed more than nearly anything else since the formation of Sheboygan County in 1835. People traveled by foot and canoe, then by ship and locomotive, streetcar, and bicycle. Finally, the automobile and airplanes entered the lives of Sheboygan County citizens, and the world became so much smaller. Because transportation is one of the most interesting topics in a city's development, it is also frequently photographed. This grouping of photos is just a small representation of the dozens taken in Sheboygan Falls.

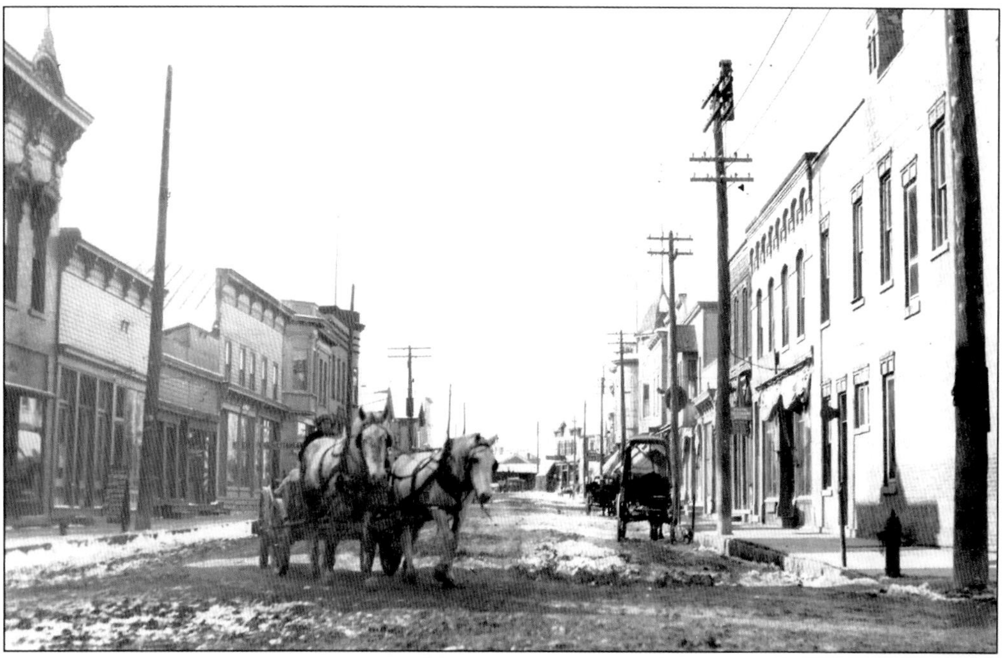

PINE STREET WEST FROM BROADWAY. Here we see a team of horses negotiating the muddy streets of Sheboygan Falls in 1917. Even though automobiles were used, many people found it easier and less frightening to continue to use their reliable horses. This wagon is turning north onto Broadway from Pine. Note the fire hydrant and utility poles, recent marks of progress.

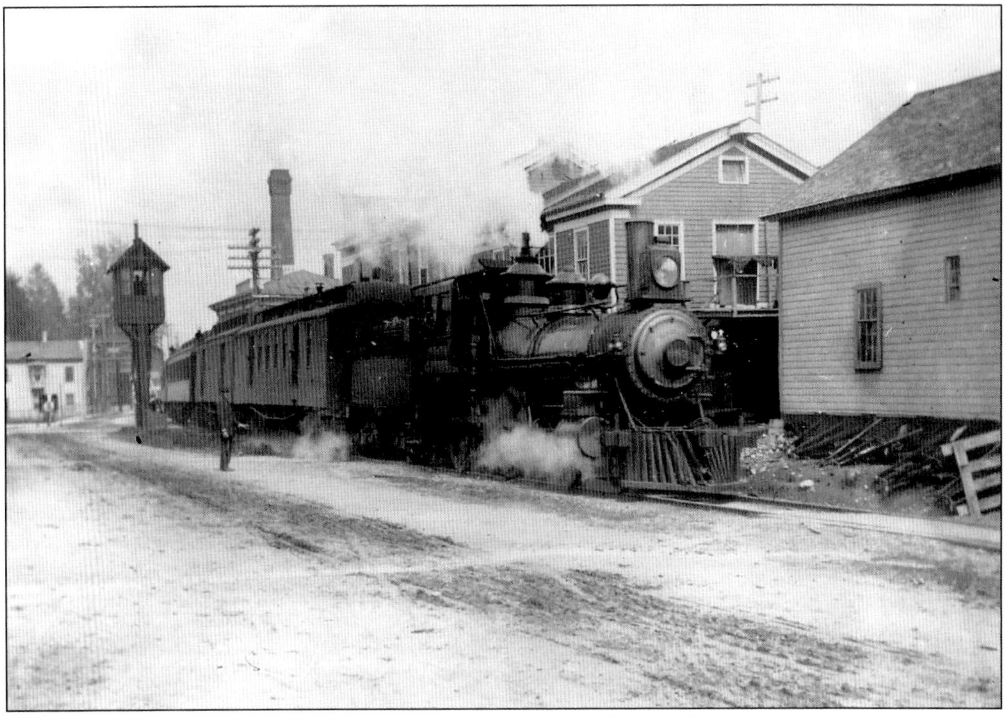

TRAIN TRAVEL. Early transportation in Sheboygan Falls was by horse or ox cart, ship, or canoe. The first train to the Falls was January 17, 1859. That was as far as the Sheboygan and Mississippi Railroad reached in that year. The little engine 'Sheboygan' stopped at the side of the L.P. Hill building that day, and was a marvelous sight to all the citizens. H. Gaylord was the engineer and B. Hinckley the conductor.

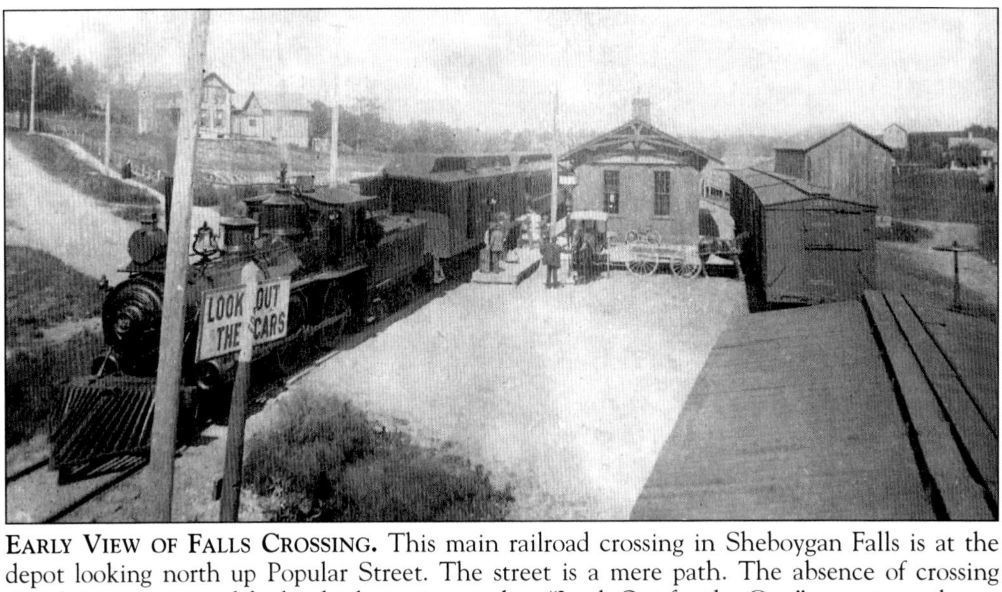

EARLY VIEW OF FALLS CROSSING. This main railroad crossing in Sheboygan Falls is at the depot looking north up Popular Street. The street is a mere path. The absence of crossing signals is compensated for by the large sign reading "Look Out for the Cars" meaning rail cars. Passengers wait to get on the train, while a horse-drawn carriage waits to gather incoming passengers. A bicycle leans up against the depot, and another delivery cart awaits use.

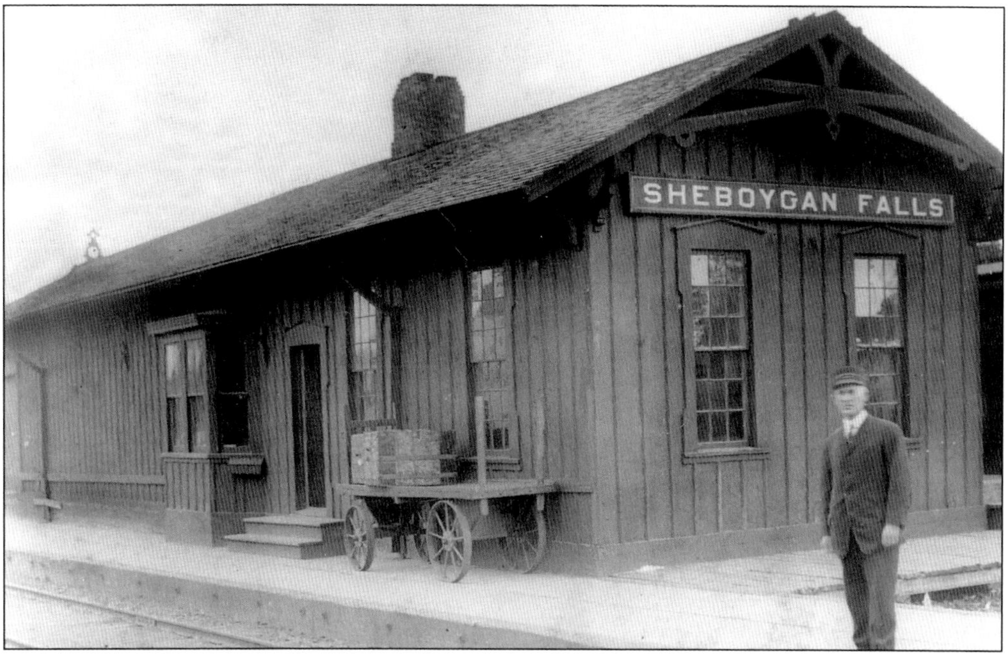

SHEBOYGAN FALLS RAILWAY DEPOT. The original and only Sheboygan and Mississippi railroad depot in Sheboygan Falls was built in 1858 and was razed in 1969. This building stood beside the tracks on Monroe Street, near today's B B Ford. Agent Snyder is the man in the picture.

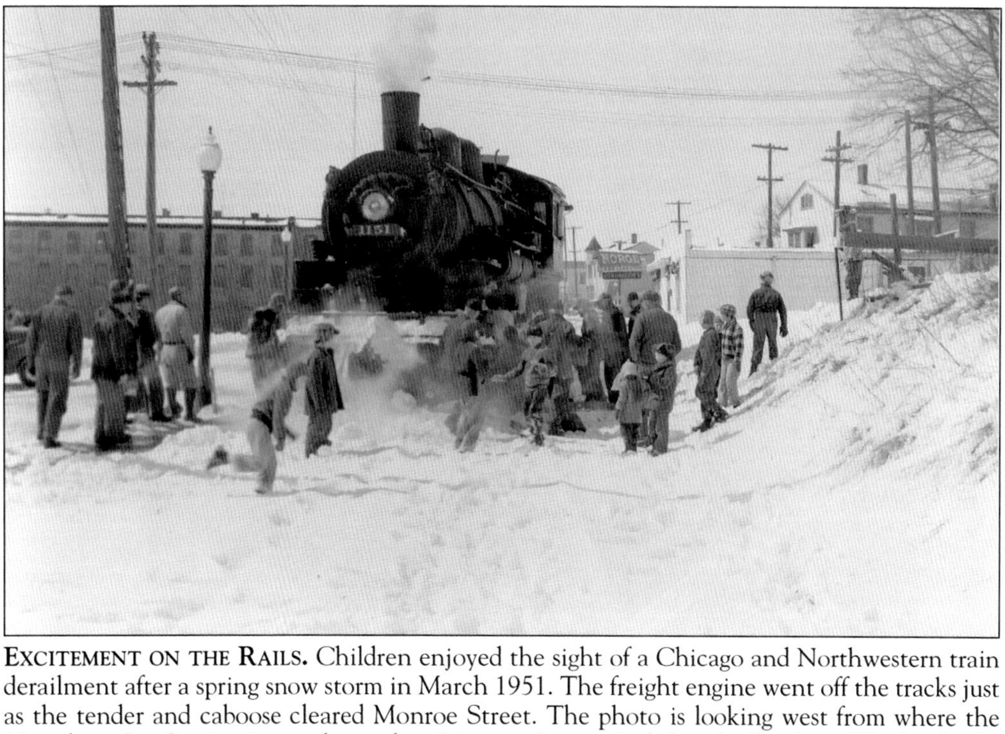

EXCITEMENT ON THE RAILS. Children enjoyed the sight of a Chicago and Northwestern train derailment after a spring snow storm in March 1951. The freight engine went off the tracks just as the tender and caboose cleared Monroe Street. The photo is looking west from where the Marathon Gas Station is now located on Monroe Street. At left is the Brickner Woolen Mills. Just right of the engine is Norge Appliance Company.

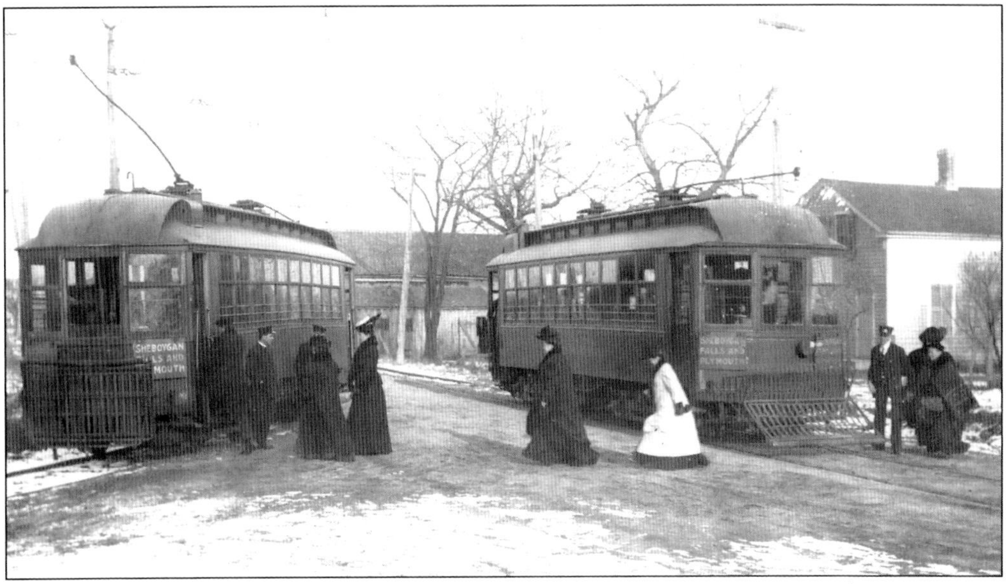

TRACK CONVERGENCE. Sheboygan Light, Power and Railway Company interurban passengers traveling farther west than Sheboygan Falls had to switch lines, and they did so here at the track convergence located on Fond du Lac Avenue at Popular Street. They got off one trolley walked a few feet and boarded another that would take them via a different line to their destination. The photograph is c. 1904.

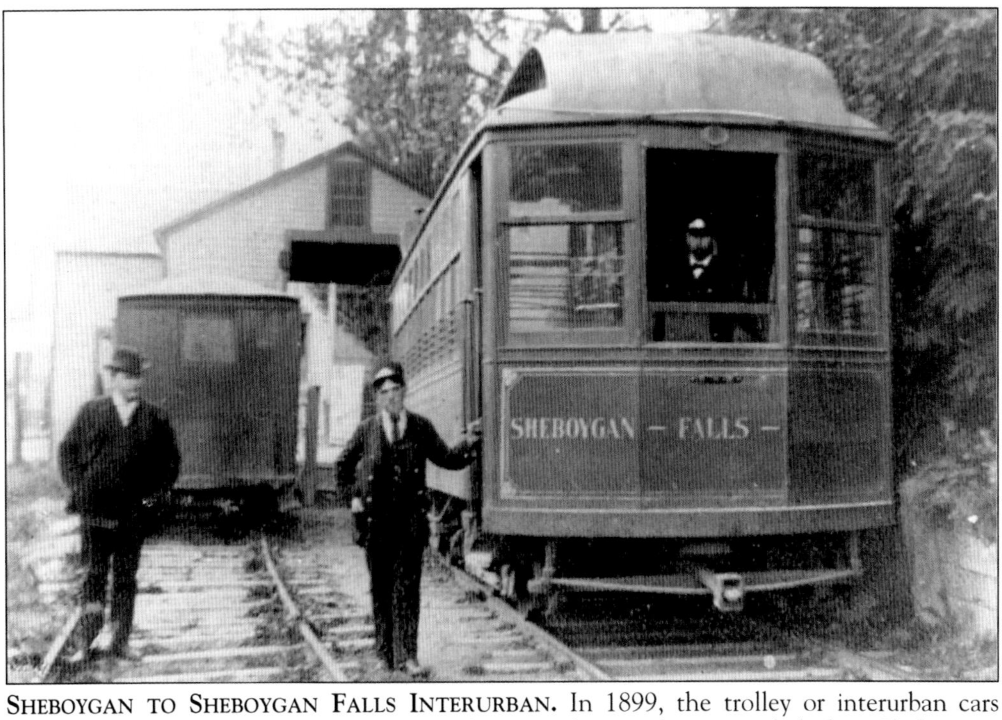

SHEBOYGAN TO SHEBOYGAN FALLS INTERURBAN. In 1899, the trolley or interurban cars reached Sheboygan Falls from Sheboygan. The interurban made 18 runs daily from Sheboygan, from 6:05 a.m. to 11 p.m. The Depot motorman was Fred Rabe. Service lasted until 1938, when such travel was replaced by buses.

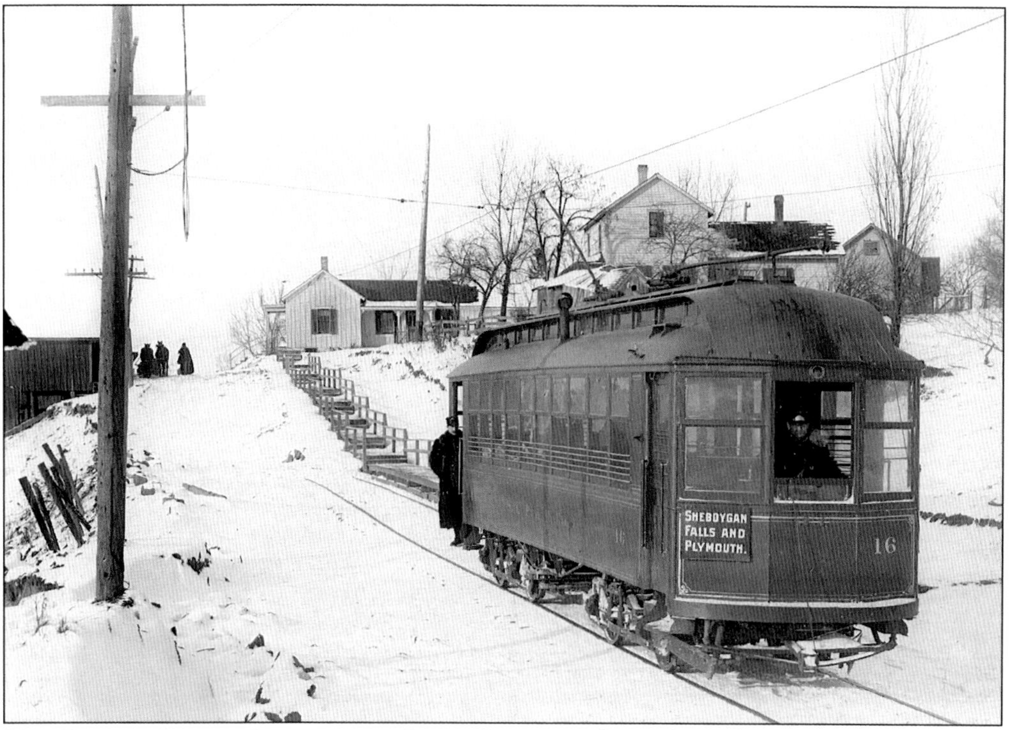

THE POPLAR STREET INTERURBAN SPUR. A spur track was built down Poplar Street. This January 16, 1904 picture shows the Sheboygan Falls-Plymouth interurban on Poplar Street with motorman Fred Rabe and conductor August Larson standing in the back.

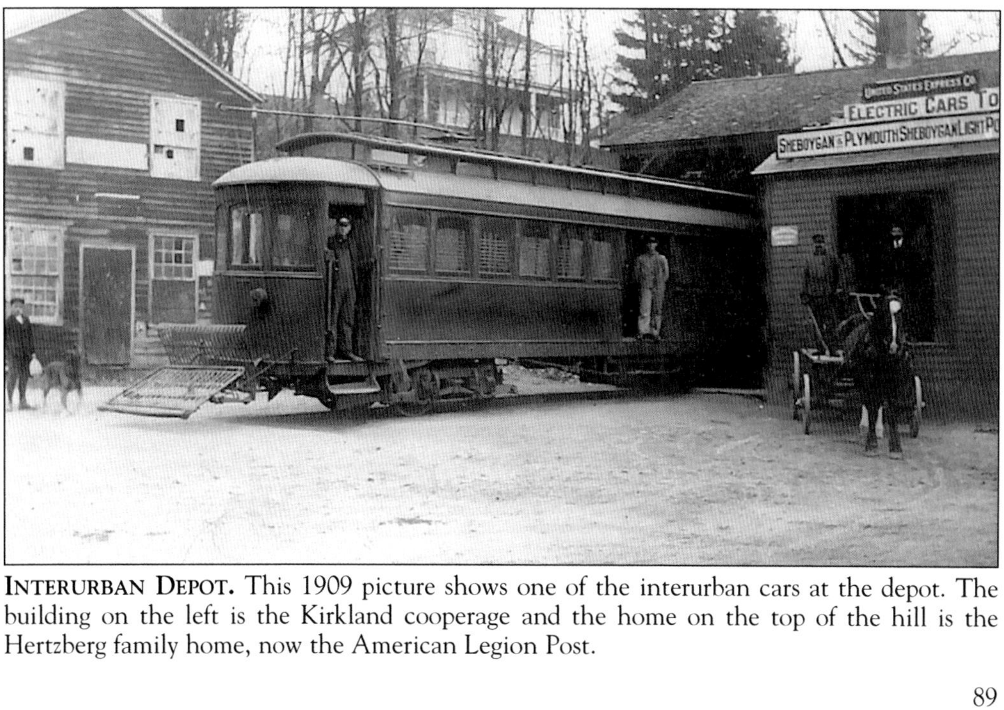

INTERURBAN DEPOT. This 1909 picture shows one of the interurban cars at the depot. The building on the left is the Kirkland cooperage and the home on the top of the hill is the Hertzberg family home, now the American Legion Post.

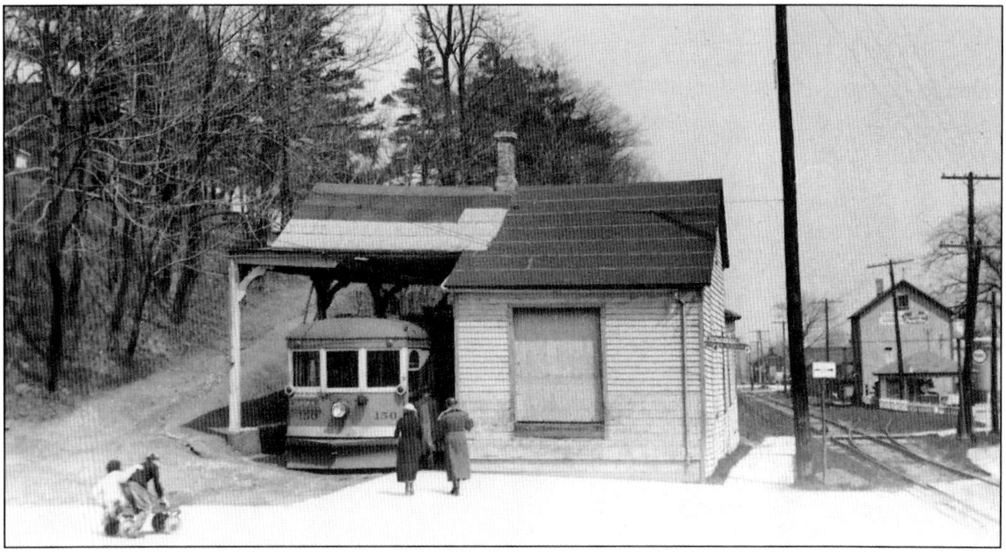

INTERURBAN DEPOT. This is the western view of the streetcar depot. The location at 500 Water Street is the site of one of the oldest businesses in Sheboygan Falls, and was originally the land offices of Silas Stedman and David Giddings. Toward the end of its life, the depot became an eyesore. People would consider going inside only if the weather was very cold. Between the restrooms, the coal stove, the spittoons, and the tobacco smoke, many times the depot's air quality left a lot to be desired.

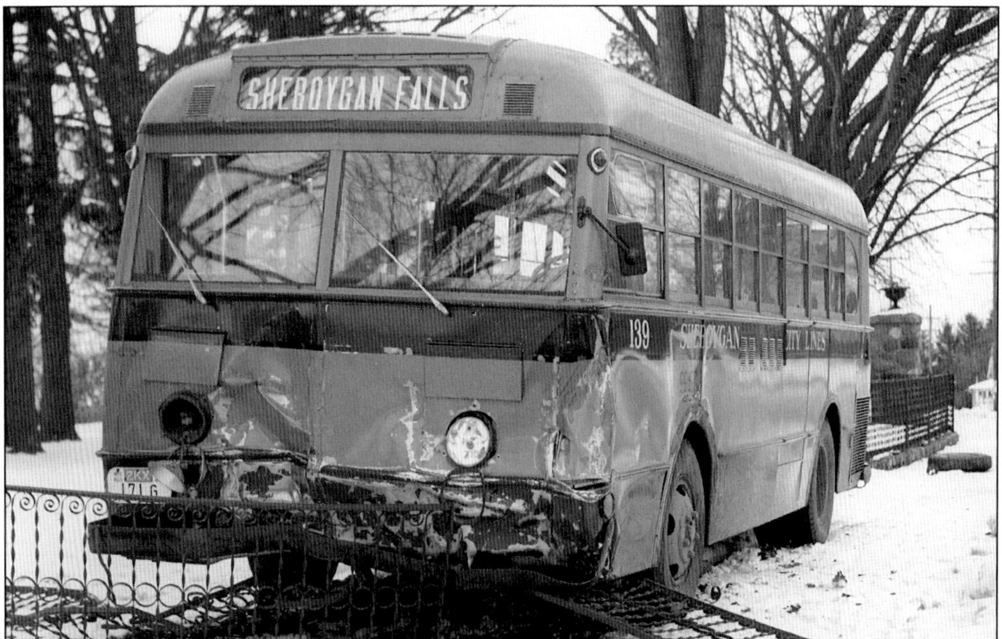

BUS TRAVEL. Bus service replaced the interurban cars in the 1930s. This bus was involved in an accident on Fond du Lac Avenue in 1947, taking down the fencing in front of the Curt G. Joa property. Today cars have mostly replaced the bus service, but daily routes still run between Sheboygan Falls and Sheboygan.

Nine

STREET SCENES

Photography is a fickle thing. In the world of street scenes, many main avenues are photographed time and again. Many other side streets, though equally interesting may never be photographed. We find this very problem with Sheboygan Falls. The main streets, Pine, Broadway, Monroe, and Main have dozens of images available. Once off these main thoroughfares good photography may be hard to find. The photos that follow are just a few examples of some of the changes in the street scenes of the city.

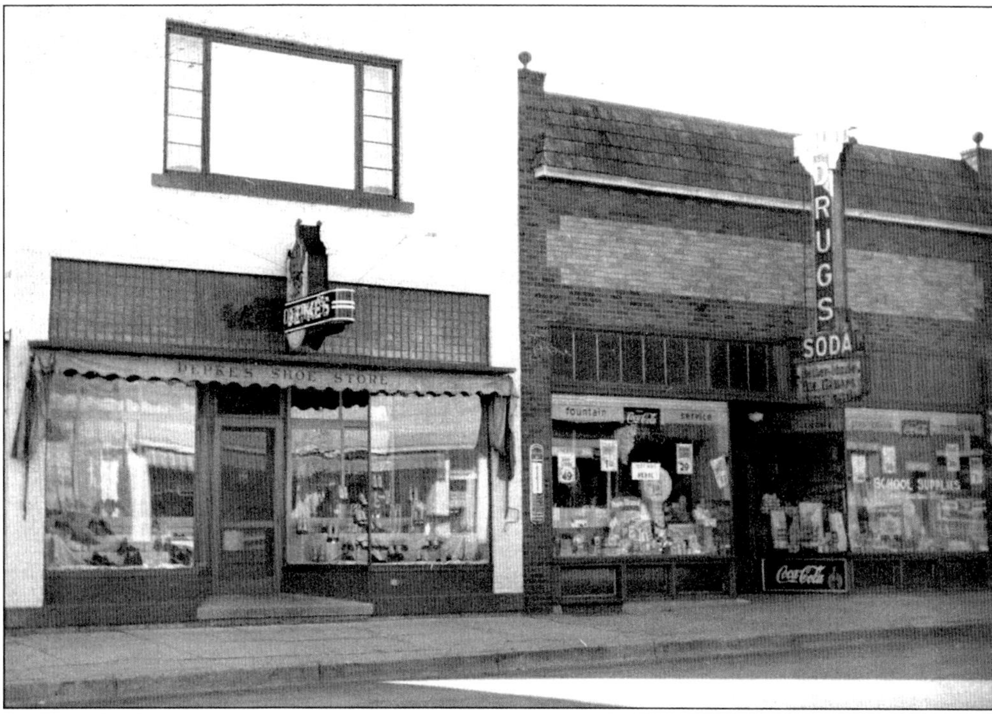

SOUTH SIDE OF PINE. Depke's Shoe Store and Boldt Drug Store were located on Pine Street west of Broadway. Depke's building was the Fidelity Lodge of the Odd Fellows in 1879. A new brick building was constructed after a fire destroyed the Lodge. In May of 1897, John Roska started his boot and shoe business at this location. The Roskas continued in business until 1945, when Herbert Roska sold the business to William Depke. The Depke Shoe Store remains in business today, and is run by the Gelstardt family.

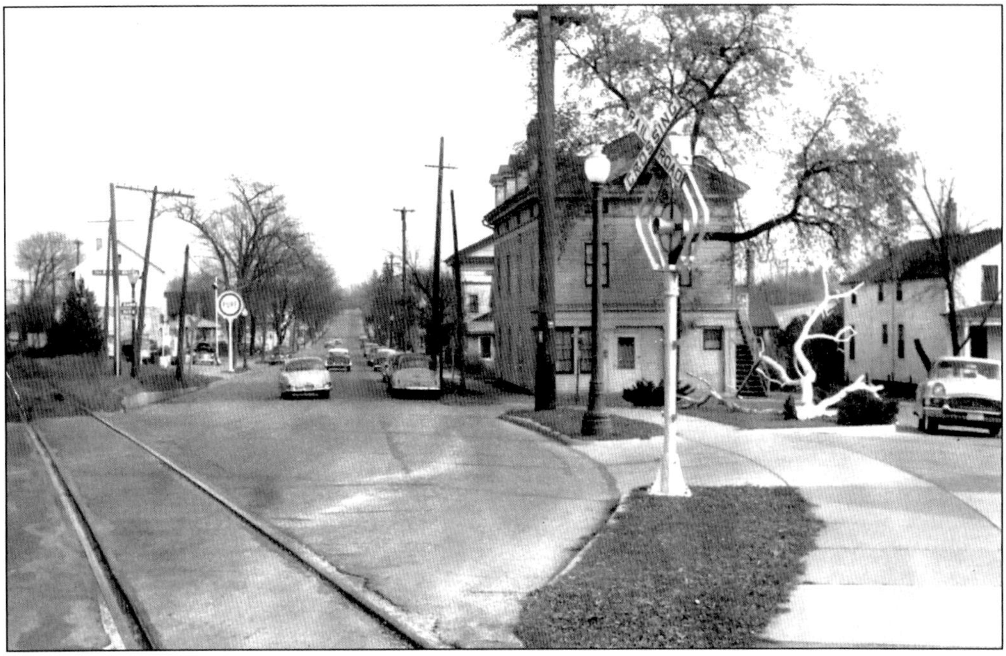

MONROE STREET EAST FROM THE BRIDGE. This 1950s scene shows the building that now houses the Rochester Inn before its rehabilitation on the right. At this point it was a private residence. Sopettos Restaurant and Bowling Alley is just beyond. The Pure Oil filling station is on the left.

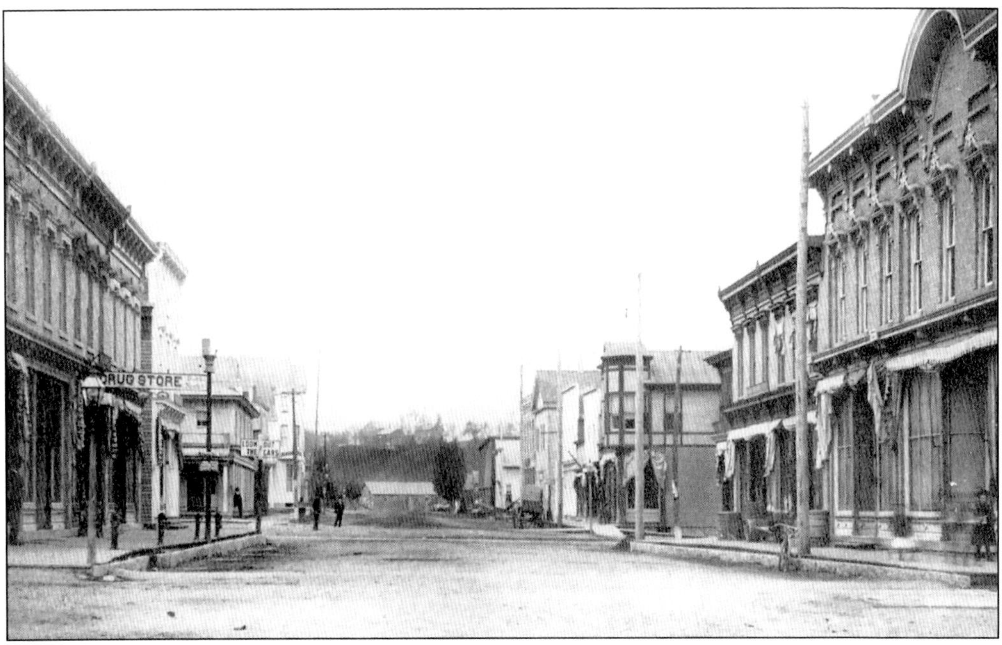

LOOKING NORTH ON BROADWAY FROM PINE STREET. Note the awnings on each building, and the hitching posts for horses located on the raised walkways. At the intersection with Monroe Street there is a sign on the left which warns, "Look out for cars." It means train cars, not automobiles.

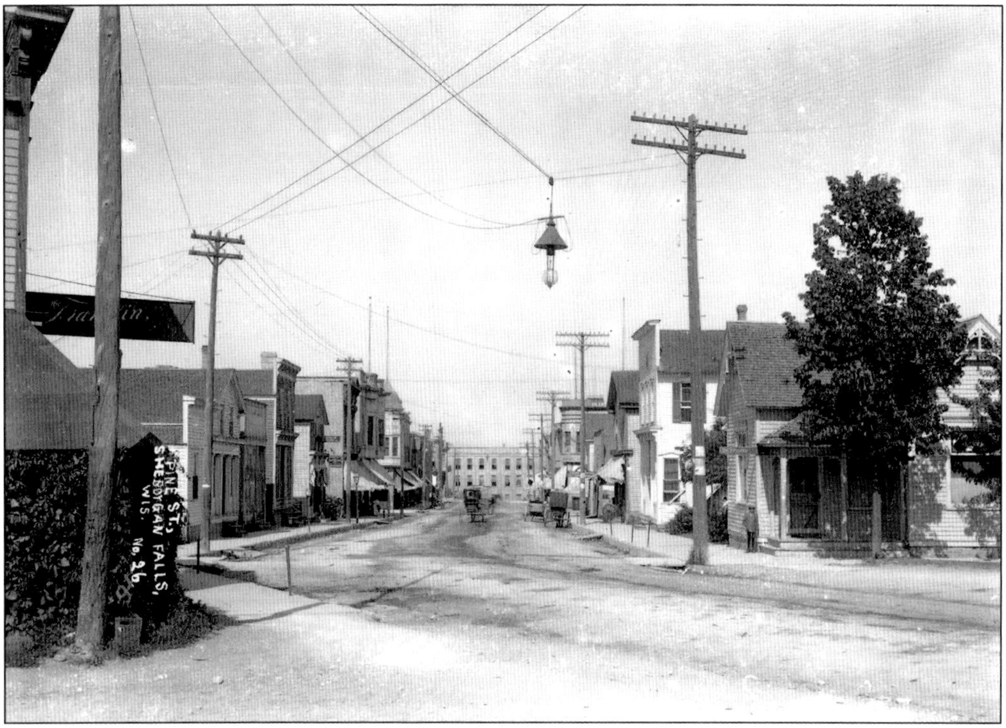

LOOKING EAST ON PINE FROM DETROIT. This view of Sheboygan Falls was found on a turn of the last century post card. The Franklin House sign can be seen on the very left. Dr. Pfeifer's office is seen on the right. Note the street light overhead and the horse-drawn buggies up ahead on the dirt roads. Also, note the many lightning rods attached to buildings.

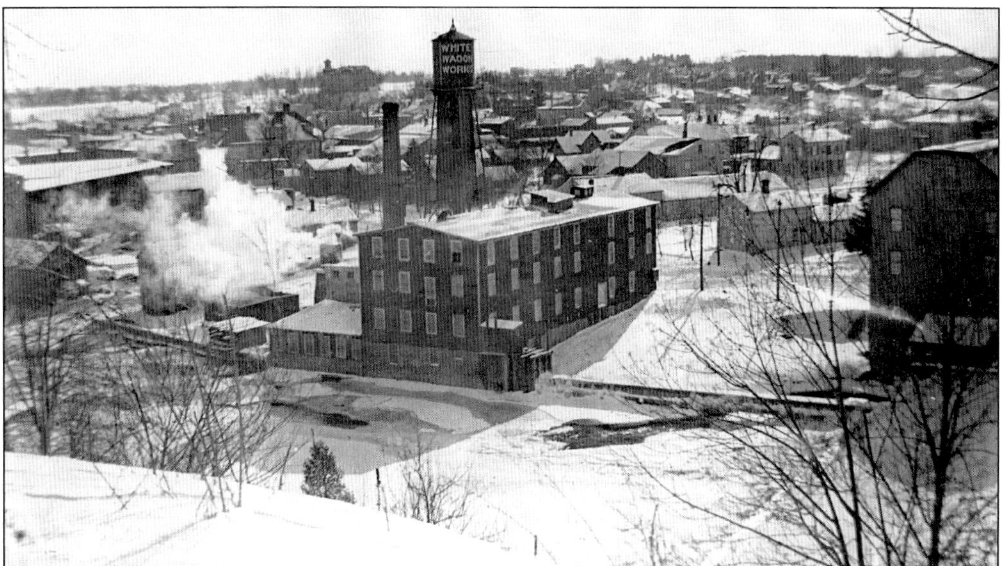

WATER STREET HILL. This view is looking southwest from Peck's or the Water Street Hill past the White Wagon Works factory. To the left of the White Wagon Works tower on a far hill is the old school.

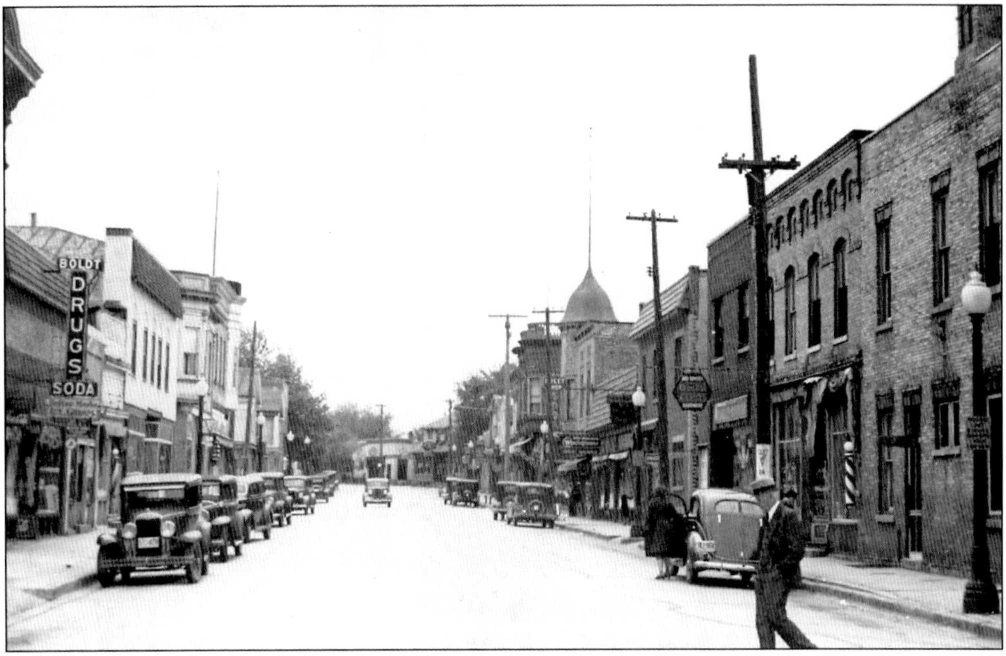

WEST ON PINE FROM BROADWAY IN THE 1940S. This streetscape is looking west on Pine Street from its beginning at Broadway. Mr. Never the tailor is the man crossing the street towards his store. Boldt Drug is on the left. The building with the dome on the right is Bill Wolf's Saloon, today the Villager Restaurant. Next to it is Schlichtings Grocery, now the Richardson Furniture Emporium. Once again, note the very tall lightning rods.

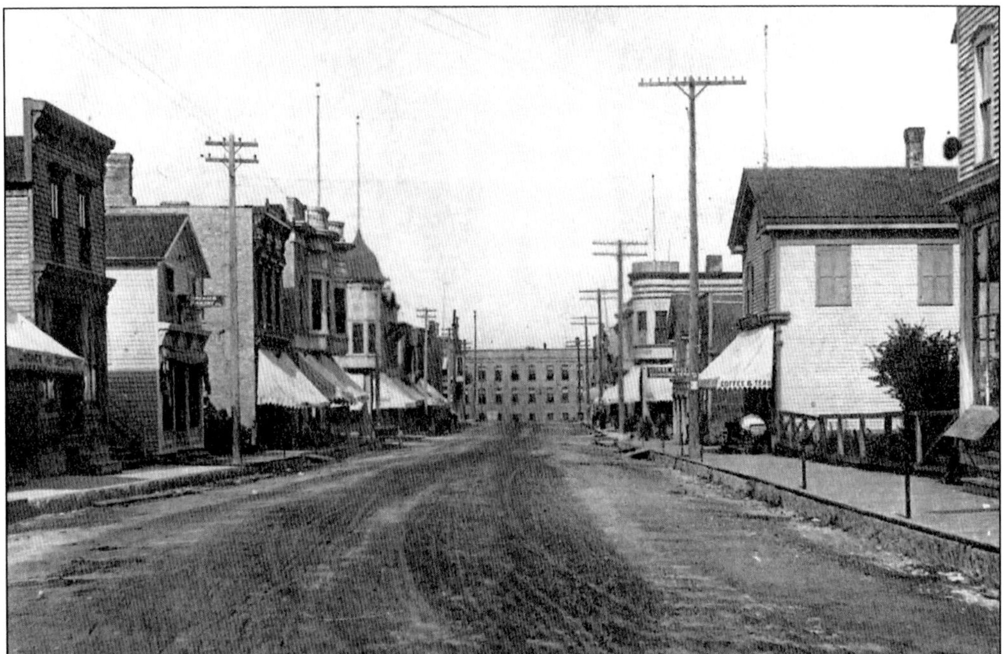

EAST ON PINE FROM JUST WEST OF BUFFALO. This is another view of Pine. The main streets of villages and cities tended to be heavily photographed, but side streets seldom were documented.

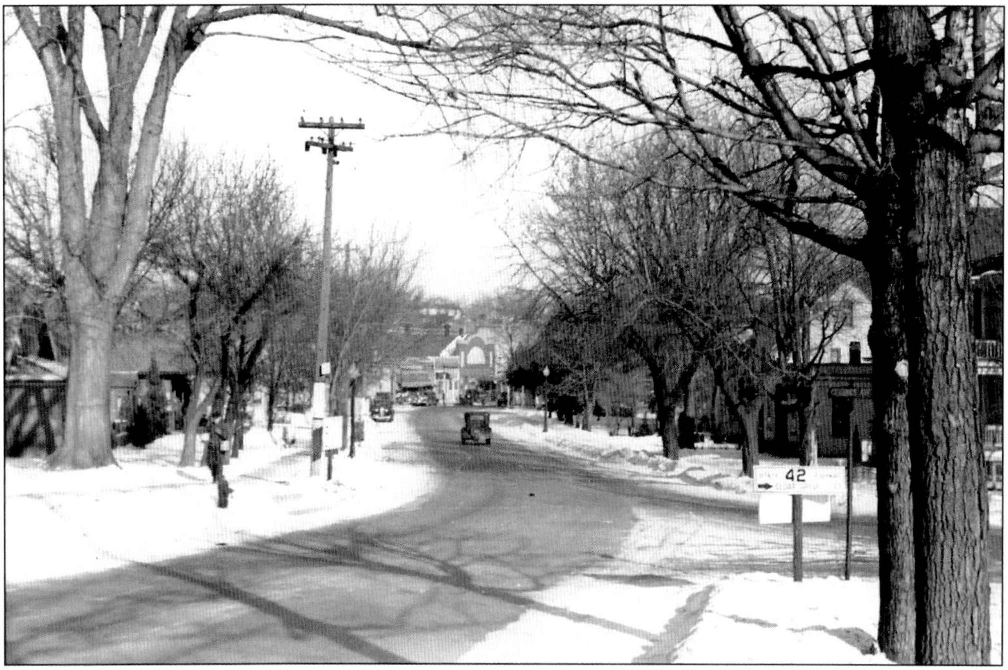

INTERSECTION OF PINE AND GIDDINGS. This view finds us looking east down Pine Street from its intersection with Giddings Avenue where it Giddings goes south. The road sign on the right still lists the main highway as Highway 42, not Highway 32. It also notes that Cedar Grove is 13 miles distant. The Falls Theater is seen at the end of Pine Street.

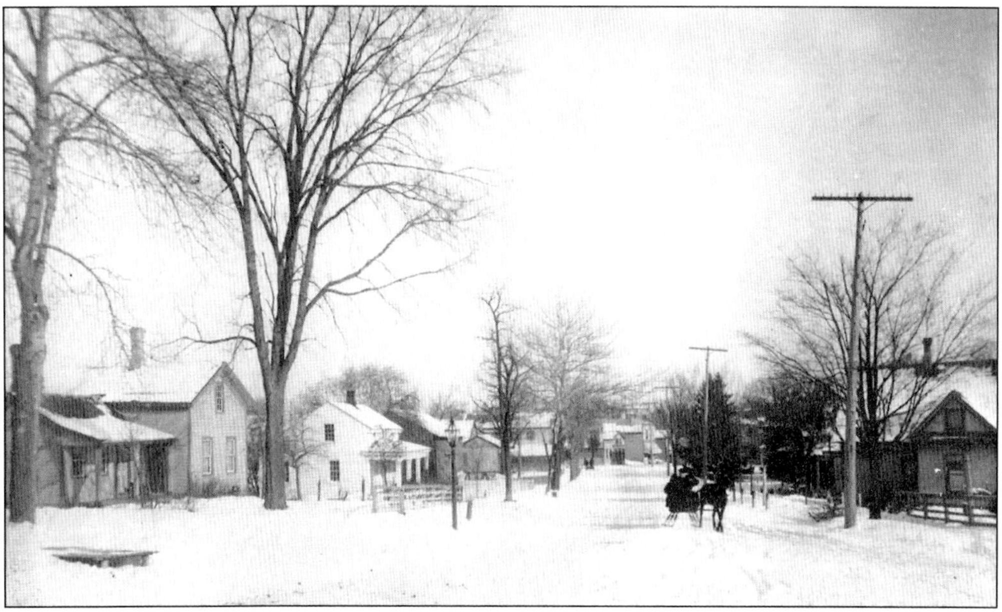

WINTER SCENE. This is a much earlier winter scene of western Pine Street near Giddings. Horse-drawn sleighs were commonly used as winter transportation, even in town.

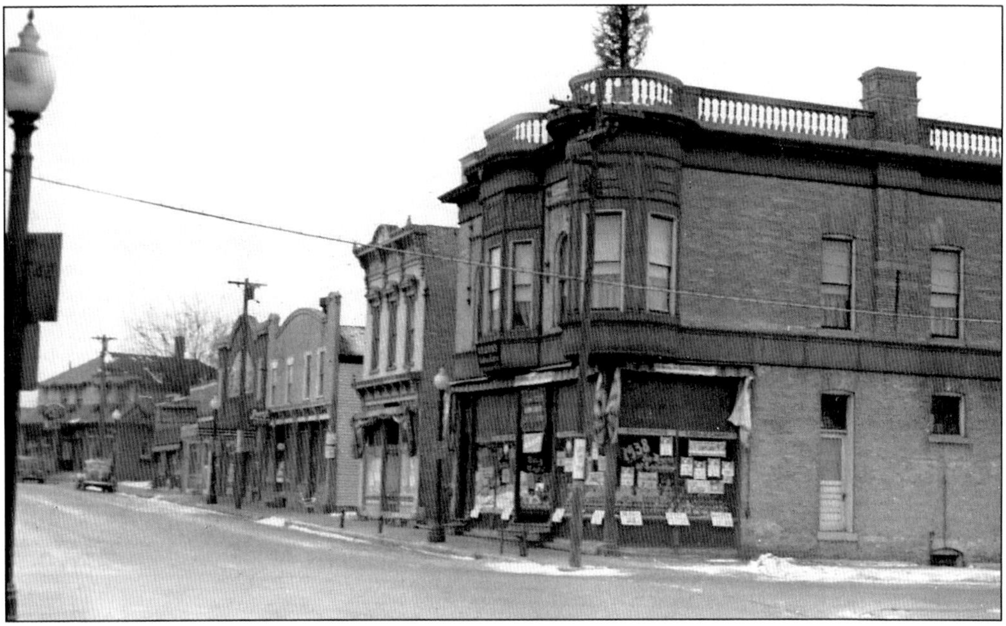

CORNER OF PINE AND BUFFALO. This image of the northwest corner of Pine and Buffalo Streets starts with Schlichtings Market, moves west past the movie theater and then toward the Franklin House.

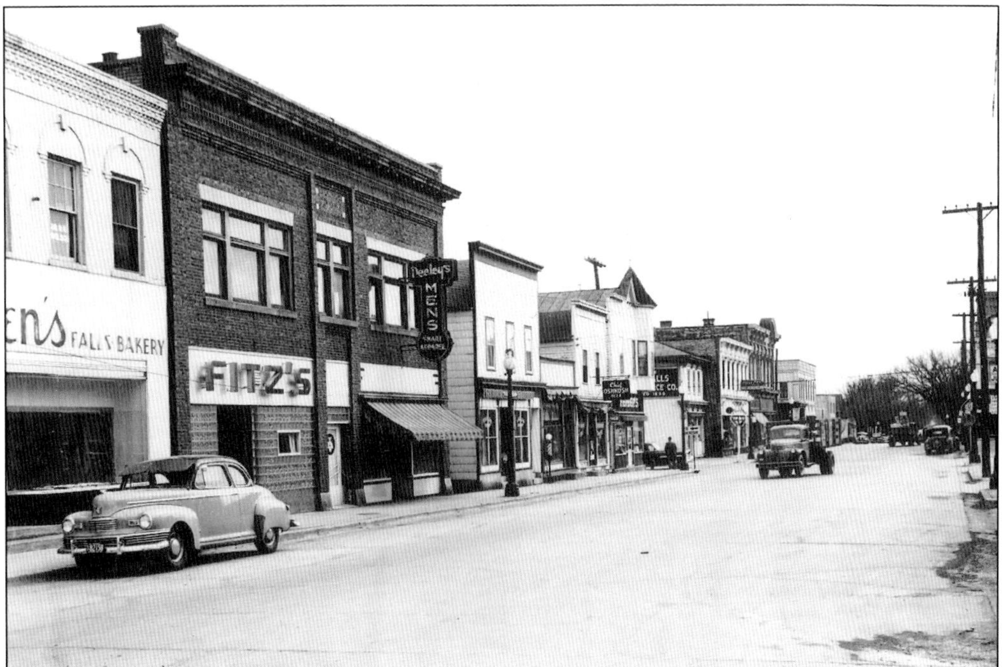

BROADWAY LOOKING SOUTH. This view is of the east side of Broadway looking south. Seen are Falls Bakery, Fitz's Tavern, Deeley's Men's Clothing, a tailor shop, a tavern, and Herber's Confectionary.

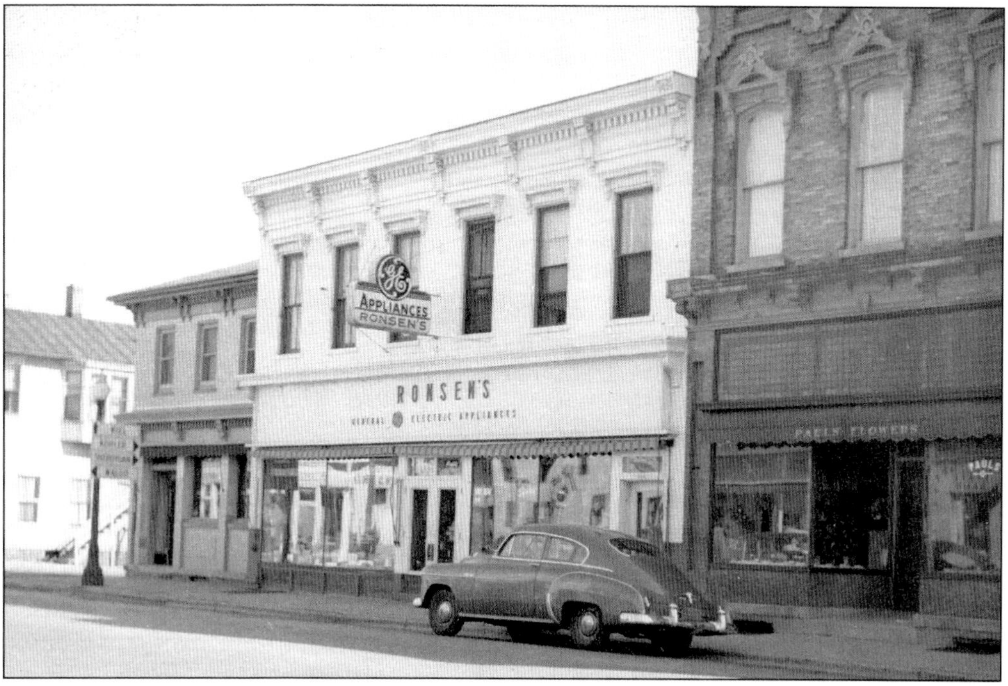

BROADWAY'S EAST SIDE. This is the east side of Broadway south of Monroe. On the left is the old German Bank, Ronsen's Appliance Store, and Paul's Flower Shop.

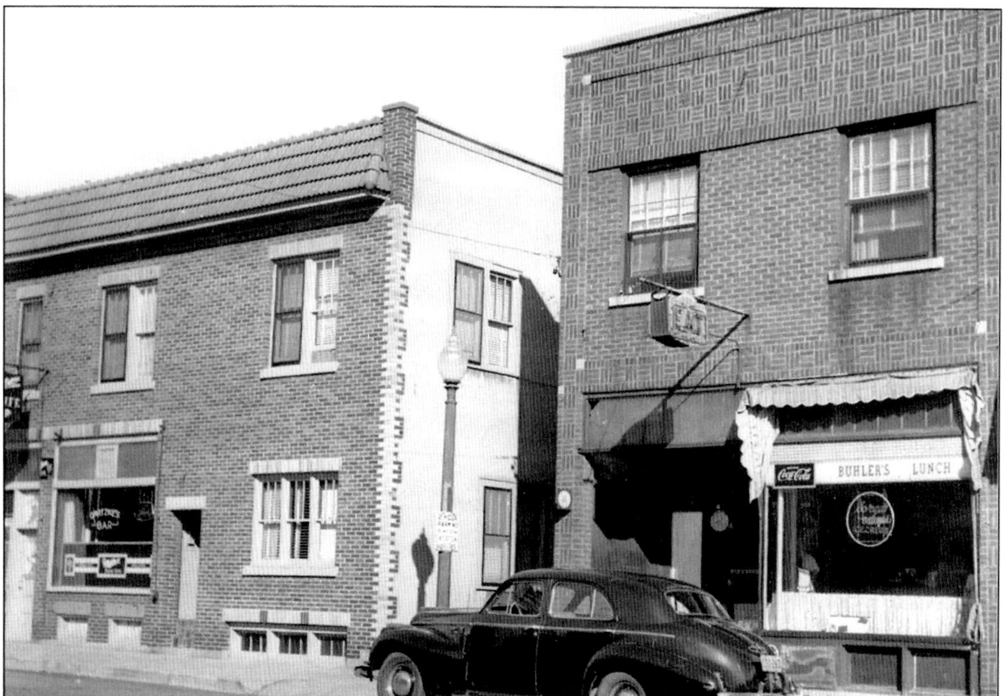

NORTH SIDE OF PINE STREET. Here we see the north side of Pine Street between Broadway and Buffalo. From the left are Gartzke's Bar and Buhler's Lunch.

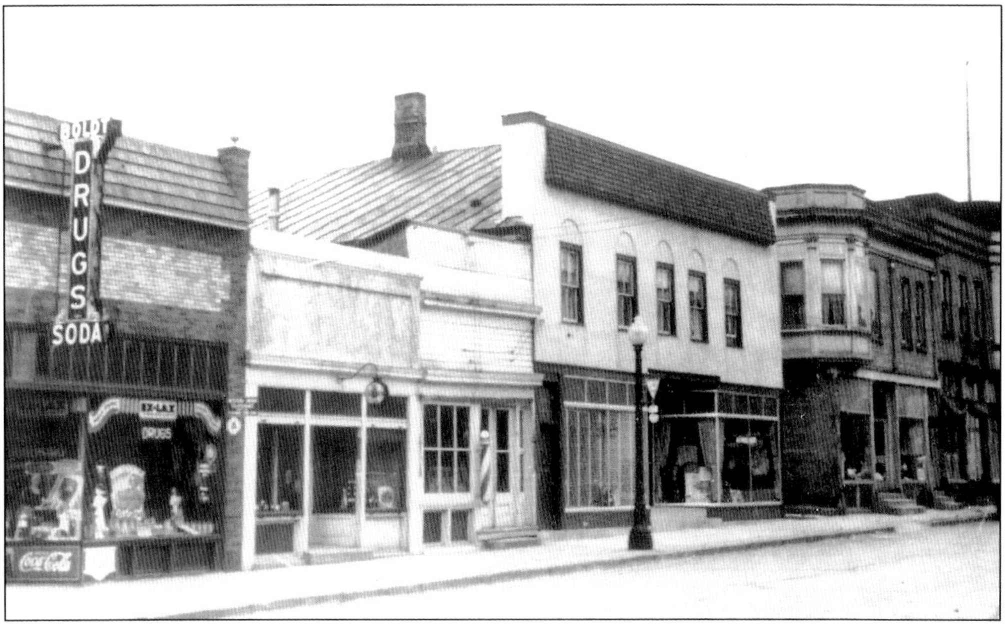

SOUTH SIDE OF PINE STREET. Shown here is the south side of Pine Street between Broadway and Buffalo from Boldt Drug Store west to the Hertzburg building.

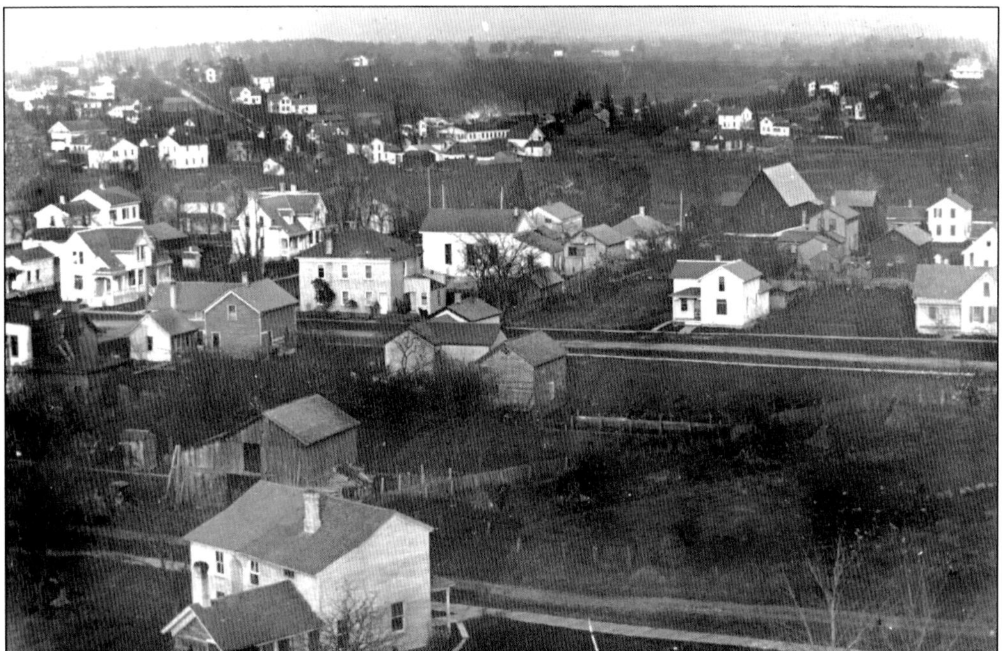

HILLTOP VIEW OF SHEBOYGAN FALLS. This view is looking east from the western highlands of early Sheboygan Falls. The old Episcopal church is to the center right, and the road going up Main Street is at the far left.

Ten

BUSINESS AND INDUSTRY

Business and industry has always been central to Sheboygan Falls' development. From the first days of settlement sound and ambitious decisions were made by the Yankee settlers. There was no time taken to adjust to their new surroundings. Commerce was the key to success, and the sooner a business was established the better. The variety of businesses found here is remarkable. The earliest businesses in Falls included: Stedman Lumber Mill, 1836; Edmund Quinlan Rake Factory, 1859; Littlefield and Leighton double sawmill, 1844; John Bryant Jewelry Store, 1859; A.P. Lyman General Store, 1846; Jacob Kehl Cigar Factory and Store, 1881; William Servis Carriage Factory, 1854; J.D. Gould Tannery, 1855; Rock Mills, 1848 and the list goes on. The images and stories about the entrepreneurs of Sheboygan Falls are vast. The most difficult thing about composing this chapter is that there is too much information, too many great images available. The goal of this book is to present the featured businesses in a new and curious manner, teaching something novel, helping the reader to gain fresh insight into the commercial dynamo that was and is the little city of Sheboygan Falls. Remember, this is but a sample of the information that is available.

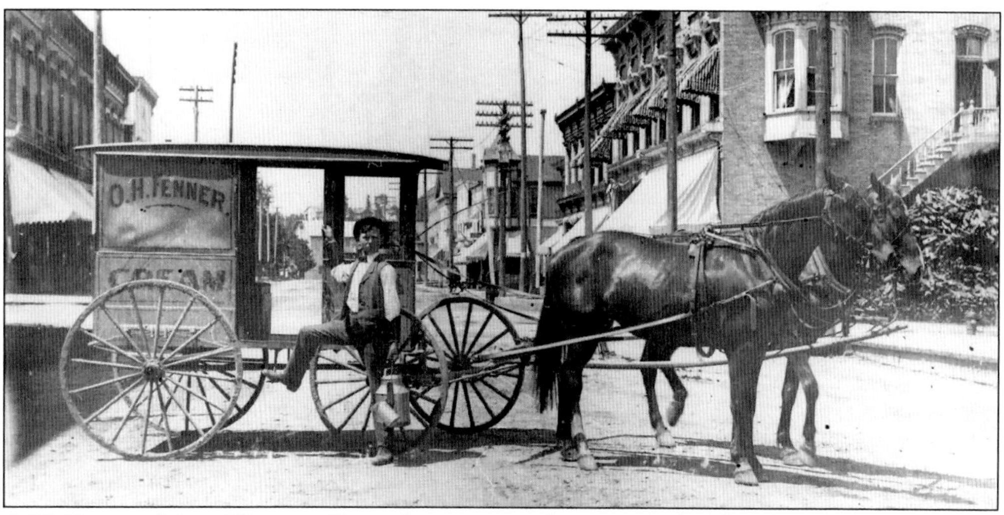

O.H. FENNER MILK WAGON. Shown here is an early cream and milk delivery wagon from the O.H. Fenner Company. This photo shows the view looking north on Broadway at Pine. The young man in the photo is Heinie (Hexel) Edler.

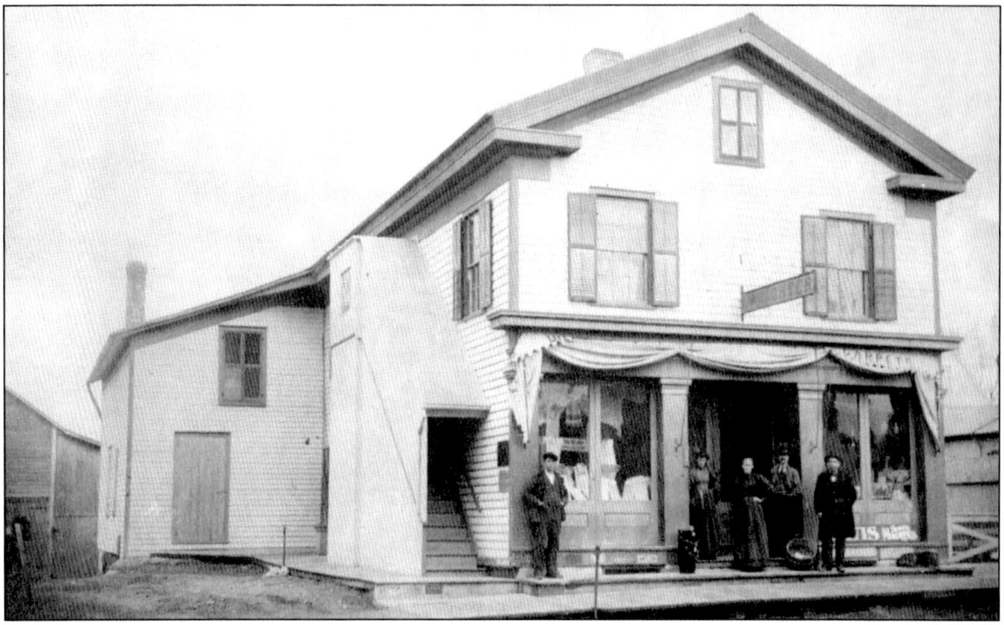

WACHTER'S STORE. Located at 215 Pine Street, Sheboygan Falls, this exterior shot of Wachter's General Store pictures, from left to right, August Wachter, Lena Wachter, Josephine Mallman, Charles A. Wachter, and Adolph Wachter Sr. Wachter's General Merchandise Store was opened in 1883 by August. He was joined in 1898 by his son, Charles. The store carried the thousand and one articles which every general store needed, including groceries, dry goods, clothing, notions, and crockery.

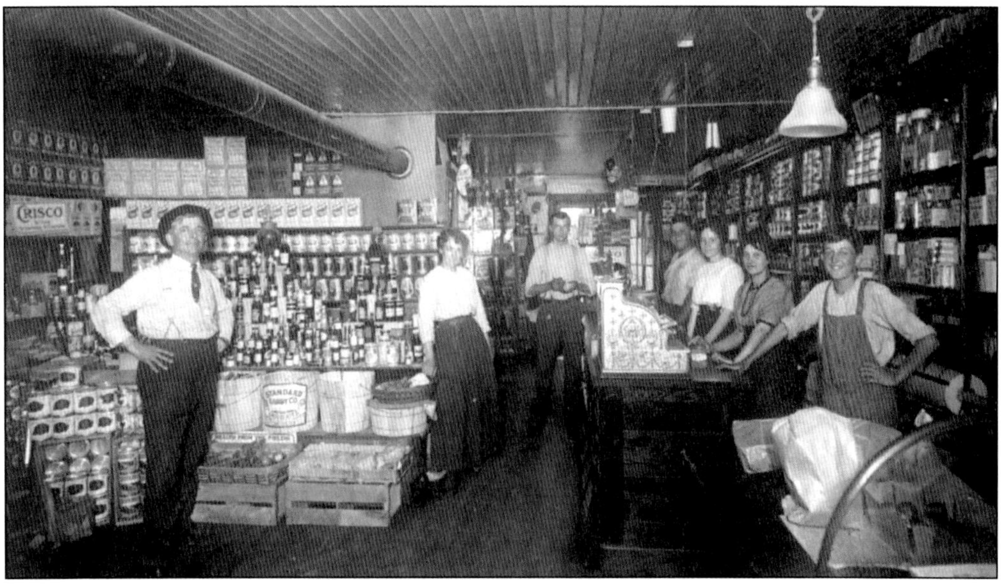

WACHTER'S STORE INTERIOR. From left to right are Charles A. Wachter, Lena Wachter, Oscar Fiedler, Raymond Wachter, Alma Mallman, Odana Henke, Mrs. Emil Heining, and Milford Wachter. During this era pickles and herring were kept in open kegs, Crisco was already a favorite in comparison to lard, the cash register required strength to "ring up" a sale, and a scoop was used to remove butter from a tub.

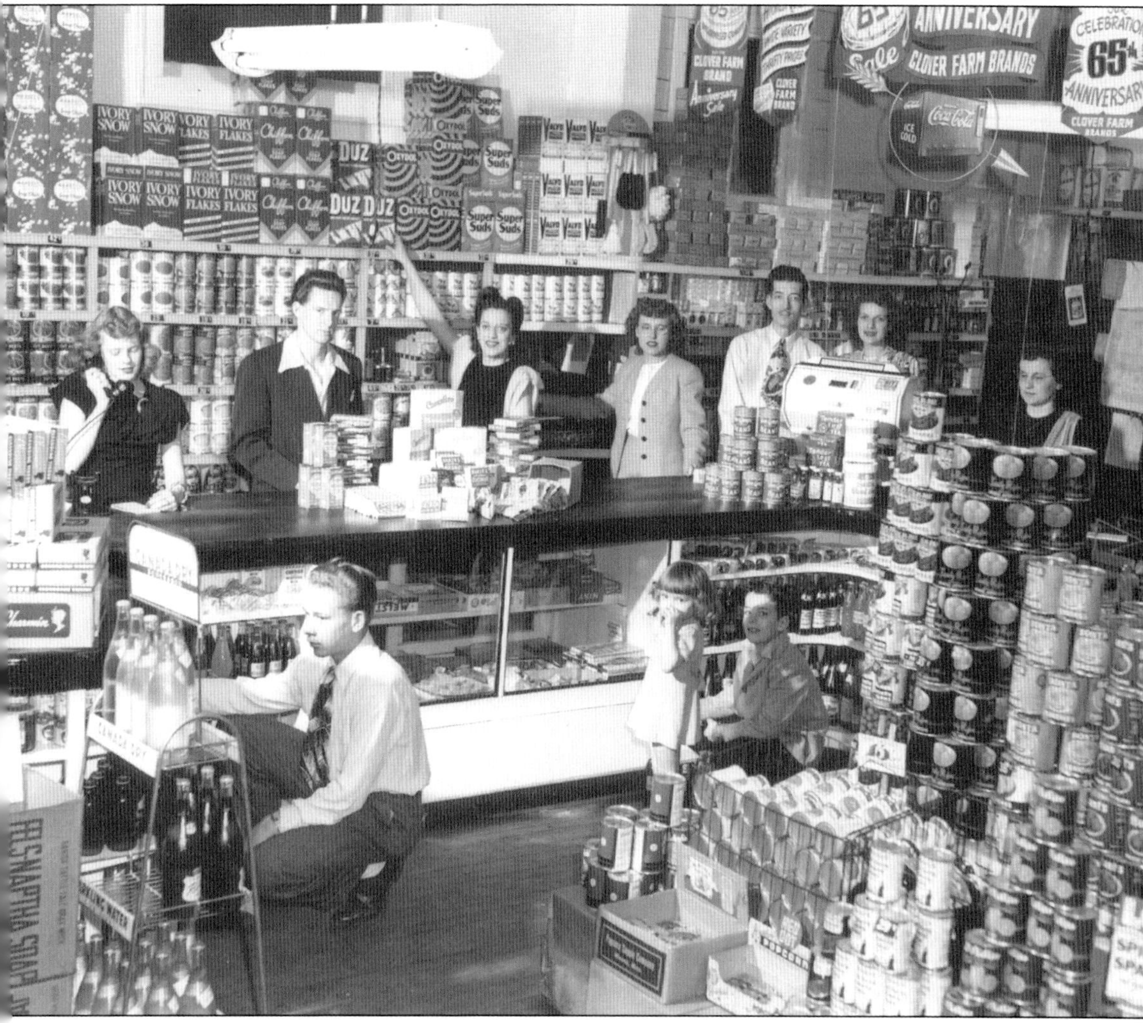

ALTMEYER GROCERY. Albert, or "Sonny," and Genevieve Altmeyer owned and operated Sonny's Clover Farm Grocery Store at 222 Pine Street from 1942 through 1958. The company was known for its large stock of canned goods and dry goods featuring the Clover Farm brand. This 1948 interior photo shows all of the favorite brands of the time: Ivory Flakes, Duz, Oxydol, Dreft for diapers, Canada Dry ginger ale, Red Dot popcorn, and Charmin bath tissue. One could phone in an order and have it delivered, or you could step into the store with your list and one of the clerks would grab the products you wanted off the shelf. There was no self-service. Pictured, from left to right, are Darlene Norgaard, Reuben Frazier, Genevieve Altmeyer, Dolores Vergouw, Albert Altmeyer, Patricia Altmeyer, and Hildegard Jacobs. The young people on the floor are, from left to right, Melvin Schelbauer, Jean Altmeyer, and Jimmy Altmeyer. Prior to becomming Altmeyer's, the building housed the Aderholdt Bakery, the Troeger Feed Store, the Bassuener Harness Shop, and the Launce Pierce Grocery Store.

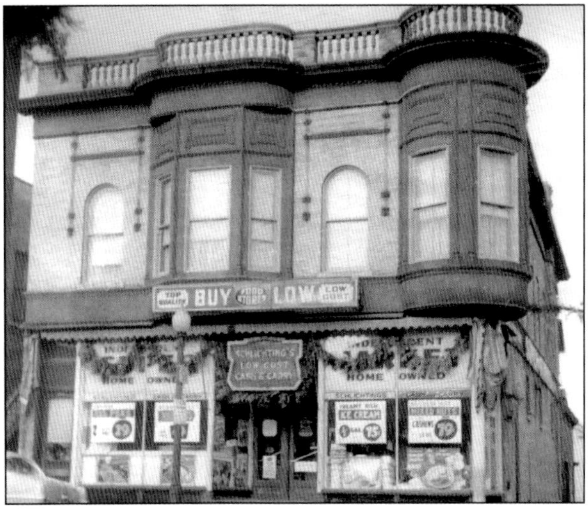

Schlichting Building. Henry Schlichting came to this country from Mecklenburg, Germany on July 5, 1835. He was initially a blacksmith. In 1894, he finished the building shown in this 1895 print of the exterior of the Schlichting block. It was located on the northwest corner of Buffalo and Pine Streets in Sheboygan Falls. The Schlichting family discontinued its grocery business in 1976, at which time the Richardson family purchased the site. Richardson Furniture Emporium now occupies the site. Note the oriel and bay windows and the wooden sidewalks.

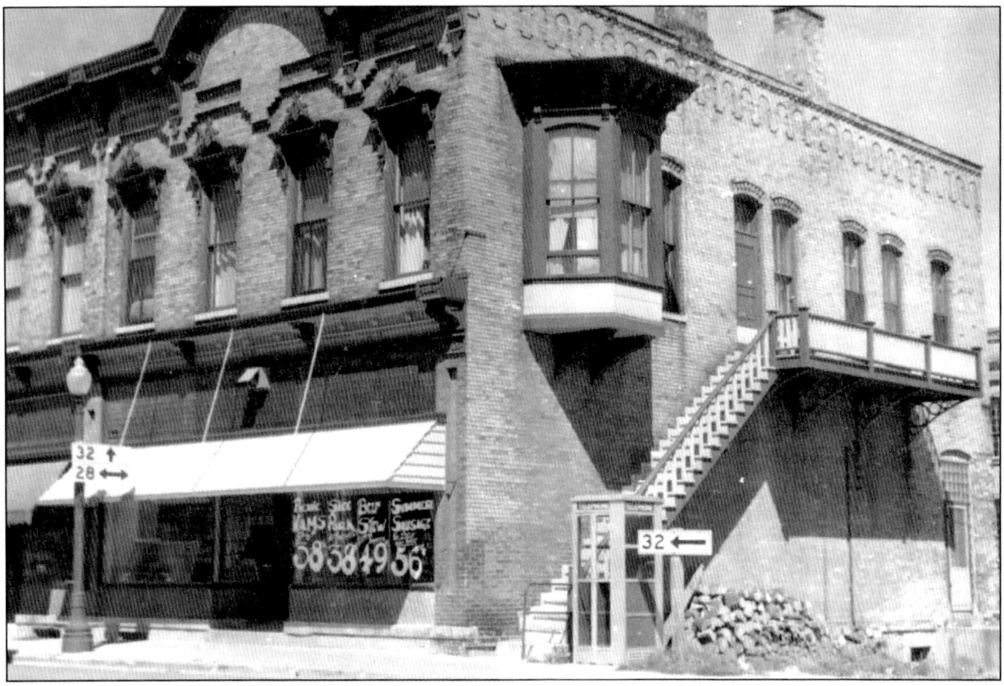

Broadway Meat Market. This 1955 photo of the Broadway Meat Market in Sheboygan Falls advertises picnic hams and side pork for $0.38 per pound, summer sausage is $0.56 per pound, and beef stew meat is $0.49 per pound. Jacob Clicquennoi owned this business from 1925 until the fall of 1947. Mr. Clicquennoi was born in the Netherlands on January 29, 1875, coming to this country at the age of nine years. At 11, he began to work in a neighborhood butcher shop. In 1899, he came to Sheboygan Falls and worked for Frank and John Blust for nine years. Those were the days, according to Jake "that meat prices were really reasonable." Beef roast was eight cents and chicken was ten cents per pound. The butcher would also give a piece of bologna to children as a treat.

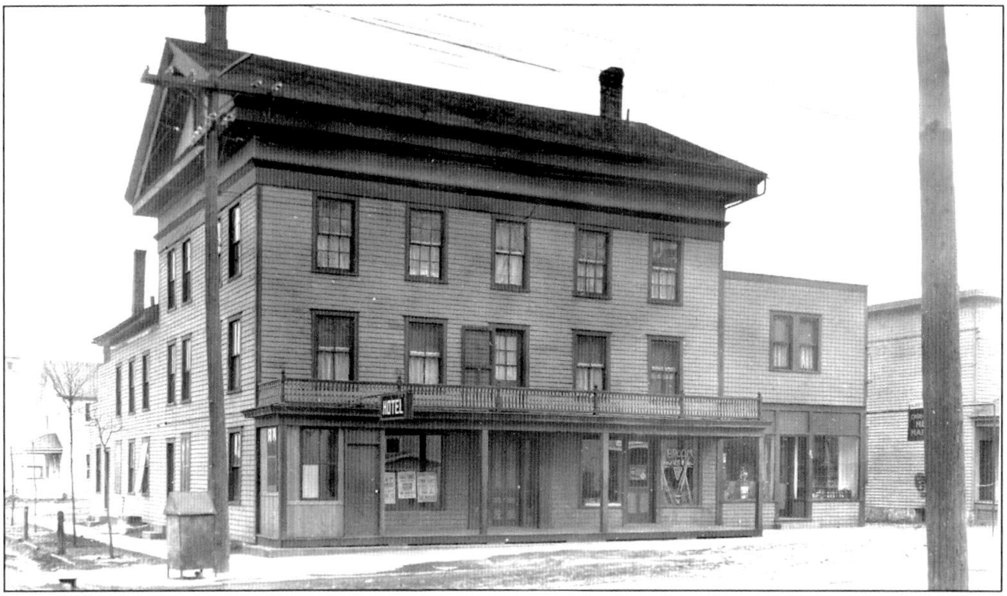

THORPE HOTEL. Originally the Thorpe Hotel, this three-story Greek Revival structure was built in 1846. It was the first hotel built in Sheboygan Falls. A ballroom was located on the fourth floor. The third floor housed seven bedrooms. During the mid-1800s, the hotel was run on a strict temperance basis as the Dixon House. Much of Sheboygan Falls was a part of the temperance movement led by Yankee settlers. The building is now home to Richard's Restaurant of Sheboygan Falls. The structure is located at 510 Monroe Street.

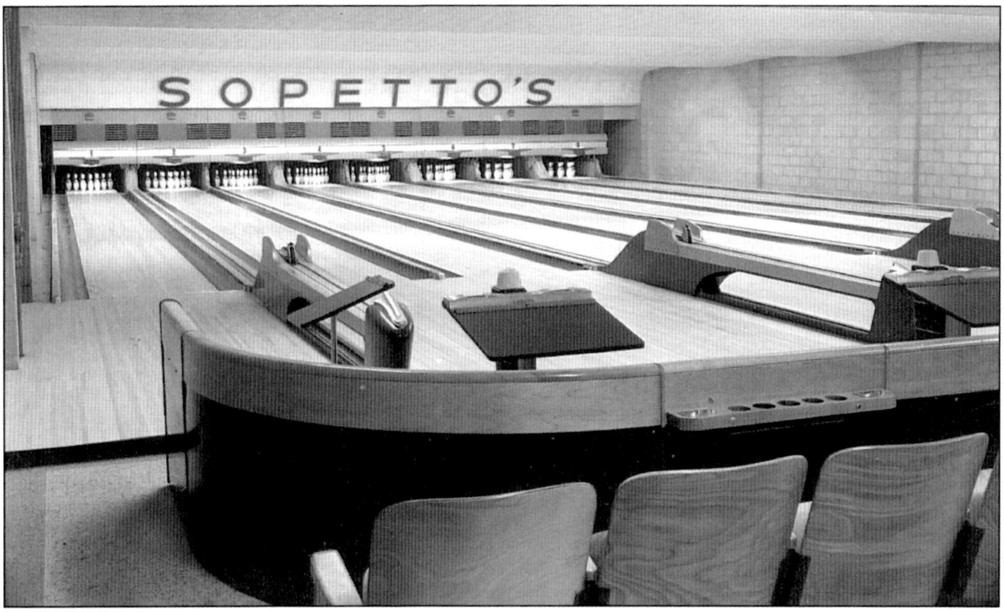

SOPETTO'S BOWLING ALLEY. In 1941, the Old Thorpe Hotel was sold to Paul and Mansueto Sopetto, and extensive remodeling was done. In 1952, a bowling alley consisting of eight lanes was added to the south of the building. The alleys were removed in 1985 and the space remodeled into banquet facilities. Richard and Darlene Kosup purchased the building in 1968, and named it "Richard's," a name it still holds today.

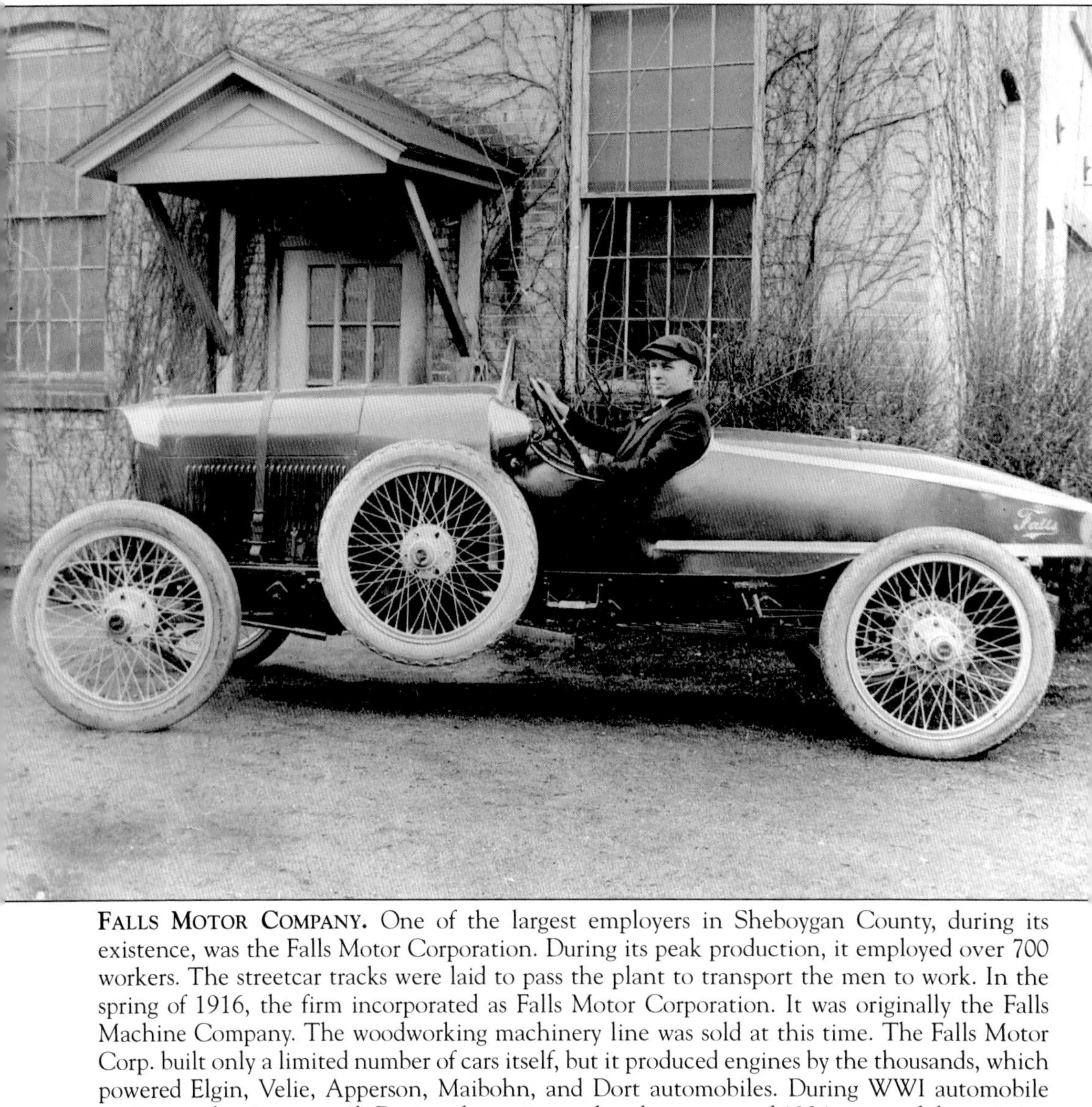

FALLS MOTOR COMPANY. One of the largest employers in Sheboygan County, during its existence, was the Falls Motor Corporation. During its peak production, it employed over 700 workers. The streetcar tracks were laid to pass the plant to transport the men to work. In the spring of 1916, the firm incorporated as Falls Motor Corporation. It was originally the Falls Machine Company. The woodworking machinery line was sold at this time. The Falls Motor Corp. built only a limited number of cars itself, but it produced engines by the thousands, which powered Elgin, Velie, Apperson, Maibohn, and Dort automobiles. During WWI automobile engine production was nil. During the spring and early summer of 1924, most of the existing automobile manufacturers, outside of Ford, GM, Chrysler, Hudson, Studebaker, Nash, and Auburn went out of business, causing Falls Motors to go into bankruptcy. The factory was located in the manufacturing plant that was also the home of Kohler General. The entire site was demolished in 2003. Seen here is an Elgin Boat Tail racecar, model year 1921-1922.

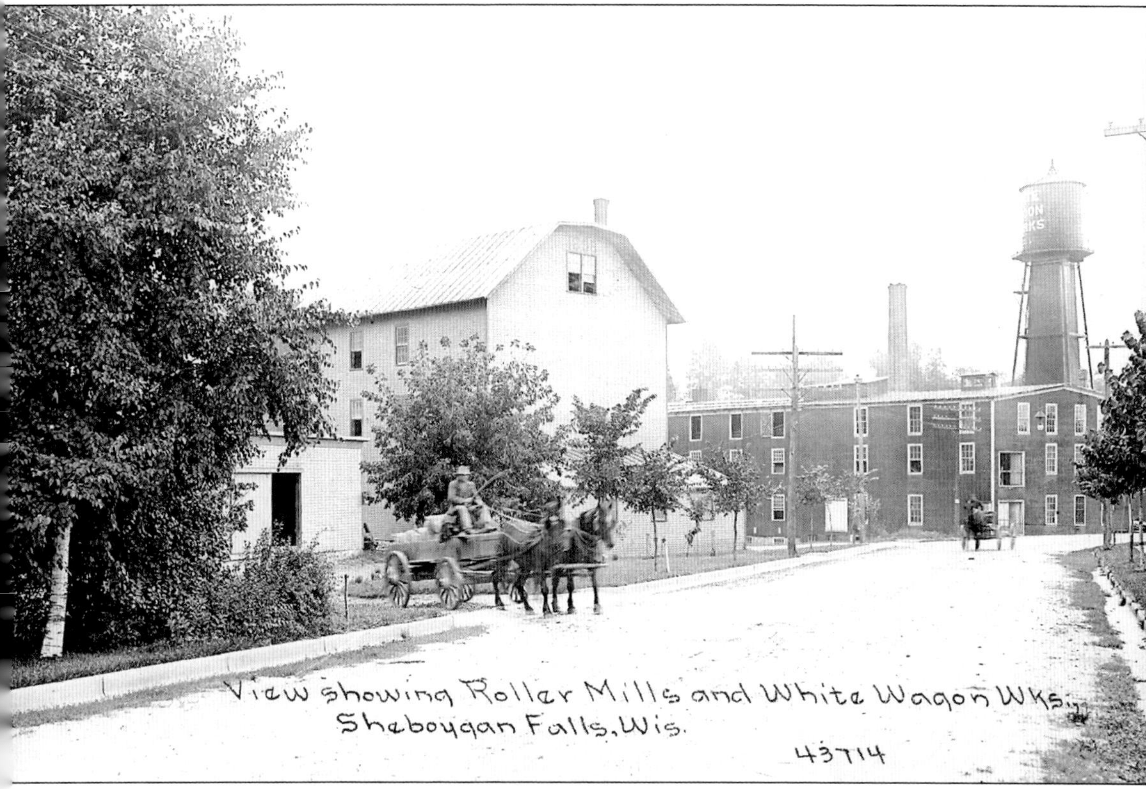

SHEBOYGAN FALLS ROLLER MILLS AND WHITE WAGON WORKS. Seen at the left is Sheboygan Falls Roller Mills, which prior to 1918 was called Rock Mills. In 1925, WP & L acquired this property and converted it into an automatic hydro-electric station. The building to the right is White Wagon Works, built in 1899 by White, Mager and Schwalbe. In its early years, White Wagon Works made wooden coaster wagons and sleds. The company later added novelty furniture to its list of products. In 1924, Albert Bemis and George Riddell bought controlling interest in White Wagon Works, changing the name to White Coaster Wagon Works. Bemis gained sole control of the business in 1928. In 1932 Albert Bemis brought Carl Jensen from the bankrupt Crocker Chair Company, along with his patents, dies, and machinery for toilet seats to Sheboygan Falls. In 1938, White Coaster Wagon Works became Bemis Manufacturing Company. These companies stood on what is today Settlers' Park on north Broadway Street.

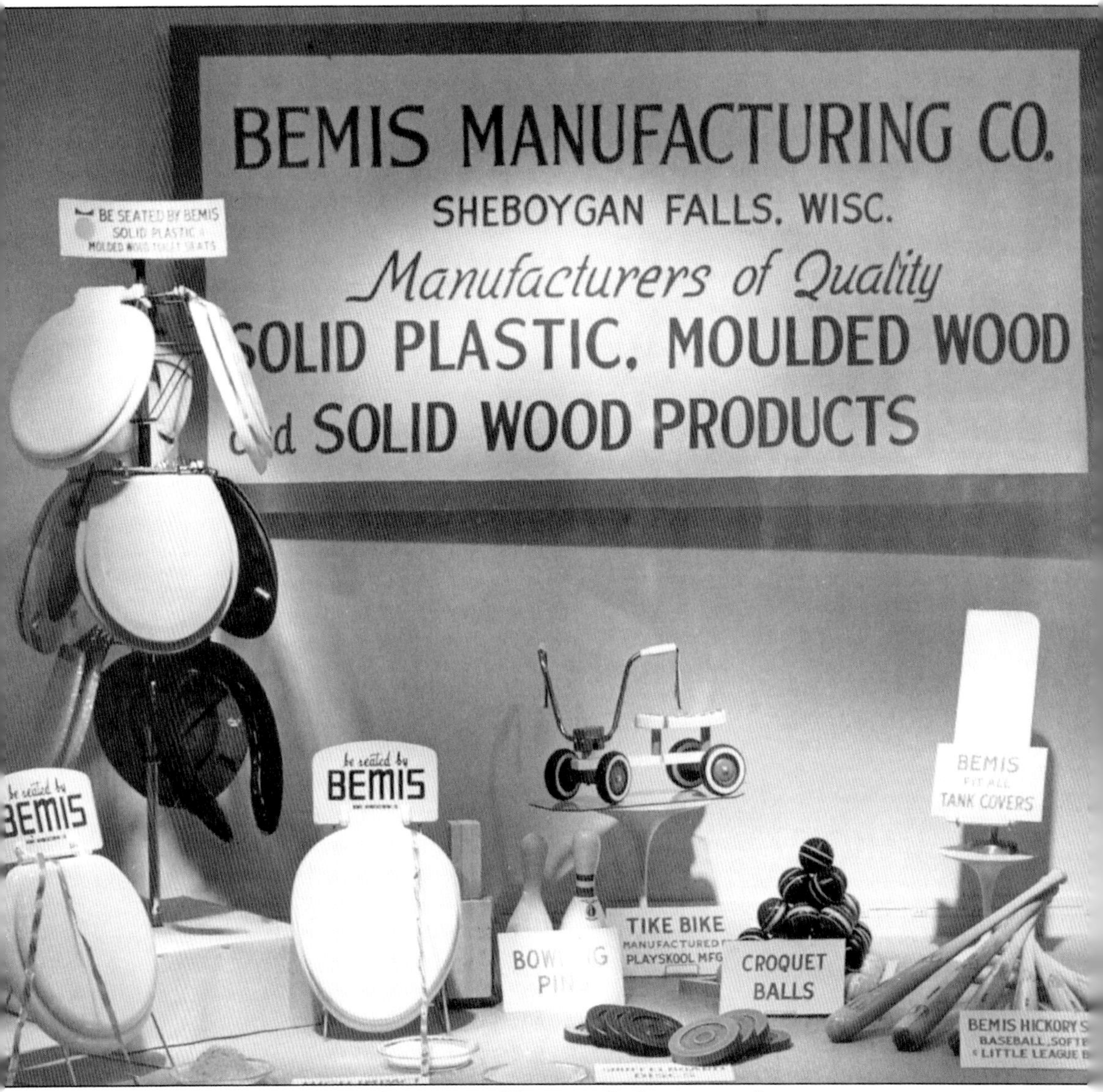

BEMIS MANUFACTURING COMPANY. The switch from manufacturing coaster wagons to toilet seats during the depression was difficult but gutsy. When Bemis Manufacturing Company secured the account to make seats for Kohler Company toilets in 1935, it was the beginning of a relationship that would provide stability and security for many citizens of Sheboygan County during the tough years of the 1930s and 1940s. The Kohler Company account meant reasonably safe jobs and income for Bemis employees, too. In 1935, Albert Bemis's son, F.K., called "Pete," joined the company after graduation from law school. He helped his father switch the company's focus from furniture to plumbing products supplier. During World War II, Bemis became a part of FDR's "arsenal of democracy" by continuing to produce the needed toilet seats for army camps, but because brass became scarce, a new hinge was created from a new petroleum-based material, plastic. This display window shows many of the products Bemis created in the 1960s. They included toilet seats, Tike Bike, bowling pins, shuffleboard discs, croquet balls, and little league bats. The main Bemis Manufacturing plant is located at 300 Mill Street.

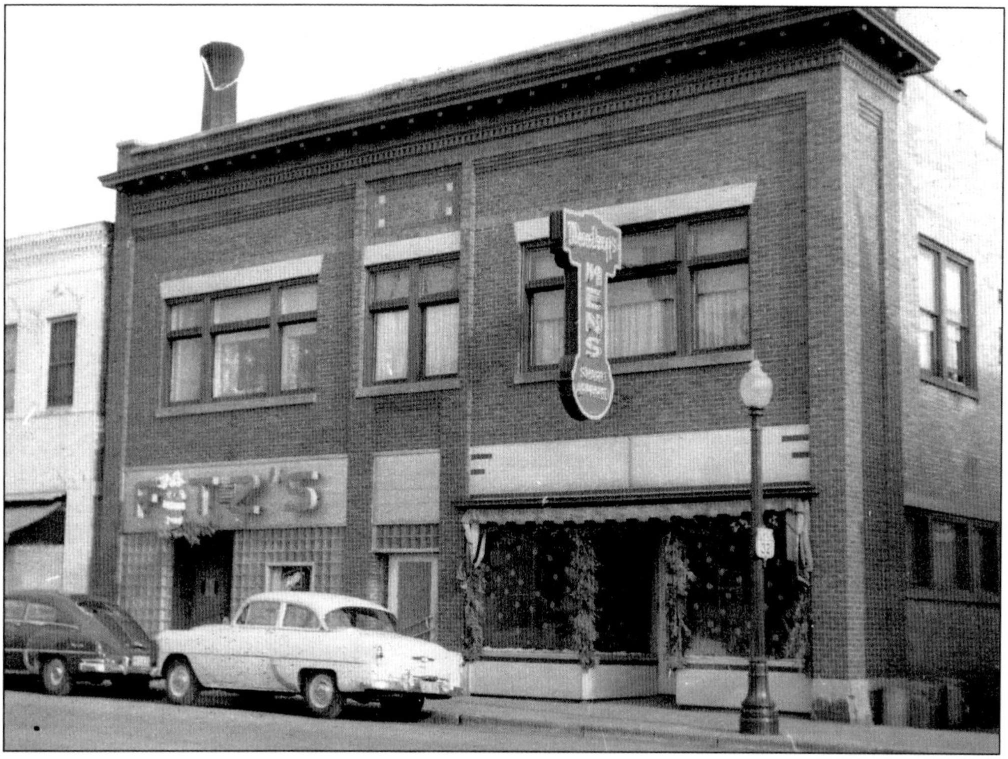

DEELEY'S MENS' CLOTHING. Deeley's Men's Clothing, 410 Broadway, was originally owned and operated by Jack Deeley. He opened for business in April of 1946. Jack leased the store from Art Fitzpatrick who operated a tavern in the other half of the building at 106 Broadway. Deeley retired in the spring of 1968 and died in 1984. He had a long military career, also serving in command of a CCC camp in northern Wisconsin during the 1930s reforestation projects.

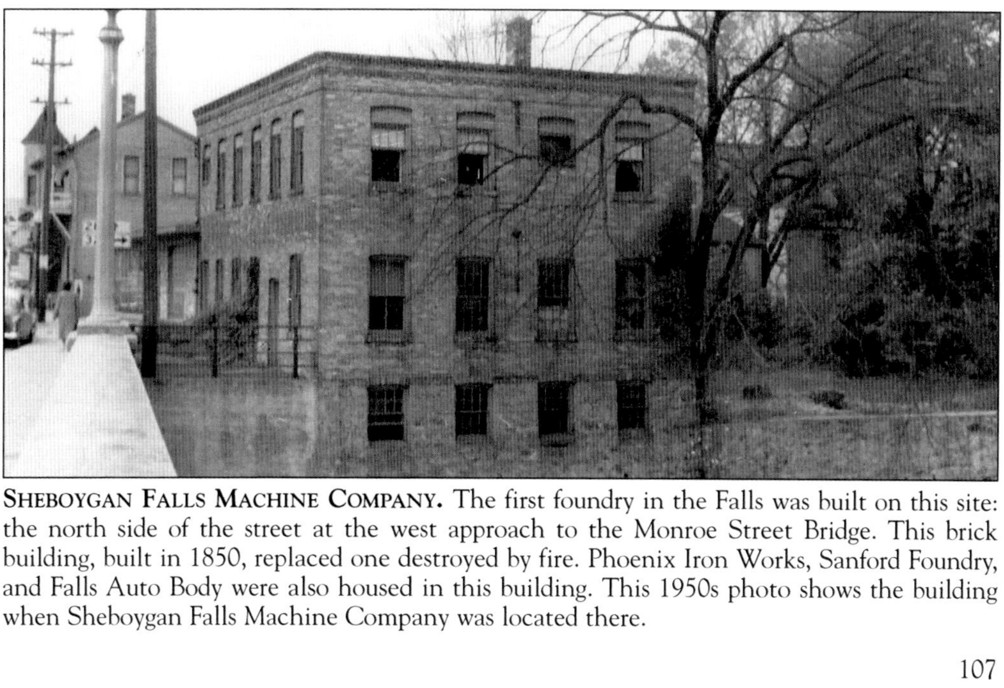

SHEBOYGAN FALLS MACHINE COMPANY. The first foundry in the Falls was built on this site: the north side of the street at the west approach to the Monroe Street Bridge. This brick building, built in 1850, replaced one destroyed by fire. Phoenix Iron Works, Sanford Foundry, and Falls Auto Body were also housed in this building. This 1950s photo shows the building when Sheboygan Falls Machine Company was located there.

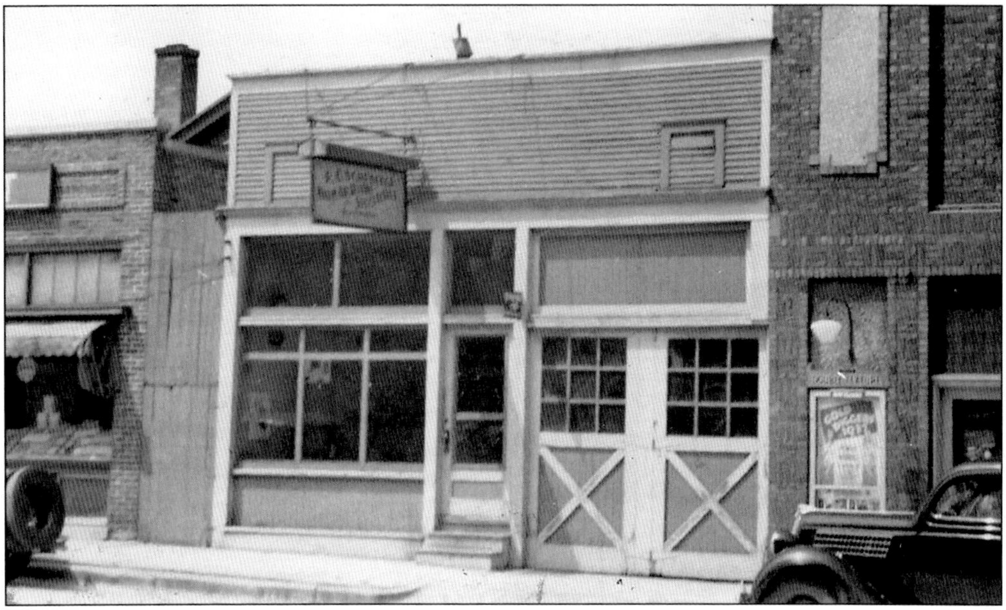

SANFORD TIRE SHOP. The Sanford Tire Shop opened on February 21, 1921. Sanford's business consisted of selling automobile and bicycle tires, and repair of tires and tubes. The building was previously used by Mr. Guyett for the "Rose Theater." The theater stayed here until the new Falls Theater on Pine Street was opened in 1916. The business was located in the 200 block of Pine Street.

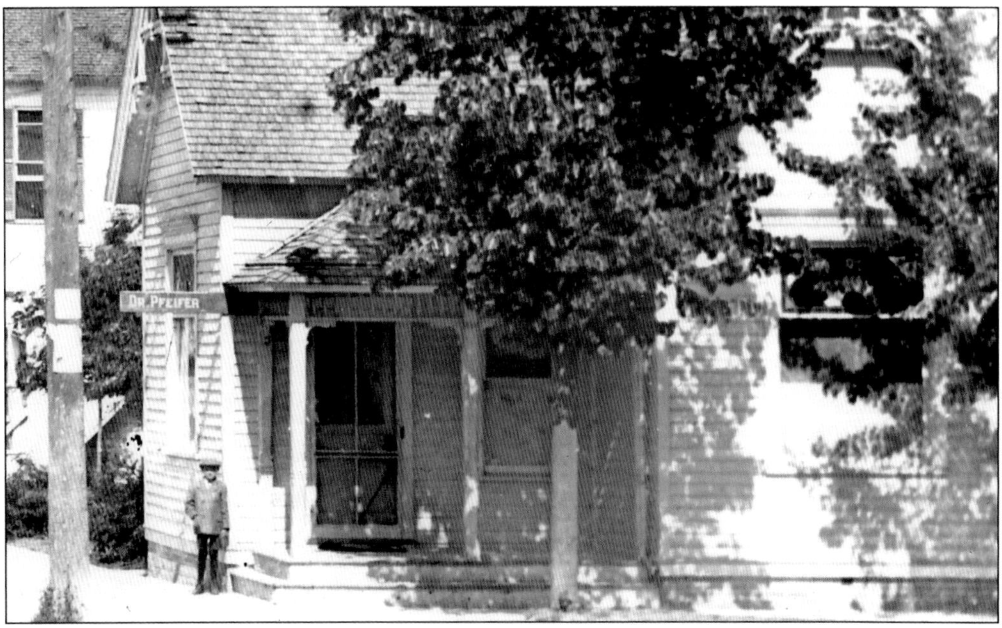

DR. PFEIFER'S OFFICE. This small building on the southeast corner of Pine and Detroit Streets was the office of Dr. Charles Pfeiffer until his death. Dr. Williard Sonnenburg replaced him and continued to use the office until he moved to Sheboygan. Dr. Frederick Leighton next took occupancy and remained until his retirement. It has also served as an antique shop, a residence, and most recently, a jewelry shop.

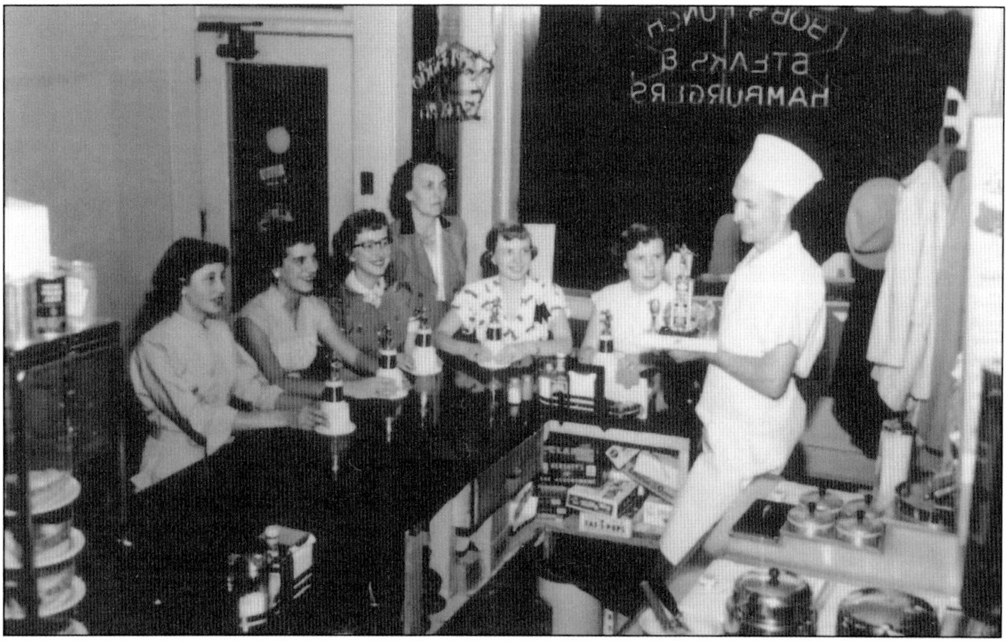

Bob's Lunch. From 1946 to 1999, Bob's Lunch was a very popular eatery in downtown Falls. Falls' natives returning to their hometown would make an effort to stop at the business for one of its famous hamburgers. Owner Bob Visser and his wife, Bea, ran the restaurant until Bob's death in 1969. Here, Bob and Bea can be seen posing with the women's bowling team they sponsored.

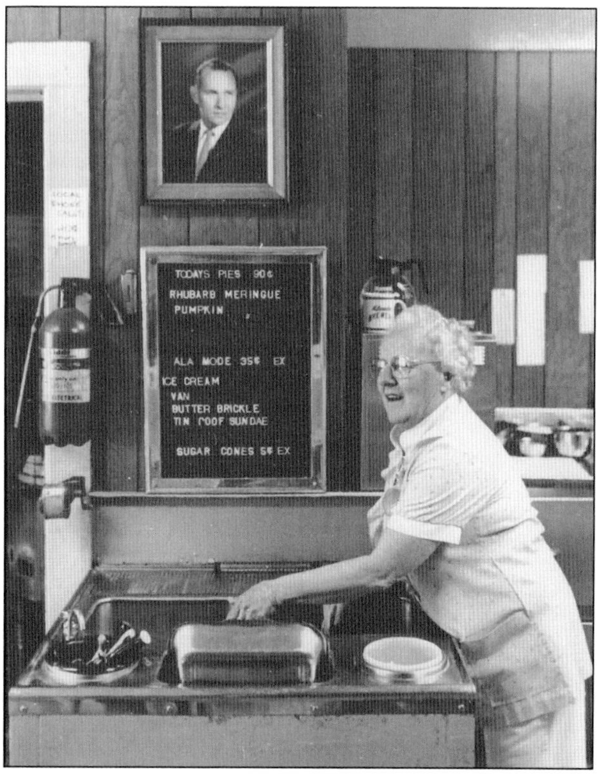

Bob's Lunch. Bea was an avid Cubs' fan and was always willing to discuss her favorite baseball team. Bea kept the business running until 1999. This photo shows Bea shortly before retirement.

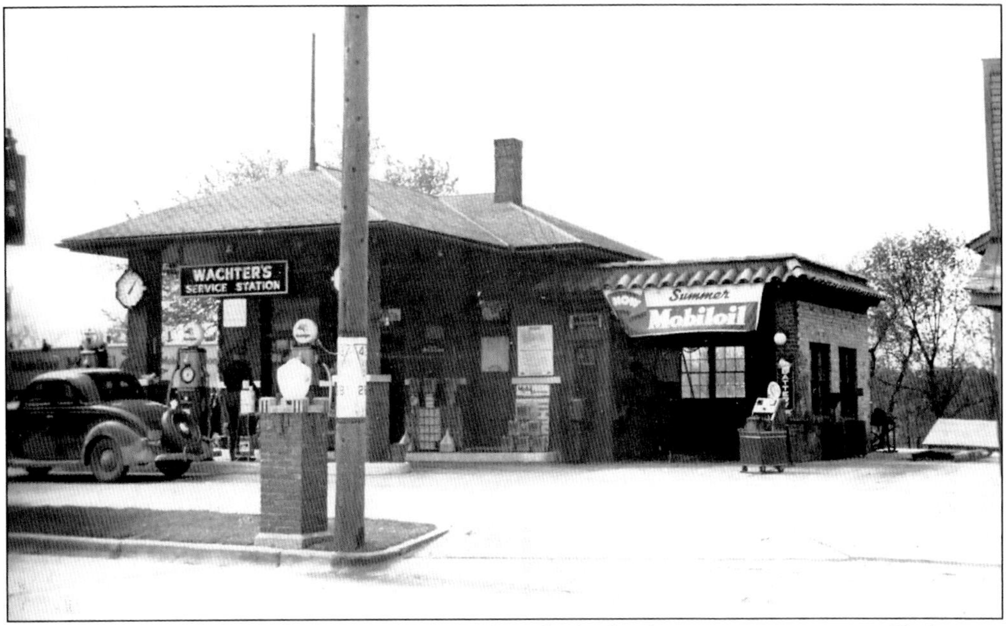

WACHTER SERVICE STATION. Raymond Wachter built the first service station in Sheboygan Falls at 326 Pine Street in 1921. He operated the station until his death in 1957 when his brother Milford took over. Milford ran the business until his death ten years later. In 1968, it was extensively remodeled for Troy Launderette.

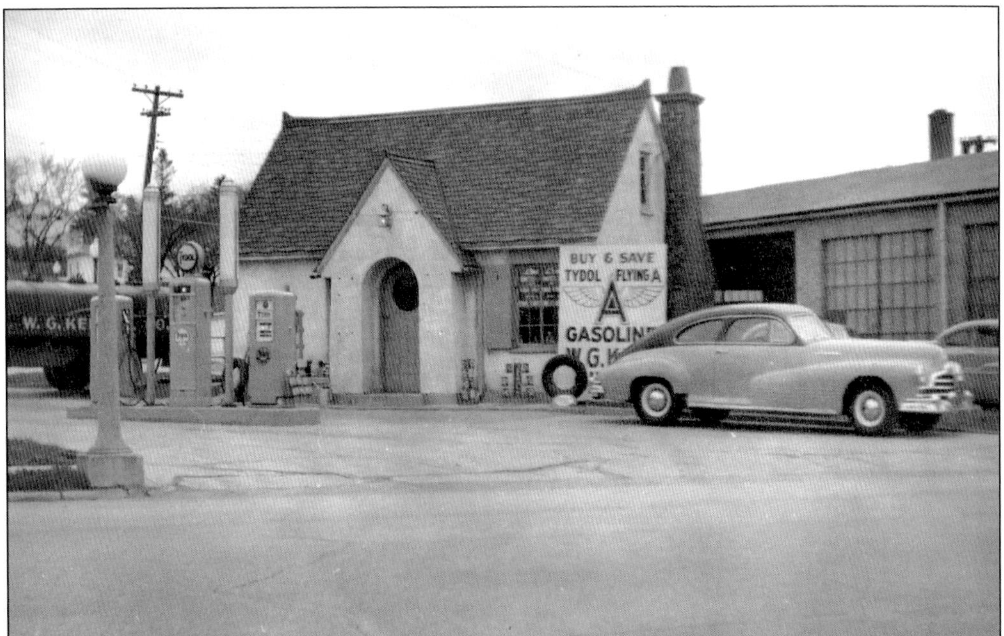

SHEBOYGAN FALLS GAS STATION. This quaint station, located on the northeast corner of Poplar and Monroe Streets, just west of the Ford dealership, urges its customers to "Buy Tydol, Flying A Gasoline and Save." The photo was taken in 1953.

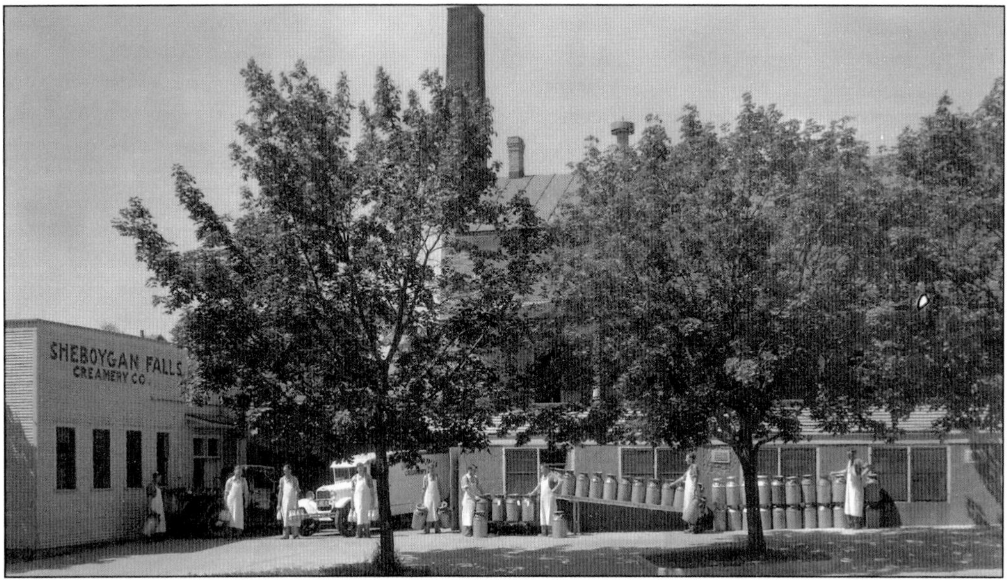

SHEBOYGAN FALLS CREAMERY. The Creamery was started by R.P. Dassow in 1915. In 1920, O.S. Damrow became a partner when the company was incorporated in June. Production was limited to butter and cheese the first year. But in 1921, a large addition was built for the handling of milk and other dairy products. In 1921, the creamery operated one wagon and employed four men. By 1929, 12 wagons and trucks were required to deliver milk, butter, cream, cooked and cottage cheese to patrons in Kohler and Sheboygan as well as in the Falls. The work force had increased to 36 individuals.

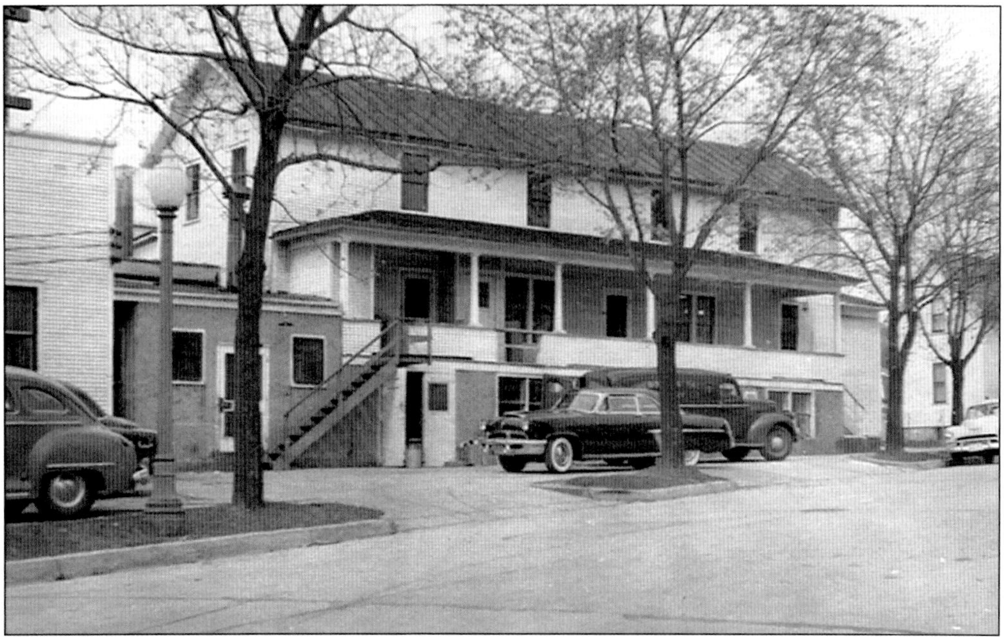

FALLS CREAMERY. Arthur Widder, who was the butter maker, William Janssen, and William Schaap all had long associations with the creamery. In 1959, Lake to Lake Dairy of Sheboygan bought the business. The buildings and equipment were removed at that time. The site was later the location of Austin's Super Market at the south end of Buffalo Street.

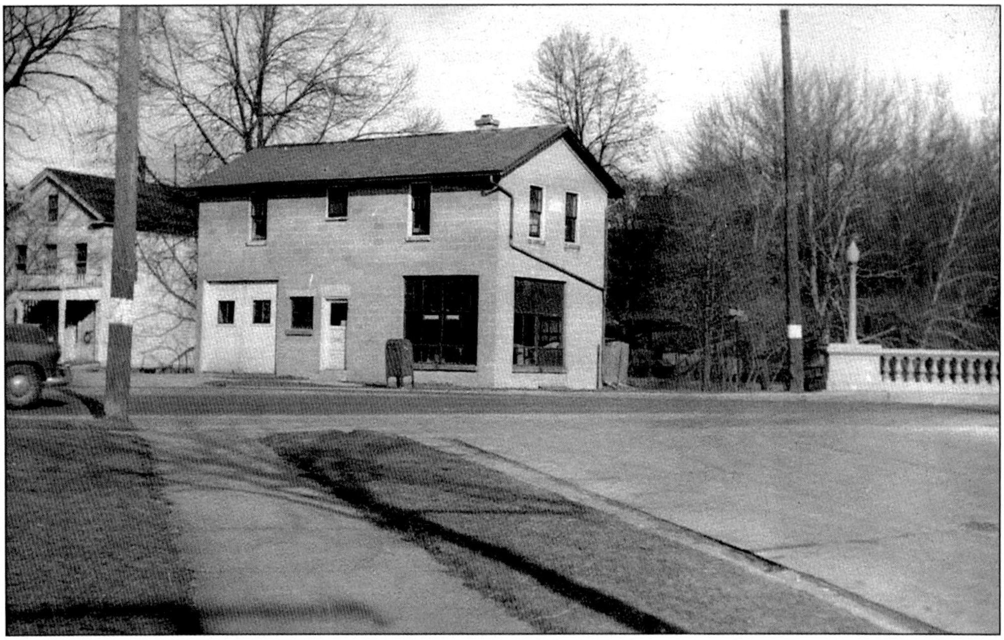

MONUMENT WORKS. Located on the eastern side of the north approach to the Broadway Bridge, the site was originally the home of the Dicke Brewery. Owned by Henry Dicke, the brewery burned to the ground on January 31, 1877. The brewery was valued at $2,000 and nothing was saved from the fire but the beer. It was not rebuilt. This building shown here housed the Falls Monument Company, started in about 1944 by Roland Veenendal. Pearl and Alan Widder purchased the company in 1969 and moved to their Fond du Lac Avenue location in 1984.

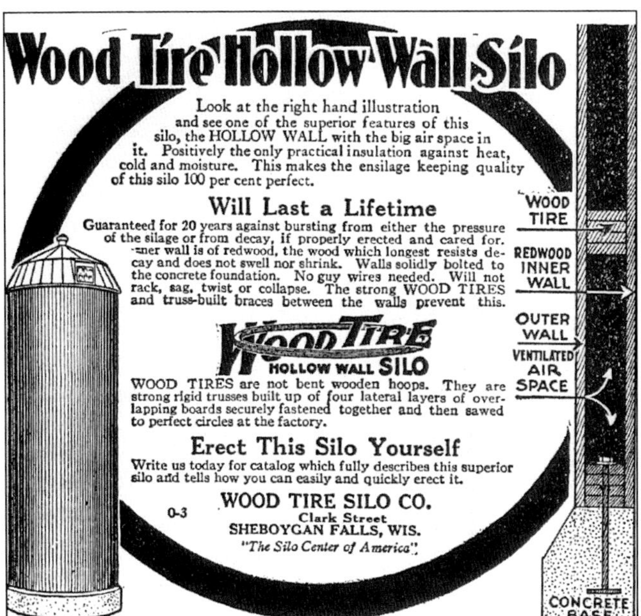

WOOD TIRE SILO COMPANY. The Wood Tire Silo Company began as the Falls Stanchion Company in 1914. The company manufactured wood tire, hollow wall silos, stanchions, bushel crates, window frames, and matched siding. The factory was located on Clark Street near the railroad tracks. Julius Widder, George Robbins, and H.E. Boldt were stockholders in the company. These were supposed to be easily erected silos that lasted a lifetime.

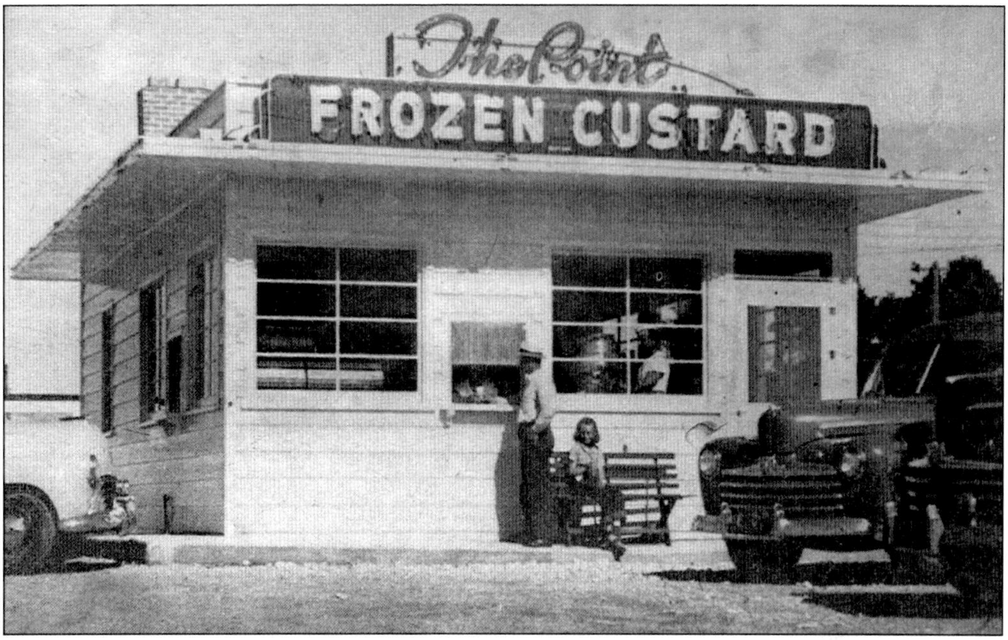

The Point Custard Stand. The first custard stand opened in Sheboygan Falls on June 23, 1949. Located on the "point" formed by the intersection of Fond du Lac and Leavens Avenues, The Point offered custard cones and the best hamburgers and steak sandwiches around. To begin with, the drive-in was open only during warm weather. It was the brainchild of Edward Kelm. The Point at one time had carhops, and for a short time, they used roller skates to get around. After 56 years, the restaurant is as popular as ever.

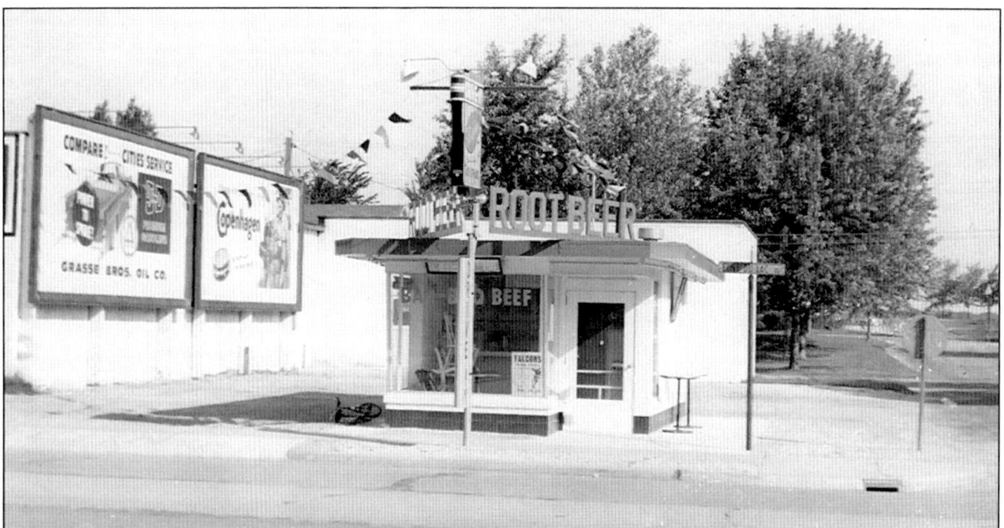

Fowler's Restaurant. The little root beer stand opened by Bert and Ceil Fowler at 404 Fond du Lac Avenue was built in 1954. It was in business until 1960 when it was rented by Richard Krauss for K-Print Publishing. Specials included Coney dogs and barbecue sandwiches.

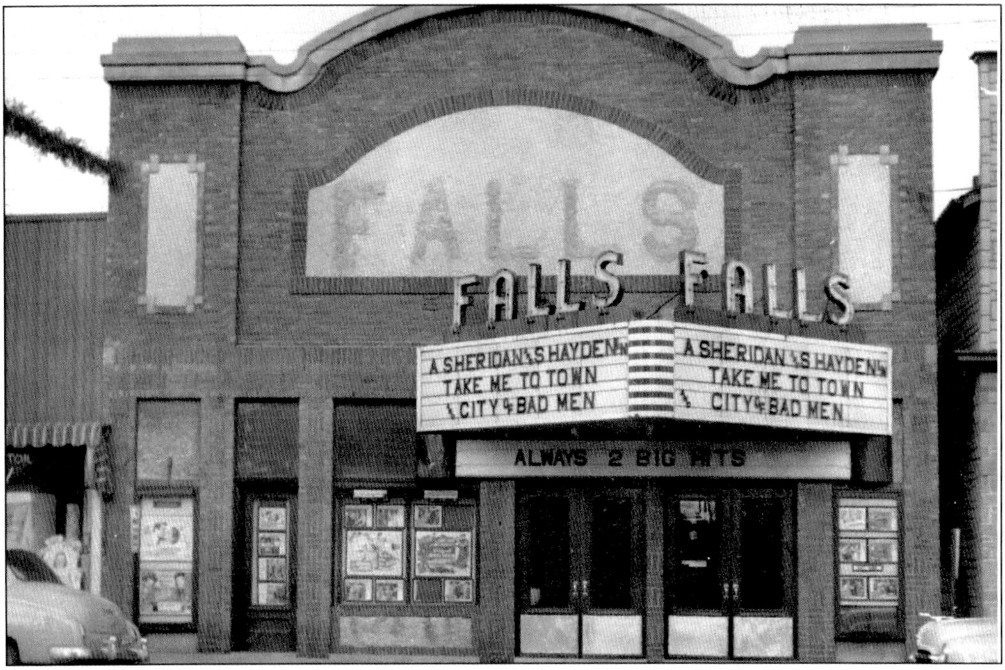

FALLS MOVIE THEATER. A good movie always packs them in. This is the Sheboygan Falls Theater showing Ann Hayden in *Take Me To Town* and *City of Bad Men*. In the 1940s and 1950s, seeing two features for the price of one was very common. Built in the 200 block of Pine Street in 1916 it ceased operation in 1959, remaining empty until 1965 when it was razed to make room for a parking lot.

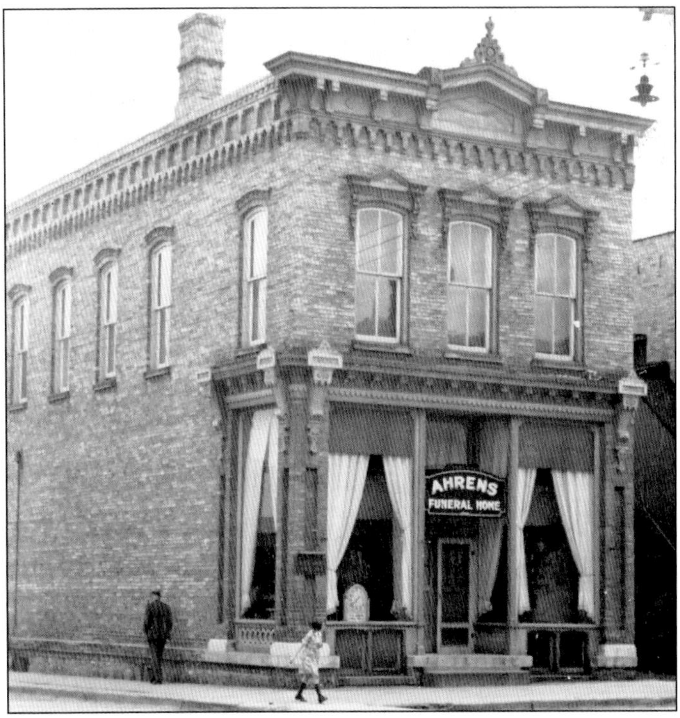

THE NEVER STORE OR AHRENS FUNERAL HOME. Built in 1882 by John Never, the building originally housed a men's clothing and custom tailoring shop. In 1936 Walter Ahrens purchased the building and used it as a funeral home. In 1944, it was sold to Mr. and Mrs. John Claerbout who operated a beauty parlor and clothing store, but then switched to the retail of furniture. He converted the second floor to living quarters. Jim and Cynthia Roberts purchased the building in 1972 and continued with the sale of furniture. This photograph is c. 1940.

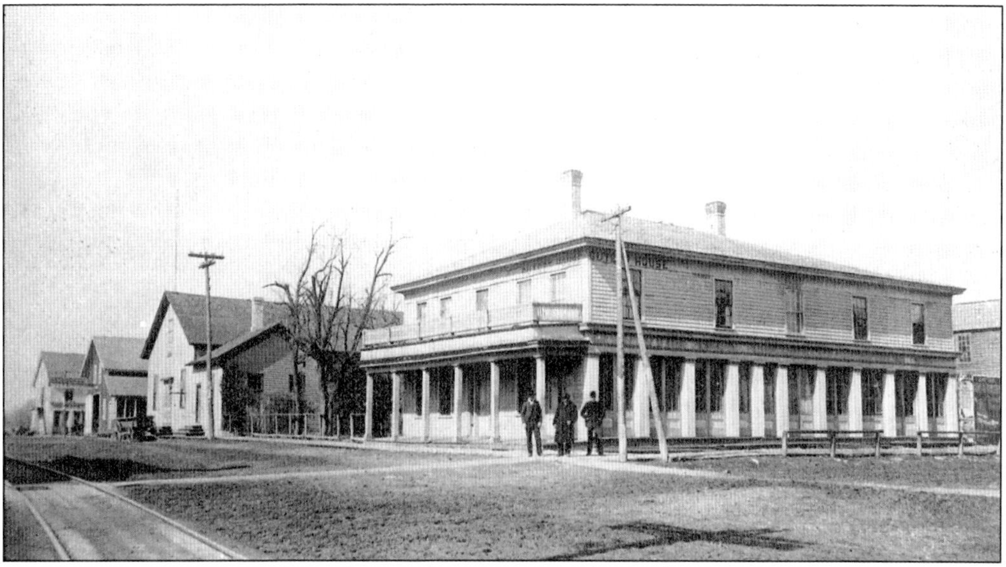

GUYETTE HOTEL. Located on the northwest corner of Broadway and Monroe Streets, Mose Guyett turned an old dry goods store into a hostelry called the Guyett House. It was a beautiful structure with colonnaded porches and elaborated entrances. This hotel ran a stage line to Weeden Station to pickup mail and passengers arriving on the Milwaukee-Green Bay railroad. The first telephone service was installed in the building. Before it was razed the building also housed Kalk's grocery store and rented living quarters on the second floor.

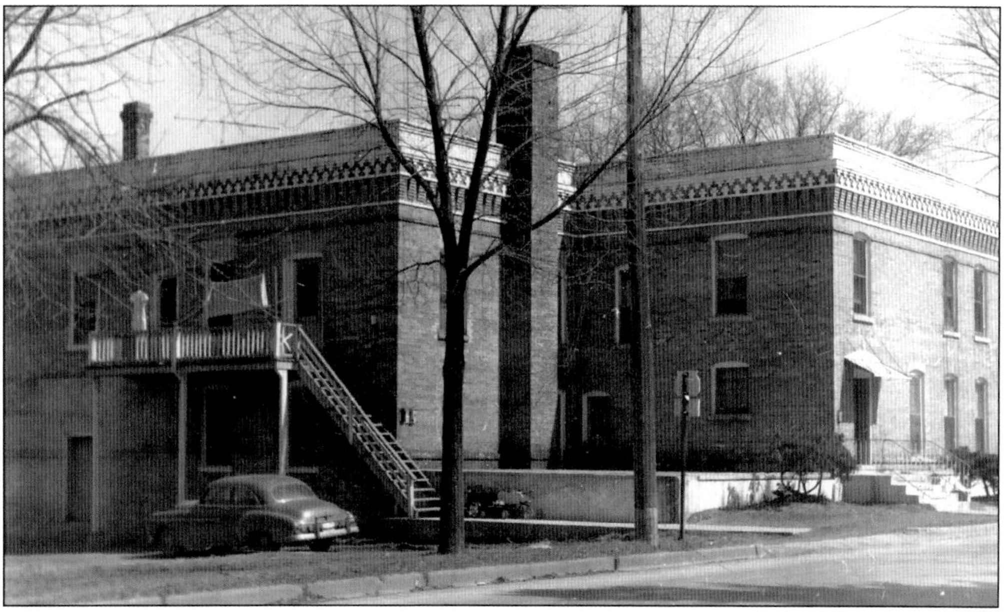

HENRY AND MCKINNON CHEESE FACTORY. Augustus Henry bought a lot in Sheboygan Falls in 1884 on the north side of Broadway just opposite the end of Buffalo Street. His cheese factory and creamery was built in 1884 or 1885. A substantial addition was added in 1905 to provide room for a cider mill. Manning McKinnon bought the factory in 1906. Otis and then George McKinnon owned the building. By 1923 no cheese making was going on. The building was later turned into apartments.

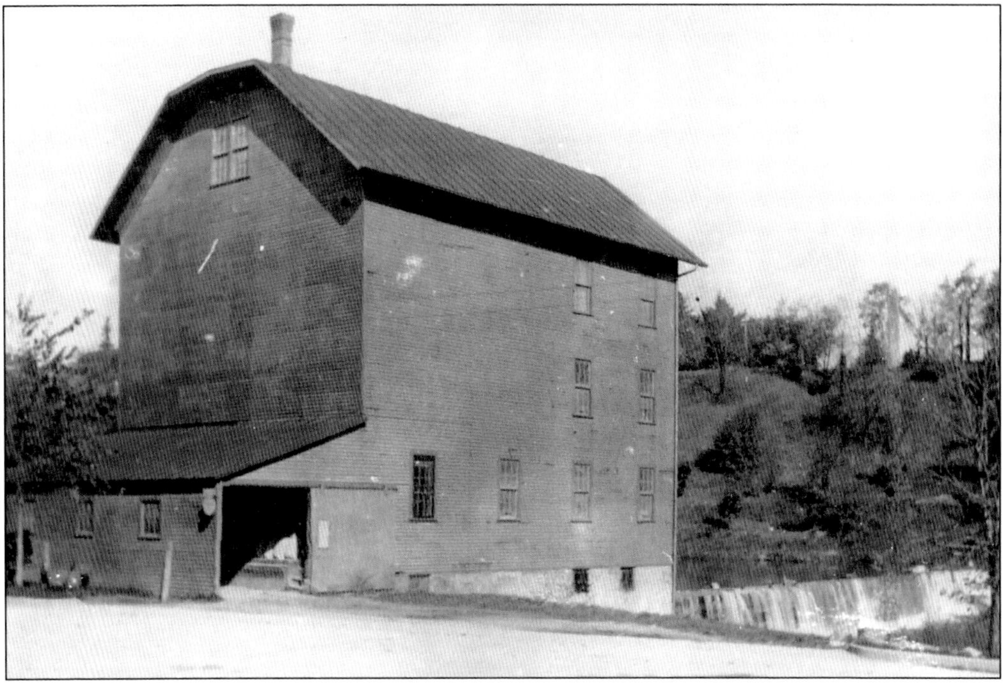

ROCK MILLS. Located on North Broadway Street near the site of the upper dam, Rock Mills was built in about 1848 by A.P. Lyman. This three story structure with a stone basement had the capacity to manufacture 80 barrels of flour a day in 1900. Power was furnished by two water wheels. The mill was lighted by electricity. The local brand of flour produced was "Golden Rod."

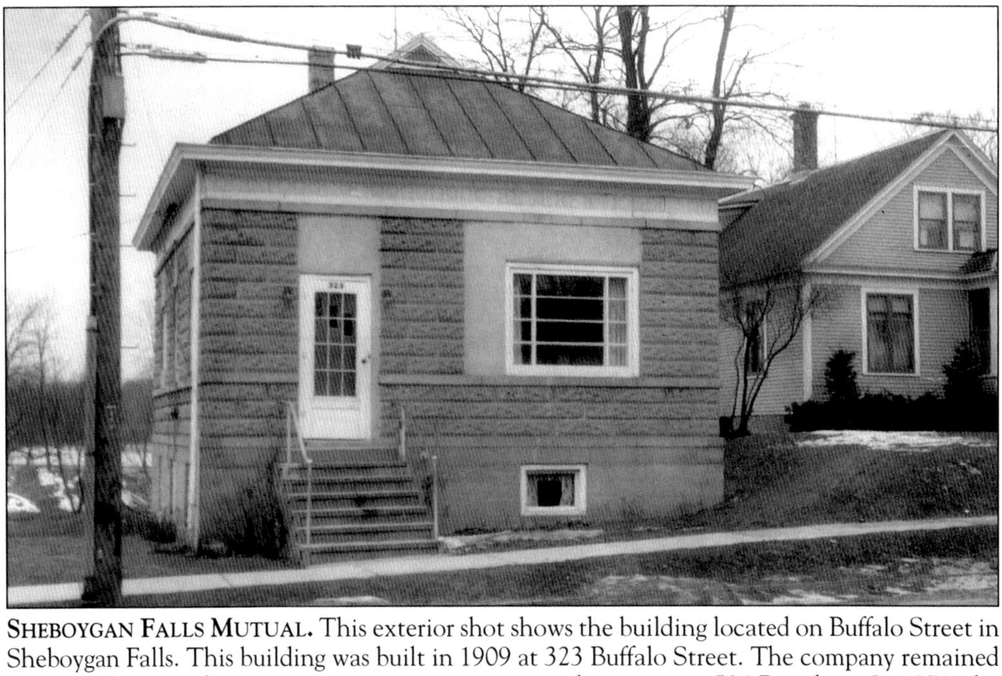

SHEBOYGAN FALLS MUTUAL. This exterior shot shows the building located on Buffalo Street in Sheboygan Falls. This building was built in 1909 at 323 Buffalo Street. The company remained there until 1937, when space requirements necessitated its move to 504 Broadway. In 1971, the company moved to "Rock Ledge" at 511 Water Street, where it remains to this day.

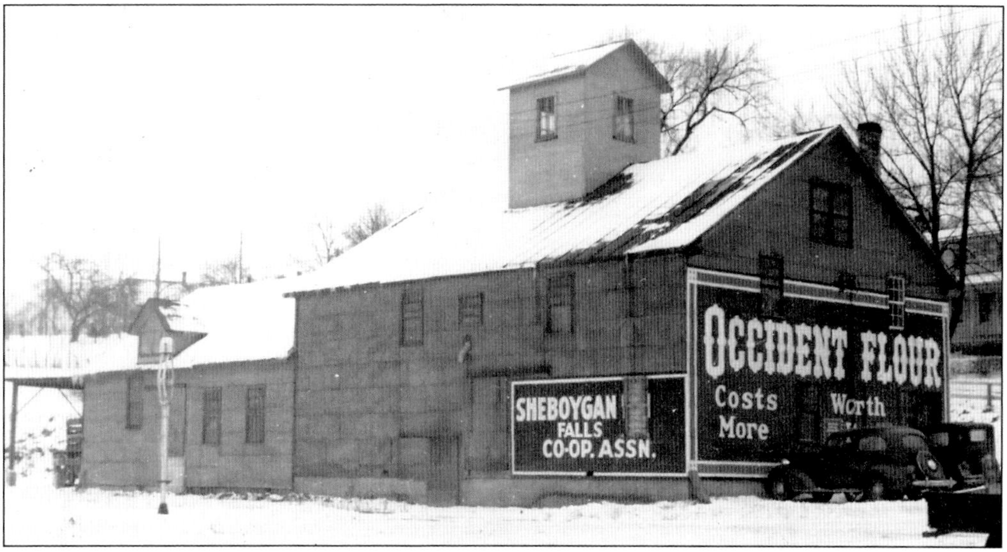

SHEBOYGAN FALLS CO-OP. This photograph, taken in 1938, shows the Sheboygan Falls Farmers' Cooperative located on the northwest corner of Monroe and Poplar Streets. Sheboygan Falls Co-op began operations in 1916. It was started by farmers to help farmers. It was initially a feed mill, but in the 1930s the co-op began to provide fuel to the farmers. A hardware line was added in the 1960s. Here it had access to the railroad and the interurban for transport and delivery. The business is still located on this spot.

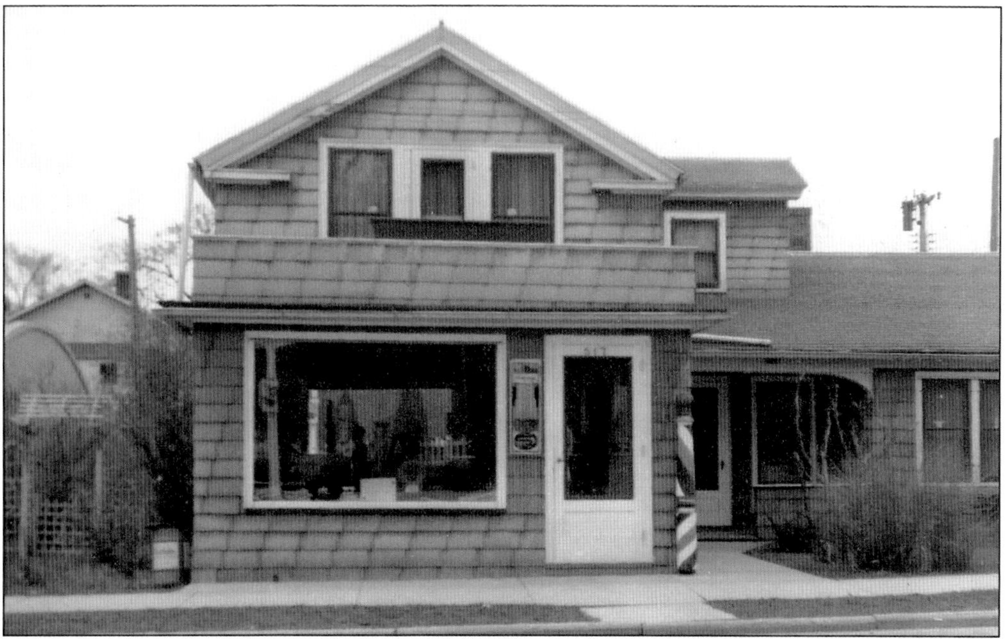

ALTMEYER BARBERSHOP. Alvin Altmeyer operated a barbershop in connection with the Sheboygan Falls Hotel, the old Thorpe hotel, owned by his father, Peter. This photograph was taken in the 1950s. The building located at 517 Monroe Street in the Cole Historic District, was completely restored to its Greek Revival beauty in the 1990s. Merseberger Financial Group now operates from this building.

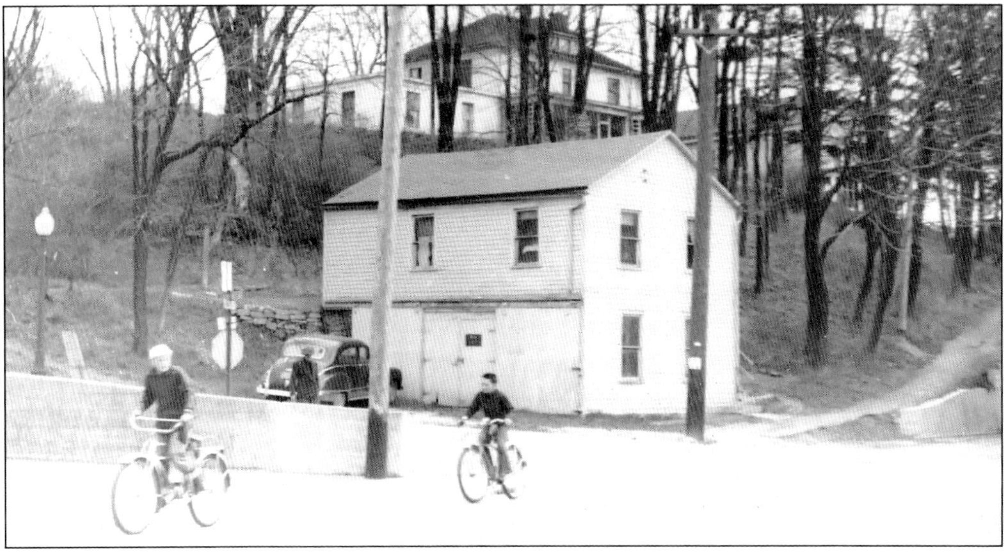

KIRKLAND COOPERAGE. This two-story frame structure stood at the corner of Water and Monroe Streets built into the Water Street hill. Here William Kirkland manufactured barrels for the fishing industry. Born in New York, his family moved to Sheboygan Falls in 1851. He became the first teacher to teach in the new school building that stood opposite the old St. Paul Lutheran Church on Broadway. The building was razed in 1966 to make a parking lot for R-Dee's Restaurant.

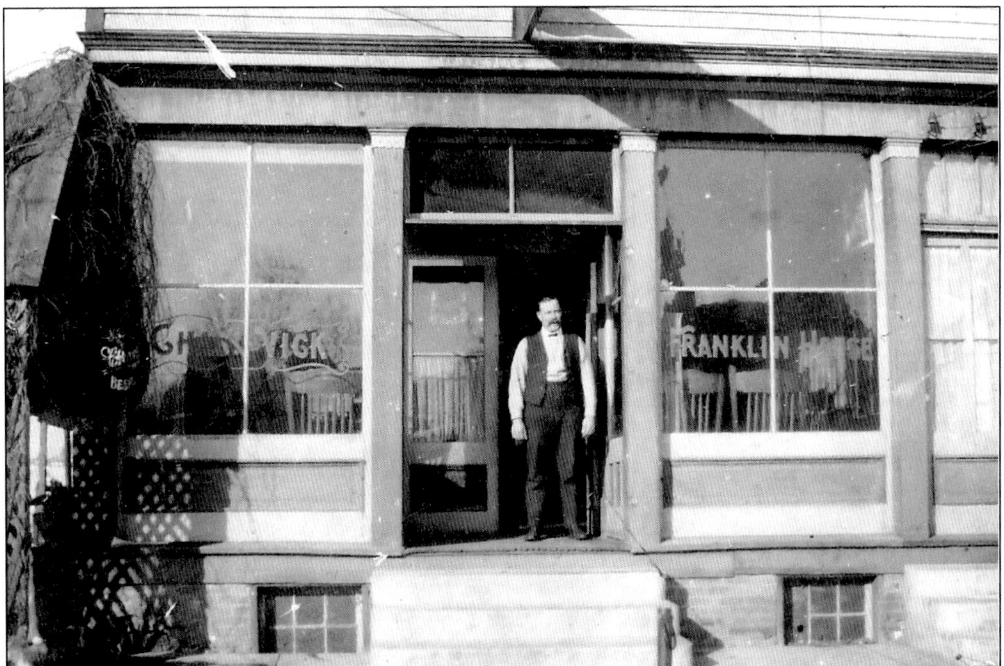

FRANKLIN HOUSE WITH CHARLES VICK. Located in Sheboygan Falls, the Franklin House was one of the earliest hotels in the area. This one and one-half story plaster house dates from before the Civil War. It was first used as a saloon and meat market.

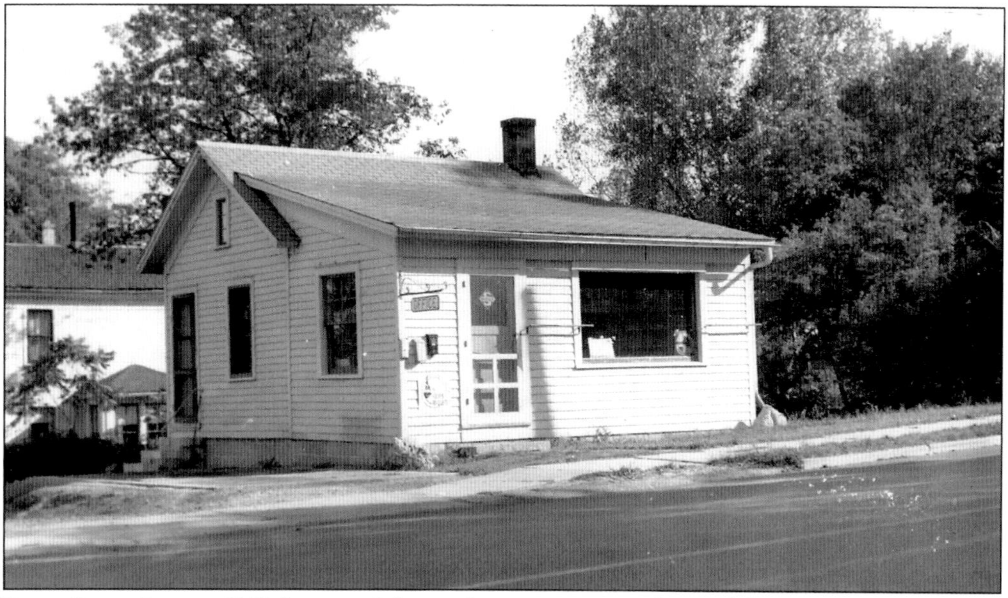

Falls Lime Office. Falls Lime and Stone Company operated out of the quarry situated north of Monroe Street on the east side of the city. The company sold not only stone, but sand and cement for the construction of walls and sidewalks. Owners of the business over time were A. Craig, William Schwessler, Henry Kohlhagen, and William and Louis Hildebrand. Operations ceased in 1938 due to a lack of profit.

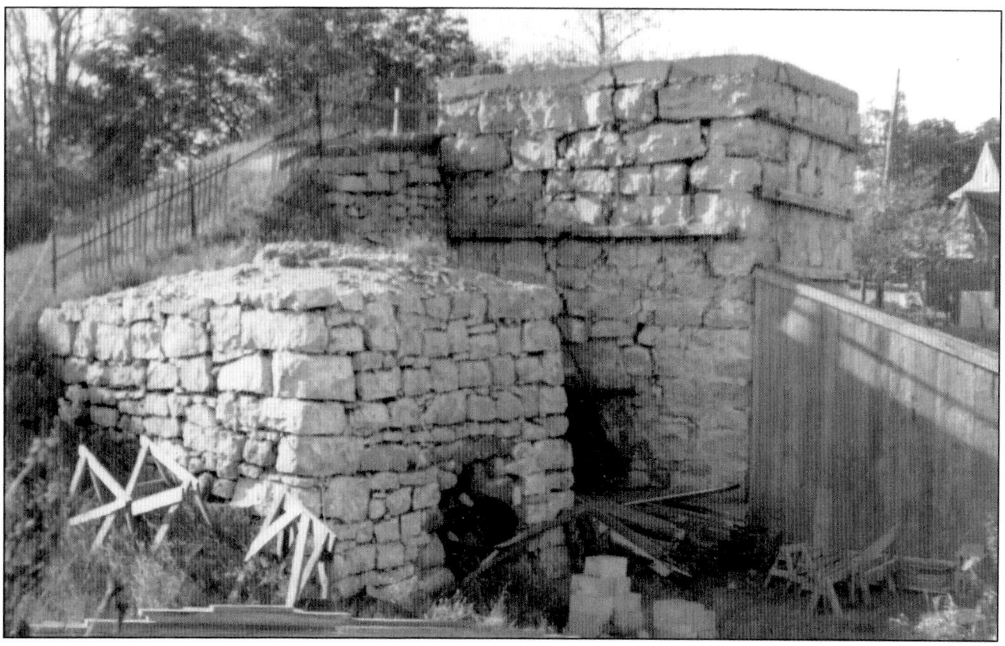

Old Lime Kiln. This old lime kiln was used to produce powdered lime from limestone rock. It is found in the quarry. The quarry became flooded with water sometime after operations ceased, probably from local springs. When the quarry was in operation it was regularly pumped out. Entrance to the old quarry property is found along the railroad tracks north of B and B Ford on Popular Street.

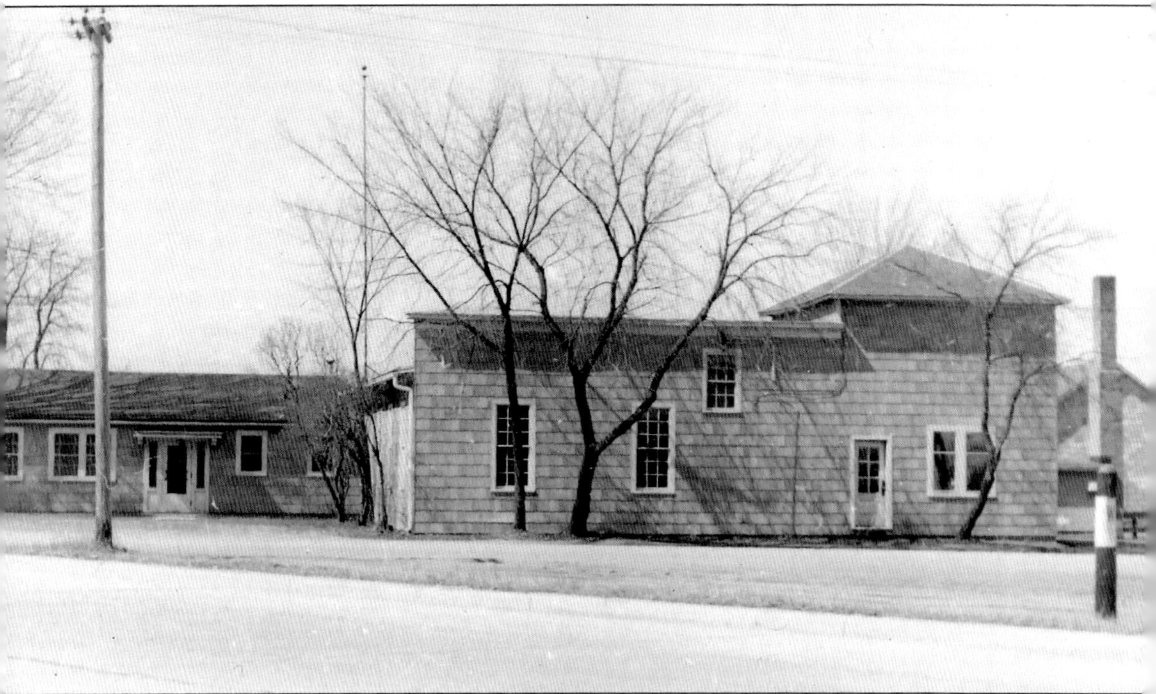

J.S. RICHARDSON COMPANY. The company located on Clark Street was organized on April 16, 1936. The company started to capitalize on the unusual mechanical abilities of Jairus S. Richardson. He developed many of the specialized woodworking machines used in woodworking. Examples were: bending machines, resaw attachments, and boring and chucking machines. During World War II, the company made gunstocks for the war effort. After the war the company did much more in the development of cutlery handle machinery. Kitchen cutlery merchandized nationally under the tradename "Flint" used handles made on Richardson machinery. By 1953, the company again turned to making of gun stock machinery, but this time more for civilian sporting arms than military models. In addition to the furniture and gun stock fields, the company has made many machines for the: cutting and grinding of fiberglass acoustical ceiling tile, machines, the turning and drilling of wooden golf club heads, sawing and shaping of coat hangars, and shaping wood parts of aircraft including helicopters. On August 18, 2000, J.S. Richardson was sold to George Ziaja who continues the machining tradition.

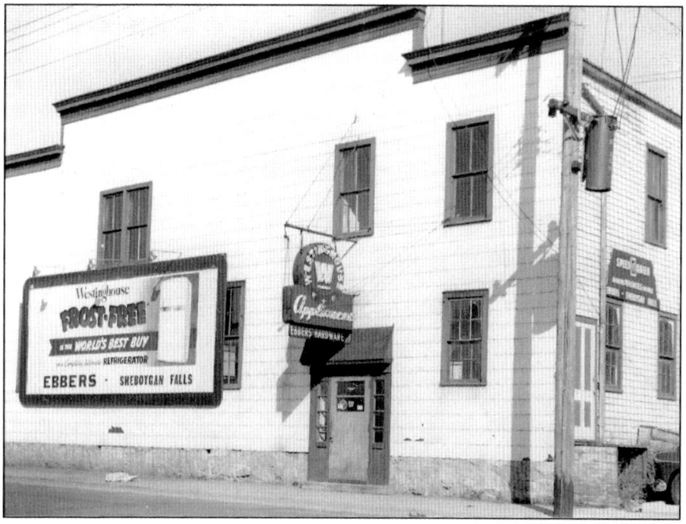

EBBERS. The G.H. Ebbers Hardware Store, shown here, burned in August of 1955, taking the life of repairman Frank Thierman and causing an estimated loss of $40,000. A spark from a machine using combustible fluid for cleaning appliance parts set off the explosion. The new Ebbers building opened in July of 1956. It was built as a business and professional building. The concrete block building was demolished in September of 2003 to make way for a parking lot.

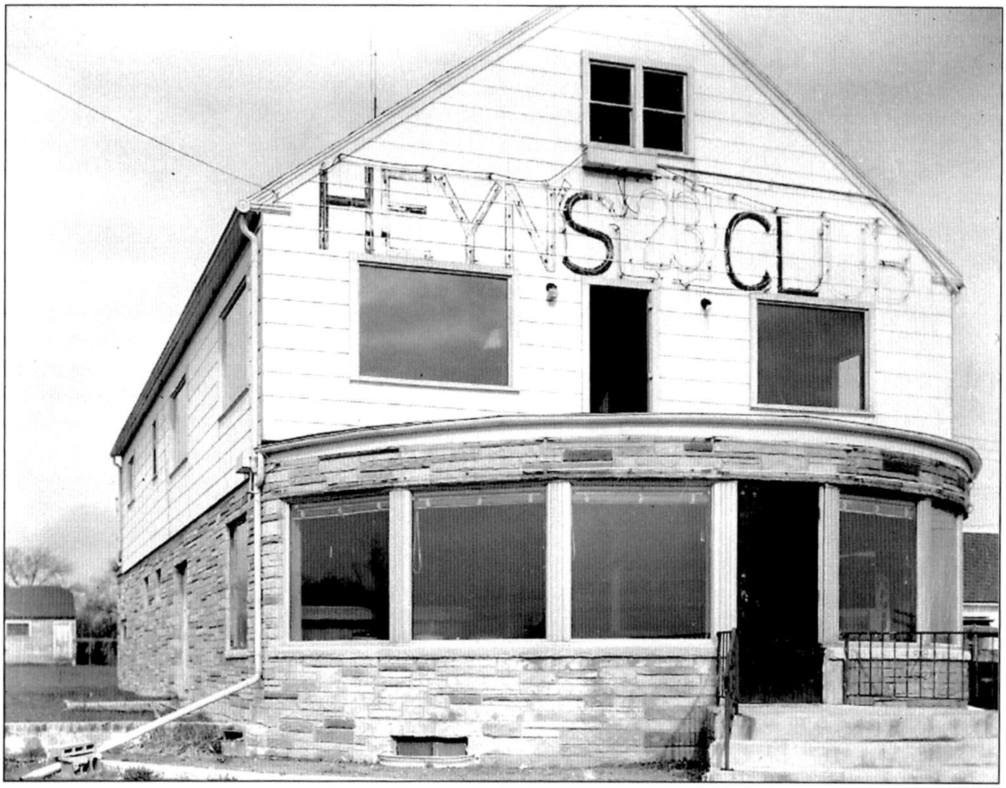

HEYN'S 23 CLUB. Heyn's 23 Club is located on Rangeline Road north of Sheboygan Falls. It was one of a handful of minor beer bars in this part of the state. Minor bars allowed teenagers from 18-21 to drink beer. At age 21 they could legally drink hard liquor. After the legal age changed to 18 in 1972 the need for minor bars ceased. Now called the Rangeline Inn, the property was purchased by Dave and Denise Schneider in 1985, the couple added a kitchen in 1988. The large banquet and ballroom was added in 1991.

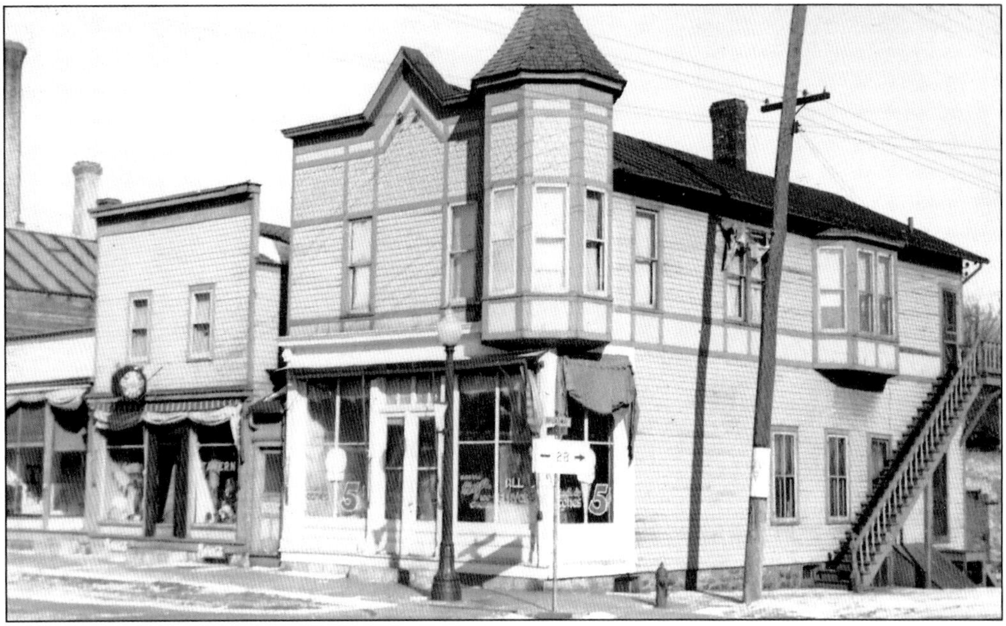

MARTHA WHIPPLE'S MUSIC STORE. Built in 1877 by Martha Whipple, she ran a music store and dressmaking business from the building. J. Kehl opened a cigar store here in 1881. The building later housed Herber's Confectionary, seen here in the 1940s. This two story building is located on the northeast corner of Monroe and Buffalo Streets. Today it houses Hy-Ryders Tavern.

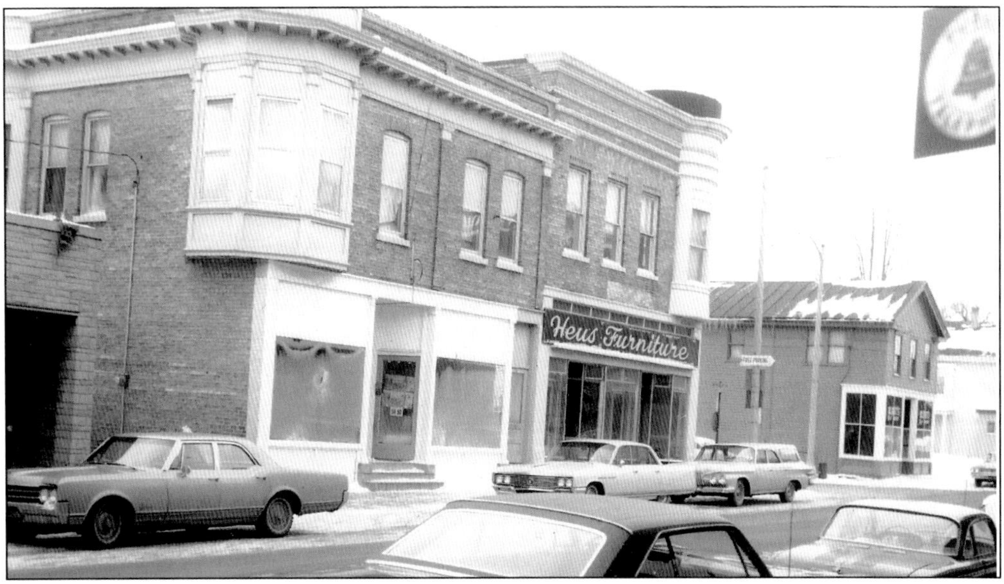

HERTZBERG HOTEL OR HEUS FURNITURE. Situated in the Hertzberg block at the southwest corner of Pine and Buffalo Streets, Heus Furniture was in business in the 1960s. Originally built as a hotel, Otto Hertzberg acquired the property in the late 1800s when he bought the business and added a livery barn and a bowling alley. The building housed many businesses including that of Arthur Rauschert who owned and operated a furniture business. Mr. Rauschert sold the business to Demo Evanoff. The building was demolished in May of 1966 to make way for a new Evans' Store.

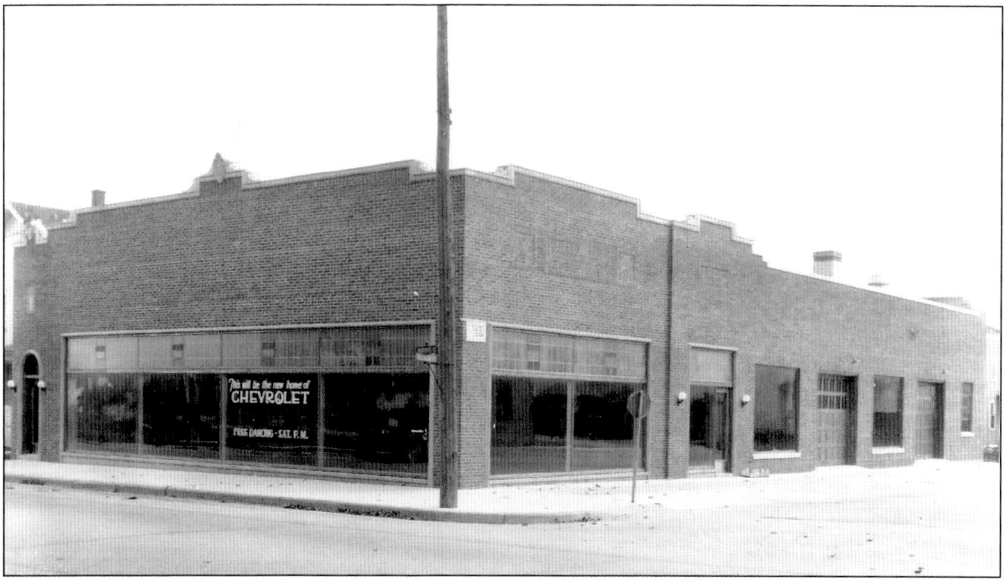

Helming Brothers Garage. Built by Gustav and Albert Helming in 1929, this building housed a large Chevrolet dealership. Located on the southeast corner of Monroe and Michigan Streets, the business ran successfully until 1938 when both brothers passed away within 12 months. The next owners were Julius and Charles Beyer, who called their business Falls Motor Sales and sold Plymouth and DeSoto cars. The building housed car dealerships until 1970 when it was vacated and boarded up. In 1997, the Selks utilized this durable building as a thriving new business, Falls Glass Service.

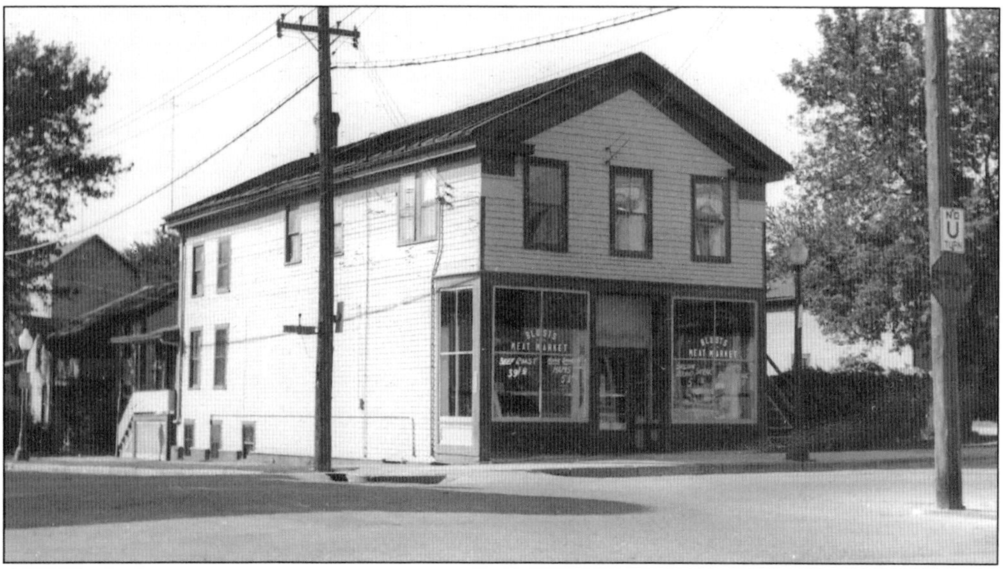

Blust Meat Market. The Blust Meat Market was an 1840s vintage Greek Revival building located on the southwest corner of Buffalo and Pine Streets. The meat market discontinued business in April of 1979. The building was razed in December of 1985 for the expansion of the Fasse Paint Company. The building had many uses over time including use as a manufacturing place, a meeting hall called Chamberlain Hall, a dealership of furniture, bedsteads, coffins, and other things.

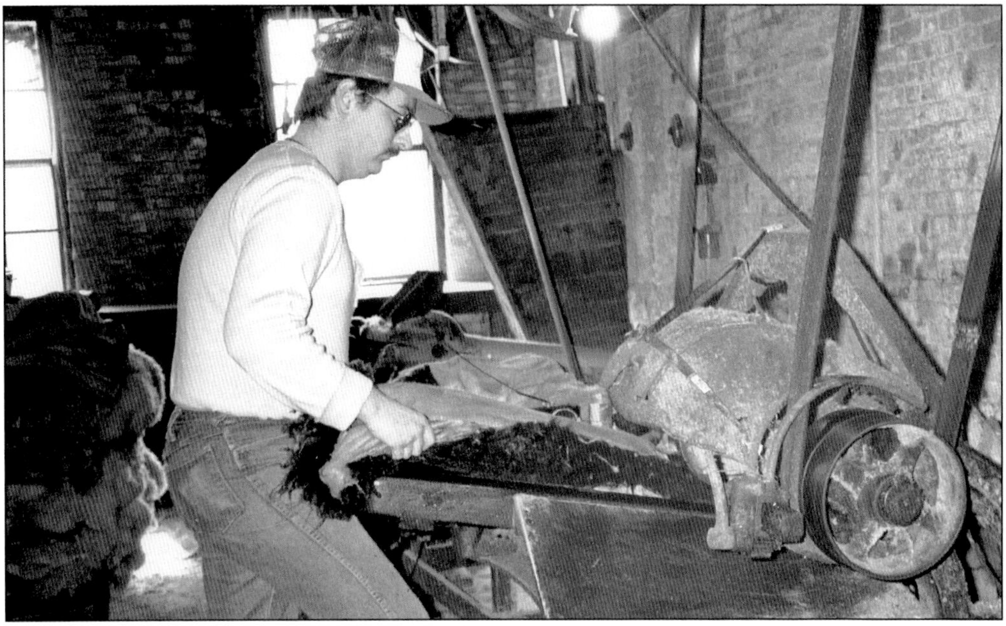

STERN TANNING COMPANY INTERIOR. Located at 334 Broadway Street, the tannery built on this site was operated by J.D. Gould in 1855. In 1866 Charles Weisse bought the business and expanded it into the four-story cream city brick structure we see today. The building burned in 1919, causing great damage. Dollar estimates of the loss were between $150,000 and $175,000. After the fire the tannery remained vacant until 1939 when it was purchased by Theodore Stern. The Stern Tannery remains in business today.

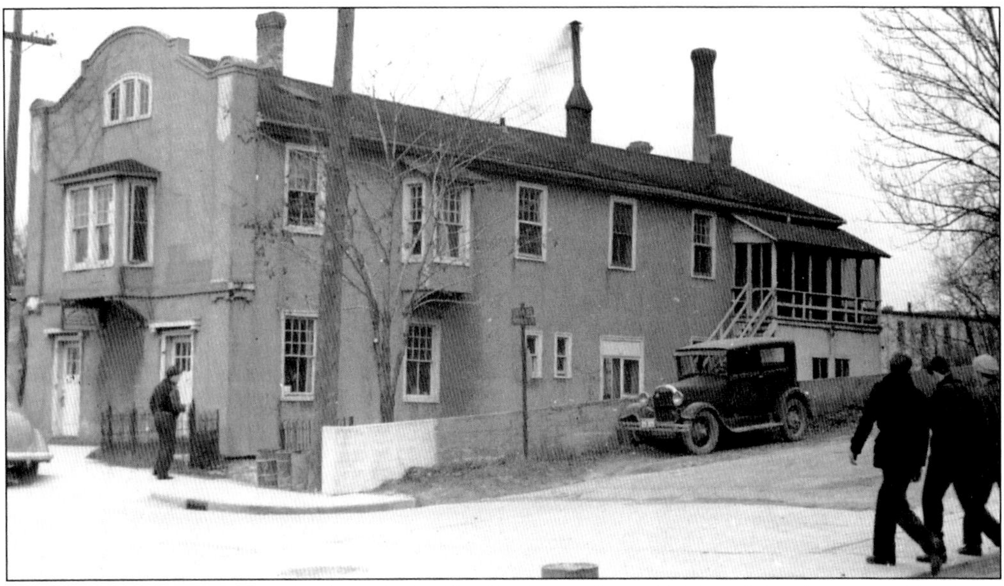

COUNTY NEWS BUILDING. Built by Col. Silas Stedman about 1840, and first known as Stedman Hall, the building served as a community hall providing a place for meetings, concerts, and celebrations for the community. It was located on the east side of the river, north of the Monroe Street Bridge, and west of Water Street. It was also home to the *Sheboygan County News* from 1878 to 1957.

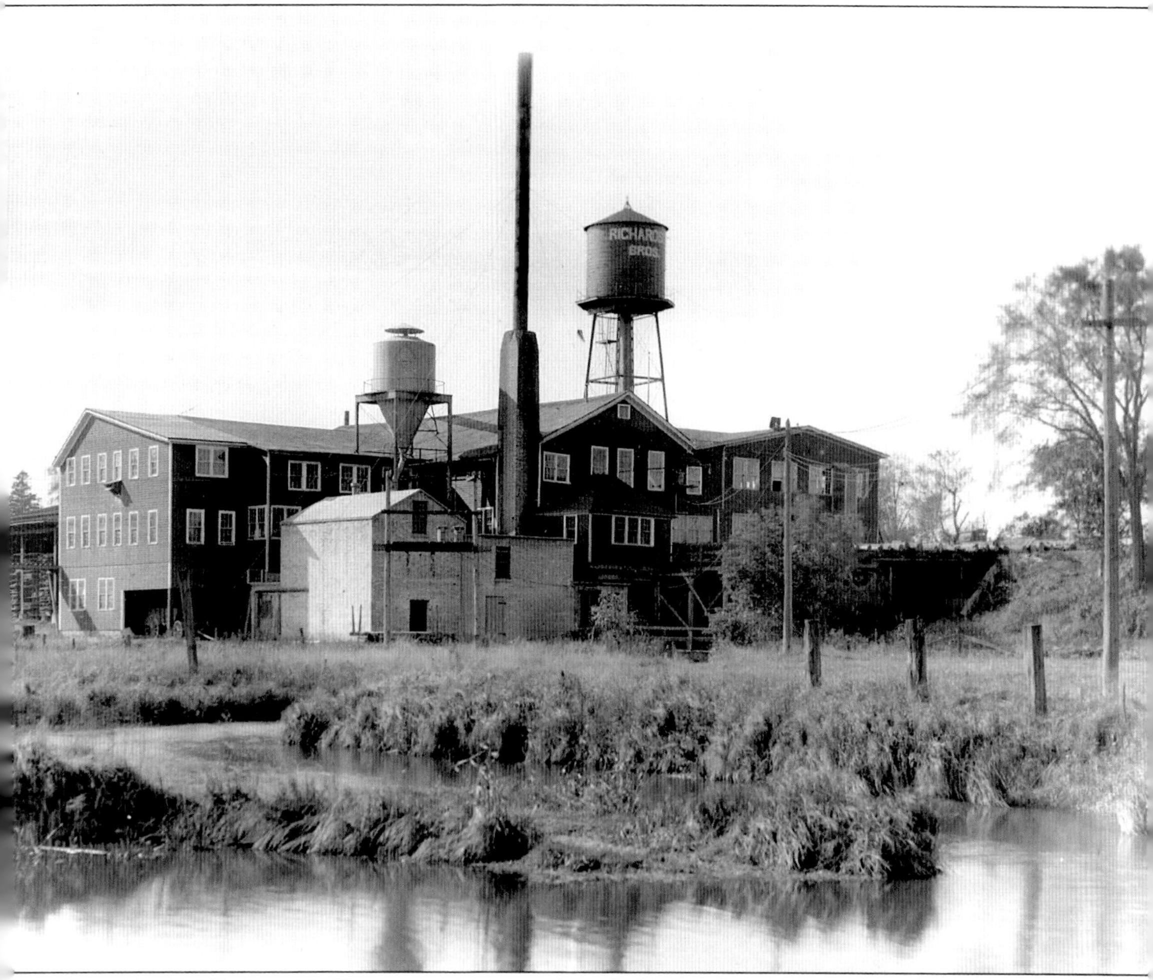

RICHARDSON BROTHERS FACTORY. In 1841, Joseph Richardson of Kinderhook, New York, moved his family west in search of adventure and greater economic promise. After spending time in Roscoe, Illinois, they decided to move to Green Bay, Wisconsin, but the Richardsons never made it to Green Bay. The road north ran through Rochester. Joe Richardson noticed that the prospects of the town looked good, deciding this was the place to settle. The family had come west to farm, but while land was purchased and cleared the family ran a small inn near the river. Richardson estimated there was a two-year supply of timber on his 200 acres of land which bordered the Mullet River, a possible source of waterpower. He saw the potential of logging and by 1848 built a dam with a swift millrace. The Richardsons had four sons who became involved and over the years the family business made Sheboygan Falls a hub of woodworking. Shown here is a photograph of the Richardson Brothers mill and factory in the 1950s. It is located west of Sheboygan Falls on Hwy. PP.

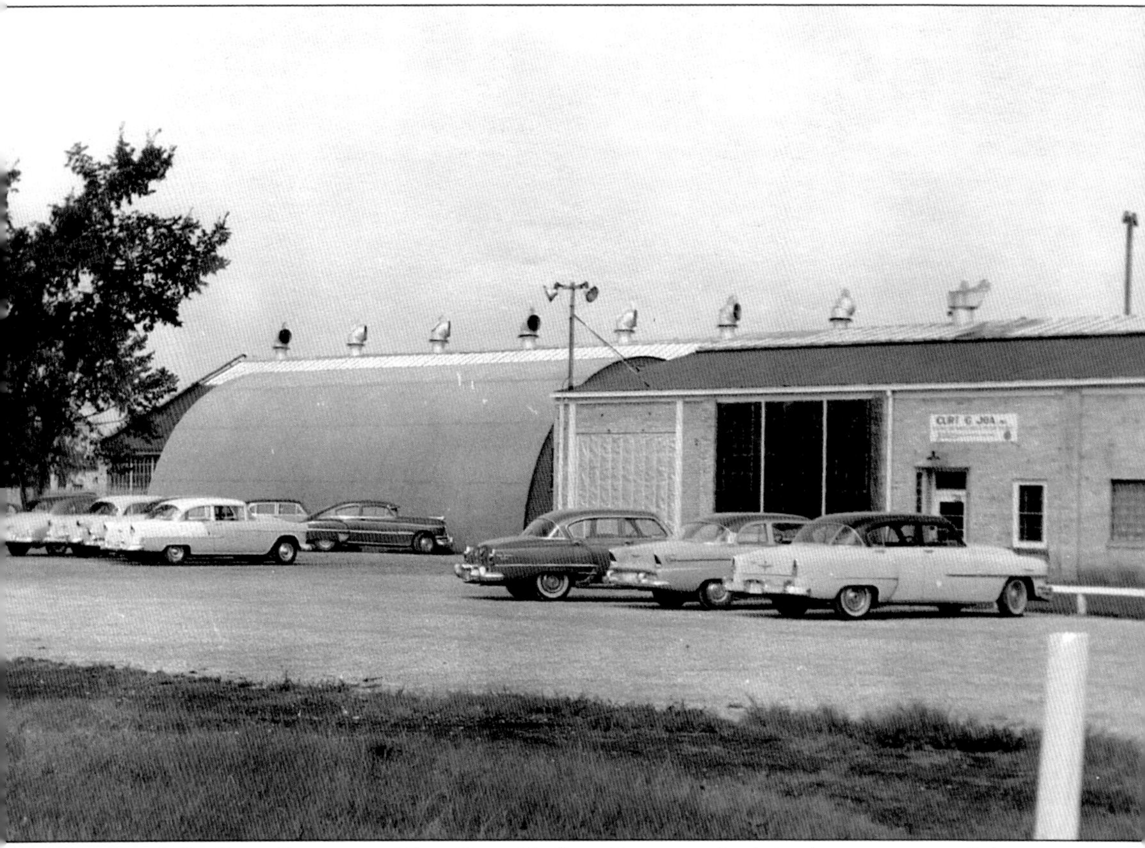

CURT G. JOA COMPANY. The Curt G. Joa Company had its beginnings in Manitowoc, Wisconsin. Joa, a German immigrant, was a tool and die designer with a skilled engineer's mind. During the Depression, he worked as a consultant for Rahr Malting and Northern Paper, A.O. Smith, and a dairy company in Chicago which asked him to design a milk bottle cap. He designed the one which consisted of an inside cap with a head cover over the cap. Soon almost every dairy company adapted the idea. He ended up working with the Diana Company of Green Bay, a manufacturer of paper products and sanitary napkins. He invented a machine that eliminated the hand operations necessary for folding the sanitary napkins. Joa's first patent application was filed on June 6, 1932, for the end-fold mechanism. Also, in 1932, articles of incorporation of the Curt G. Joa Consulting Engineer Company were filed in Manitowoc. At about the same time Jenkins Woodworking Company in Sheboygan Falls was in deep financial trouble. Joa was offered the Jenkins plant to see if he could make a success of it. He moved his operations to Sheboygan Falls in the early part of 1935. This photograph shows the Curt G. Joa plant in 1955 located on Clark Street.

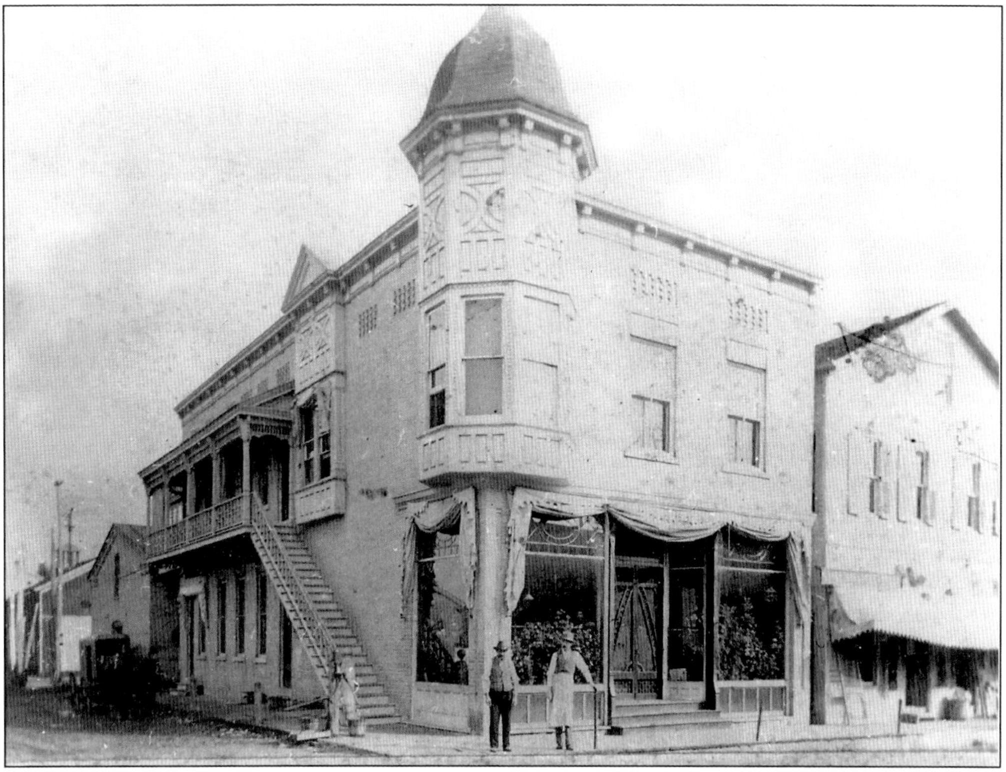

Billy Wolf's Saloon. Located on the northeast corner of Pine and Buffalo Streets, Billy Wolf's Saloon was described by the *Sheboygan Herald* as "handsomely furnished and well stocked." It was a popular resort for the socially inclined and pleasure-loving people of the village. Prohibition, which began in 1919, ended the saloon business. Today The Villager restaurant operates from this site.

Ogle Blacksmith Shop. George Ogle, a native of town of Lyndon, was born in 1860 and became an apprentice blacksmith as a young man. In 1884, he came to Sheboygan Falls and located his smithy on Pine Street between buildings that later housed Blust's Meat Market and Fasse's Paint Store. Children used to stop and watch Mr. Ogle fashion articles from red hot metal on his anvil and shoe horses. He also served four and one-half years as postmaster. He later moved to Waldo and became a merchant.

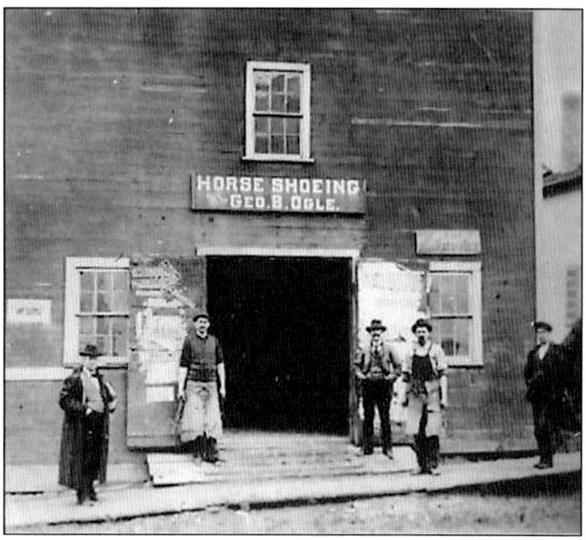

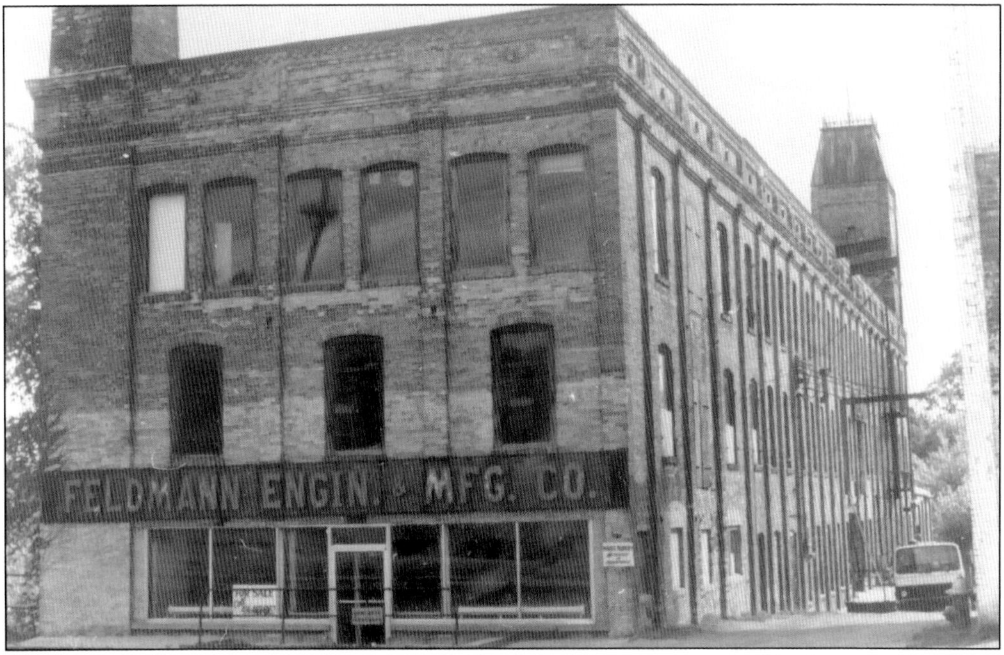

FELDMAN MANUFACTURING. The Brickner Woolen mills was just one of the homes of Feldman Manufacturing and Engineering. Marvin Feldmann has a long list of patents and inventions to his name, among them the Jiffy Ice Drill, the automatic twine tying attachment for the Case hay baler and the six-wheeled Terra Tiger ATV. The Terra Tiger was able to traverse rough terrain, rivers and lakes, as well as plunge from the lake ice into the water and propel itself back out of the water onto ice. In 1991, the Feldmanns graciously donated the structure to the city to be rehabbed into the Brickner Woolen Mills' Apartments.

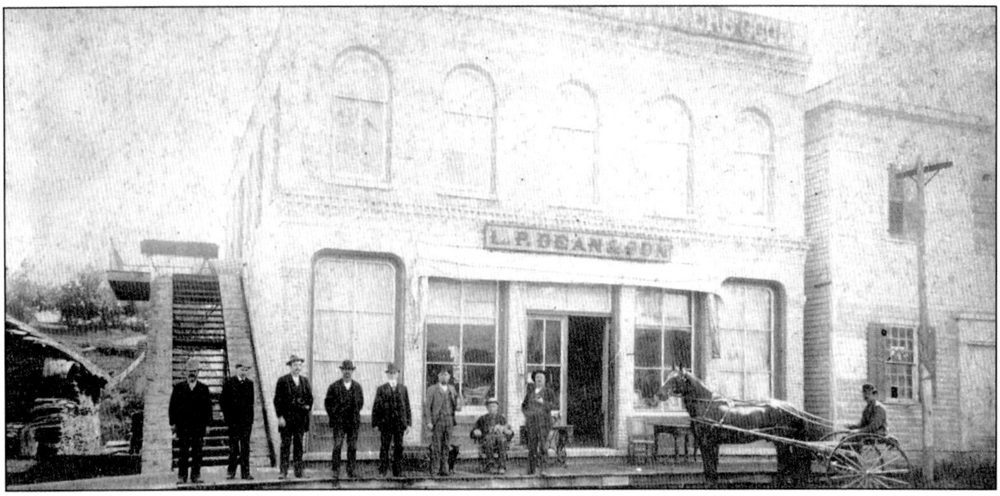

L.P. DEAN. Founded in 1886, L.P. Dean Undertaking, occupied the Benedict and Schuman building in the early 1900s. A coffin can be seen resting on supports at the top of the ramp on the north side of the building. In addition to funeral work, they were headquarters for parlor and chamber sets, tables, sideboards, couches, chairs, and upholstered goods. The building today is occupied by Walters Electric. The city's second school can be seen to the right before its move to the west side of the street.